a study of

jazz

a study of
jazz
fourth edition

paul o.w.
tanner
and **gerow** maurice

university of california,
los angeles

wcb

Wm. C. Brown Company Publishers
Dubuque, Iowa

wcb

Wm. C. Brown
Chairman of the Board

Book Team

Thomas W. Gornick
Editor

William J. Evans
Designer

Patricia L.A. Hendricks
John F. Mulvihill
Production Editors

Mary M. Heller
Visual Research Editor

Mavis M. Oeth
Permissions Editor

Wm. C. Brown Company Publishers,
College Division

Lawrence E. Cremer
President

Raymond C. Deveaux
Vice President/Product Development

David Wm. Smith
Assistant Vice President/National Sales Manager

Matt Coghlan
National Marketing Manager

David A. Corona
Director of Production Development and Design

Marilyn A. Phelps
Manager of Design

William A. Moss
Production Editorial Manager

Mary M. Heller
Visual Research Manager

Frederick W. Westphal
California State University, Sacramento
Consulting Editor

Contents

1

What is jazz?   3
Jazz interpretation/Improvisation/Rhythm/
Syncopation/Sounds associated with jazz/Form/
Summary

2

How to listen to jazz   11
Listening techniques/What to listen for in jazz/
Some musical concepts in jazz/Listening suggestions

3

Jazz heritages   20
European and African/Field hollers (cries)/
Work songs/Religious music/Marching bands

4

The blues   34

5

Early New Orleans Dixieland (1900–1920)   47

6

Ragtime (1900–1917)   56

7

Chicago Style Dixieland (the 1920s)   63

16

Jazz in television and motion pictures 148

17

Future directions 151

18

Five out of many 153
Louis Armstrong/Duke Ellington/Benny Goodman/
Charlie Parker/John Coltrane

Recorded Examples

Photographs

Preface

Even though some eras of jazz music sound extremely different from others, it is our contention that jazz has evolved logically from one era to the next. This study attempts to show the logical musical derivatives and developments of jazz and at the same time to point out the important elements that comprise the individual styles of jazz as they have evolved from era to era. The book, then, tries to define jazz as precisely as possible.

In this fourth edition of A Study of Jazz, *the text has been brought up to date by updating the resource materials, adding to the list of recordings receiving industry awards, and discussing contemporary trends extensively.*

The fourth edition delves into a number of areas that have become important in the current development of jazz. The chapter on jazz/rock has been expanded, while new chapters have been devoted to electronic advancements and jazz in television and motion pictures. Besides retaining the sections added in the third edition—jazz in other countries, Latin jazz, a profile of Benny Goodman, and a Listening Guide—a part has been added that examines the relationship between disco music and jazz.

Many features of the third edition have been retained. Suggestions on how to listen to jazz have been expanded, references and lists of recordings, as well as suggested classroom activities, are provided at the end of each chapter, the written music in the text can be heard on the record in the back of the book, and additional references for recommended reading have been added to both the chapter reading resources and the Bibliography.

This book can be used most effectively in a variety of situations, at either the secondary or college level. At the junior high school level, for example, a unit on jazz can be easily correlated with a social studies unit on American history since the Civil War. At the high school level, it can be used to supplement and extend studies of southern folk songs, Stephen Foster songs, Negro spirituals, blues, and work songs. At the college level, this book can be used as a text for a course entirely on jazz.

Much has been written about jazz, and as a consequence the references recommended for additional reading have been carefully selected for their accuracy, authenticity, and applicability to school and college use.

We would like to note that while we have used the generic he *freely, we did so for succinctness and to avoid inept wording. The term is meant to refer to both men and women when that meaning is proper.*

Paul Tanner   Maurice Gerow

a study of

jazz

1
What Is Jazz?

For more than eighty years jazz has exerted an influence upon many composers of the twentieth century both in America and in Europe. Jazz audiences listen to their favorite music with the same intense interest as the most devoted symphonic or chamber music lover. (It is interesting to note the popularity of jazz in the Far East. More American jazz records are sold in Japan than in any other country, including the United States.) Many modern jazz musicians are highly trained instrumentalists using the same complex harmonies and rhythms that classical composers use. What is jazz? What are the unique characteristics distinguishing it from other types of musical composition and performance?

In the case of many school administrators, their lack of enthusiasm for jazz reflects their lack of understanding of this type of music. Some people consider all music that is not classical to be jazz, thereby putting jazz, country and western, rock, all levels of popular music, and other types of music into one all-inclusive category. Of course, much music that borrows from jazz is hardly jazz itself. Furthermore, academia must be encouraged to distinguish good jazz from bad just as it distinguishes good classical music from bad. Writer-teacher Leon Dallin has this to say about the misunderstandings concerning jazz:

In choosing between good and evil the acceptance of the one implies the rejection of the other. This is not true in choosing between the classics and jazz, though admittedly more often than not it works out that way. I prefer to think that the two aspects of musical art are perfectly compatible and that to appreciate both of them requires only an understanding of what each is—and is not. . . . There are some parallels, and music might be divided along similar lines into "music which costs" and "music which pays." Symphonies, string quartets and the like would constitute the former; Dixieland combos, swing bands and their successors, the latter.

Symphony and chamber music players and composers would agree to this distinction. On the other hand, the very mention of the word "commercial" in jazz circles suggests Lombardo and Garber [and Welk]. Another argument against this distinction in music is that some of the more creative aspects of jazz have been the least successful financially and for a time, during the early days of the Depression, were pursued mainly, if not exclusively, for the sake of art.

Formerly the problem of pigeonholing music could be accomplished nicely by approaching the problem from the standpoint of use. There was dance music and concert music. This distinction loses validity with the invasion of "dance" bands into Carnegie Hall and the prohibition of dancing in the "Storyville" and Basin Street Clubs, traditional haunts, for lack of a better term, of the jazz men. The issue is confused hopelessly by the mixture that streams out of radio and television sets, though there is no question where the emphasis lies.[1]

As far as considering jazz to be dance music and classical music to be concert music, it should be remembered that most jazz stopped being a music primarily for dancing in the 1940s. And it should be noted that two of the greatest composers of dance music were Wolfgang Mozart and Johann Strauss, and that in 1597 Thomas Morley published very precise instructions for writing actual dance music in *A Plaine and Easie Introduction to Practicall Musick*.

It is extremely doubtful that any amount of teaching can produce a jazz performer of the quality of Louis Armstrong or Charlie Parker—too much in jazz is concerned with personal experiences and feelings. But what can be taught are appreciation and discernment, at least to the capacity of each student. Incidentally, it must be emphasized that it is the capacity of the student, certainly not of the teacher, that sets the limit. In regard to the study and teaching of jazz, Charles Suber, editor of a leading jazz publication, *Down Beat*, has best expressed certain pertinent views:

To be a successful professional performing musician you need three basic things. First is a strong, outgoing ego—something inside of you that must speak out. Second is ambition—a strong, almost ruthless drive that makes everything besides music insignificant. The third, and the most elusive to define, is talent. Talent has many ingredients, such as mastery of instrument, thorough knowledge of the theory and literature of music, and the ability to communicate your music and personality to an audience. Talent is a quality that is usually regarded by others as a relative value—"He's the best (or worst)." To the top pro, talent is more of an absolute. He sets his own standard of excellence and consequently is his own best (and worst) critic and judge. You can be sure that Ellington or Parker or Heifetz set his own (seldom or never-to-be-achieved) standard and did not accept the criteria of others.

The same three things—ego, ambition, and talent—are needed to be a successful music educator; especially today, when there is a very thin line between

professional teacher and professional performer. It is no longer true, if it ever was, that "only unsuccessful musicians teach." Being able to make it as a full-time working professional is denied to many musicians because of many other factors. (Remember that less than 5 percent of the 240,000 union musicians in the U.S.A. earn their full-time living from music.) It is fortunate that in today's education market there is a place for talented professional musicians to teach and perform in the jazz idiom. To be involved in school jazz as student or teacher is becoming a requirement for acceptance as a complete musician in all idioms.[2]

Along with many others, author-critic Henry Pleasants has tried to define jazz: "The influence of a variety of indigenous musical styles originating in the Negro communities of New Orleans and other American cities, in the Negro communities of the rural South, and in the Negro or mixed communities of the Caribbean islands and some areas of South America in the early decades of the twentieth century has been felt and reflected in the popular music of most of the civilized world."[3] Pleasants's formula, emphasizing the contribution of the American Negro and the geographical origins of jazz, is really no formula at all. He does, however, invalidate several of the misconceptions concerning jazz:

Prevalent assumptions are: (1) that the distinguishing feature of jazz is syncopation; (2) that the distinguishing feature of jazz is improvisation; (3) that jazz cannot be played from notes; and (4) that jazz is a Negro music and can be played properly only by Negroes. All are easily disposed of: (1) If syncopation were the distinctive element in jazz, then much European [classical] music would be jazz. (2) Improvisation was common in European music well into the 19th century, and most church organists improvise to this day without producing anything that sounds like jazz. (3) The time has long passed when an astigmatic jazz musician could get by without spectacles. (4) While the Negro has certainly been the decisive contributor

1. Leon Dallin, "Classics and Jazz: An Eternal Conflict?" *Music Educators Journal* 45, no. 2 (November-December 1958):32.

2. Charles Suber, "The First Chorus," *Down Beat* 35, no. 18 (September 1968):4.

3. Henry Pleasants, *Serious Music and All That Jazz* (New York: Simon & Schuster, 1969), p. 51. Copyright © 1969 by Henry Pleasants. Reprinted by permission of Simon & Schuster, a Division of Gulf and Western Corporation.

to jazz, there is no jazz in Africa that was not brought there by Americans or Europeans, white, black and mixed.[4]

Many individuals who write about music state that improvisation is the *only* type of jazz or that jazz is strictly improvisation. Improvisation is the art of composing original music while performing the music, with or without the aid of written music. Most improvising musicians, however, make up their individual parts based on an overall plan that has been previously agreed upon by all the participating performers.

We contend that all jazz is *not* improvised, because if it were much of what is classified as jazz would not fall strictly into this category. To illustrate this point, look to the music performed by the smaller groups within the Benny Goodman orchestra. Very few would argue that the Benny Goodman trio, quartet, and other small ensembles are not playing jazz. In a particular composition or performance these smaller groups continuously alternate between music that is improvised and music that is notated or at least planned. The two- and three-part harmony strains played by the clarinet, piano, and vibraphone on "Avalon," for example, could not possibly be performed unless they had been previously contrived.[5] Hence, to those who hold the view that jazz consists exclusively of improvisation, the Goodman groups would seem to fluctuate continually between jazz and some other style of musical performance.

Writers constantly refer to the use of improvisation in dixieland music. Those who have never been involved in the actual performance of dixieland music seldom realize the musical techniques used by performers of this type of music. (These techniques are explained in chapter 5.) Regardless of the feeling of spontaneity perceived by the listener, there is actually very little improvisation in the ensemble portions of dixieland music. The better dixieland players have performed their repertoire for so long that during the ensemble sections they usually play established lines or at least planned patterns instead of improvisation.

Count Basie's orchestra is generally accepted as a jazz organization; yet this musical group plays written arrangements with parts left open for improvisation by solo instruments. It cannot be maintained that such small groups as those led by Charlie Parker and Dizzy Gillespie and the early Miles Davis groups play music containing a few bars of jazz followed by a few bars of something else. It is the authors' opinion that everything these groups perform is jazz.

Therefore, it is clear that jazz can be both written (planned) and improvised and that jazz and improvisation are not synonymous.

It is also our opinion that certain elements are generally found in jazz that distinguish it from other music, and that all of these elements may not be equally present in any one jazz performance. These elements are jazz interpretation, improvisation, rhythm, syncopation, sounds associated with jazz, and particular musical forms. Only by understanding and identifying the elements that comprise jazz can the listener develop an appreciation and understanding of jazz itself.

Jazz Interpretation

The interpretation of music in the jazz style originally came about when Afro-Americans attempted to express themselves on European musical instruments. The natural way for these early instrumentalists to think of their musical lines was as the lines would be treated vocally. Eventually, the attitude developed that *what* was played was not as important as *how* it was played.

In jazz interpretation, the player restricts his interpretative ideas to his conception of the melody, coloring it by the use of rhythmic effects, dynamics, and any other slight alterations that occur to him while performing. He remains enough within such melodic restrictions as would allow a listener to easily recognize the melody regardless of the player's interpretation. Almost any kind of a melodic line can be performed with jazz interpretation. Most jazz musicians will agree that to write down an exact jazz interpretation is next to impossible, and all will agree that only a musician who has played jazz can even approximate the notation.

Another way of explaining jazz interpretation is to speak of the jazz "idiom." Classical music and jazz music differ primarily in idiom. A classical musician plays the notes, but his playing lacks the same idiomatic execution usually found in jazz. The European system of musical notation cannot represent this kind of expression. "The conventional symbols could, in other words, indicate in a general way *what* should be

4. Pleasants, *Serious Music and All That Jazz*, p. 62. Copyright © 1969 by Henry Pleasants. Reprinted by permission of Simon & Schuster, a Division of Gulf and Western Corporation.

5. Benny Goodman, "Avalon," *Benny Goodman Carnegie Concert*, Columbia Records, OSL–160.

played, but could not indicate [precisely] *how* it should be played."[6] Idiomatic expression in jazz is the result of the black American musicians interjecting African music into European music. However, ". . . when jazz compromises its own characteristics of pulse, contour and cadence, to accommodate a more nearly European frame of expressive reference, calling upon strings, or employing its own European instruments in a European [classical] manner, it jeopardizes its idiomatic identity."[7]

This technique is illustrated by examples 1A and 1B, the first without jazz interpretation and the second with suggested jazz interpretation. Listen to the differences in the performances on the record included in the sleeve at the back of this book.

Today, two completely diverse directions in jazz interpretation are very active. One kind of interpretation seems to be closer than ever to classical music. This trend started about 1950 and continues as more schooled musicians enter the jazz field. The other direction is toward *avant-garde* jazz, in which some players disregard all earlier approaches to musical lines. These musicians maintain that instead of interpreting lines per se they are playing emotions such as rage or pain. (This topic is discussed further in chapter 13.)

Improvisation

Improvisation is similar to interpretation, but without melodic restriction. When a jazz player improvises, the "standard" procedure is to use the original as a point of departure and to invent a new melodic line while still fairly well restricted by the harmonic structure of the original melody. However, as discussed in chapter 13, there is a contemporary style called "free form" or "free improvisation" in which the player's only restriction is that he compose lines related to the musical sounds made by the other musicians in the group.

6. Pleasants, *Serious Music and All That Jazz,* p. 32. Authors' brackets. Copyright © 1969 by Henry Pleasants. Reprinted by permission of Simon & Schuster, a Division of Gulf and Western Corporation.

7. Ibid., p. 44.

Example 1A
(Side 1, Band 1A)

Example 1B
(Side 1, Band 1B)

Example 1C

(Side 1, Band 1C)

Improvisation did not come into being with jazz nor is the technique confined solely to jazz, as many authorities state. The Greeks improvised two thousand years ago,[8] and at one time improvisation was extremely important in baroque and classical music. Bach, Mozart, Beethoven, Liszt, and many others were superb improvisers. Therefore, listeners who say they cannot understand jazz because of improvisation also cannot understand much of the great traditional classical music. Improvisation in classical music can be heard today performed by groups such as the Improvisation Chamber Ensemble.[9] In contrast with interpretation, example 1C is an improvisation (written out) of the same melody used in example 1A. Listen to the record and compare examples 1A, 1B, and 1C.

Rhythm

An emphasis upon rhythm has always been an integral part of jazz. One reason is that for many years jazz was considered primarily music for dancing. While jazz players have found that a steady, unbroken beat is necessary for dancing, it also aids in developing the emotional pitch identified with jazz, even though in some cases the pulse is merely implied rather than obvious.

The jazz player does not always play exactly in rhythm with the pulse. He sometimes feels the need to be slightly ahead of (on top of) the beat, sometimes to lag a trifle behind the beat. This is more a feeling than something that can be measured accurately; it varies from one style to another and indeed from one individual to another. But throughout the development of most jazz, performers have felt the need for this pulse in order to play what they consider jazz. However, recent experiments in jazz have not used a steady beat.

(These experiments toward rhythm are discussed further in chapter 13.) For years it was thought that all jazz must be played in 2/4 or 4/4 meter. This attitude changed, however, when 3/4, 5/4, 9/4, and other meters began to be used in performing well-accepted jazz works. Dave Brubeck first brought newer meters to public notice with an extremely popular 5/4 recording of Paul Desmond's "Take Five."[10]

Syncopation

To syncopate means to accent or to extend the note value of a normally weak beat or weak part of a beat. It can be done in many ways. The following two examples of the same melody illustrate this technique: example 2A has no syncopation, example 2B does.

It can be seen that the syncopated notes in example 2B fall on weak beats, namely, beats 2 and 4. There is also a lengthening of the note values of the weak part of the beats, namely, the second half. Certainly there is syncopation in all musics, but in jazz, syncopation is used often and becomes highly intricate. There is very little jazz that does not use syncopation. As a consequence, syncopation is more natural for the jazz musician and is more closely connected with jazz in the mind of the public. Of the many examples, we

8. Leroy Ostransky, *The Anatomy of Jazz* (Seattle: University of Washington Press, 1960), p. 50.

9. Improvisation Chamber Ensemble, *Studies in Improvisation*, RCA Victor Red Seal Records, LSC–2558.

10. Dave Brubeck Quartet, *Time Out*, Columbia Records, CL–1397 and *Time Further Out*, Columbia Records, CS–8490; Don Ellis Orchestra, *Live at Monterey*, Pacific Jazz Records, PJ–19112, and *Live in 3²ᐟ³/4 Time*, Pacific Jazz Records, PJ–10123; Elvin Jones Quartet, "That Five-Four Bag," *The Definitive Jazz Scene*, vol. 3, Impulse Records, A–9101.

Example 2A

Example 2B

suggest something like Count Basie's "Jumpin' at the Woodside."[11]

Gunther Schuller has defined the syncopation of jazz as "no more than an idiomatic corruption, a flattened-out mutation of what was once the true polyrhythmic character of African music."[12]

Sounds Associated with Jazz

In classical music, each instrument has an "ideal" sound or tone, or at least there is a consensus as to what the ideal sound is. The jazz musician, though, finds that conformity is of little importance. As long as his sound communicates well with his peers and his listeners, the jazz musician appreciates the individuality of personal sounds. This situation, in which personal expression is more important than aesthetic conformity, often causes listeners not tuned to jazz to question the sounds that they hear. Frankly, the quality of much great classical music is lost in the search for authenticity instead of for beauty and emotion.

There are certain sounds peculiar to jazz that are a consequence of jazz having originated from oral tradition. Many of the sounds are the result of instrumentalists attempting to imitate vocal techniques.

Jazz singers and instrumentalists use all the tone qualities employed in other music and even increase the emotional range through the use of growls, bends, slurs, and varying shades of vibrato, employing any artifice available to assist their personal interpretation of the music. Jazz musicians have always had a great affinity with good singers, especially those whose interpretation closely resembles their own. Such singers include the early great blues singers (to be discussed later) and other talented performers such as Bing Crosby, Ella Fitzgerald, Billie Holiday, Frank Sinatra, Sarah Vaughan, Billy Eckstine, and Betty Carter.

Distinctive jazz instrumentation produces unique sounds. A featured saxophone section or rhythm section, for example, are seldom found in other types of music. And while some authorities are mistaken when they claim that mutes are indigenous to jazz (mutes were used in the 1600s), it is true that a larger variety of mutes is used in jazz.

To many listeners the sounds of jazz are personified and identified through the musical interpretation of specific artists. Listeners who have not heard much

11. Count Basie Orchestra, "Jumpin' at the Woodside," *The Best of Basie*, Roulette Records, R–52081.

12. Gunther Schuller, *Early Jazz* (New York: Oxford University Press, 1968), p. 15.

jazz are often surprised that the well-initiated can recognize a soloist after hearing only a few notes—at least within the listener's preferred style. Talented jazz musicians seem to have their own personal vibrato, attack, type of melodic line, choice of notes in the chord, indeed, their own sound. Very few classical connoisseurs can say for sure who is conducting a standard work, let alone identify the individual soloists or section leaders.

Form

Form is the construction of the music; in classical music, for example, the sonata allegro, fugue, and rondo are typical forms, or constructions. Jazz is usually written in certain forms: the twelve-bar (measure) blues strains and the sixteen- and thirty-two-bar choruses, usually AABA or ABAB. Since the 1940s, some jazz players have combined the AABA and blues forms. The performer does this by playing the first strain (A), repeating it (A), following with a different strain of usually only eight measures (B), and ending with the original strain (A). The first, second, and fourth parts all have twelve measures.

Since the advent of the long-playing record, modern jazz players have tended to adopt extended musical forms such as the theme and variation, fugue, and rondo.[13] The Modern Jazz Quartet offers several albums with examples of extended forms such as the excellent recording titled *Collaboration* in which they perform Bach's "Fugue in A Minor" with guitarist Laurindo Almeida.[14] In fact, jazz players have used the theme-and-variation form since the beginning of this art. The tune is established and then each repetition is given a variation, whether improvised or planned, in order to constantly create new interest as the work progresses. This form is often compared to the chaconne, in which a series of improvisations is played from a predetermined chord progression.

The authors have considered the possibility that the most important element in all jazz—that of emotion—is overlooked. There is no question that emotional force has been the strongest ally of jazz throughout its history. Jazz can make one dance with joy, weep with sadness, and contemplate deeply. However, since both authors are involved in the performance of music, we are totally convinced that emotion is too necessary an element of all types of music to be considered the exclusive element of any one kind of music—any music without emotion simply does not seem worth listening to.

Summary

In summary, a listener must decide whether a specific performance contains enough recognizable jazz elements to make it jazz. Identical melodies can be played or sung in a jazz or another musical style. A good example is "Empty Bed Blues" as sung on the Leonard Bernstein record *What Is Jazz?*[15] The melody is sung by both Sherry Ostrus and Bessie Smith. Miss Ostrus's interpretation lacks jazz elements, while Miss Smith utilizes the jazz elements we have discussed. There can be no question in any listener's mind which rendition is jazz.

In contemporary classical music, the composer remains the focal point. In general, a performer of classical music follows the conductor and what the conductor understands the composer to have intended. In a jazz performance, on the other hand, if the performer does not integrate something of himself, his personality, and his background into the music, the audience (which is itself a part of the performance) rightfully feels cheated. In classical music, *how* a work is performed is rarely considered as important as the work itself. In jazz, the work itself is never really as important as the *way* in which it is played. Even more unusual is that in jazz the *way* a performer plays determines *what* he plays. That is, the strong as well as the weak aspects of an individual's abilities on his instrument cause stylistic directions to appear in his playing, which in turn dictate both *what* and *how* he plays, and *what* and *how* tend to merge. For example, what Charlie Parker played on "Parker's Mood" or "Bird Gets the Worm" or "Merry Go Round" *was* precisely how he played the saxophone;[16] there is no way of separating style from content. This approach, this attitude, distinguishes jazz from most other music.

13.   Gunther Schuller, "Variants on a Theme of Thelonious Monk," *Jazz Abstractions,* Atlantic Records, 1365; "A Fugue for Music Inn," *The Modern Jazz Quartet at Music Inn,* Atlantic Records, 1247; "On Green Mountain" (chaconne form), *Modern Jazz Concert,* Columbia Records, WL127; Dave Brubeck Quartet, "Blue Rondo a la Turk," *Time Out,* Columbia Records, CL1397.

14.   Modern Jazz Quartet with Laurindo Almeida, "Fugue in A Minor," *Collaboration,* Atlantic Records, 1429.

15.   Leonard Bernstein, *What Is Jazz?* Columbia Records, 919.

16.   Charlie Parker, "Parker's Mood," "Bird Gets the Worm," "Merry Go Round," *Charlie Parker Memorial Album,* vol. 1, Savoy Records, MG–12000.

Perhaps Bryce Jordan has one of the clearest definitions of jazz:

Jazz, then, is not a composer's art. The particular melody and harmonies which formed the basis of a performance, improvised or arranged, are of secondary importance. Rather jazz is the art of the performer, the performing ensemble, the arranger. And the quality of the art is dependent upon their creative ideas.[17]

Suggested Classroom Activities

1. Name the six elements of jazz that distinguish it from other types of music.
2. Give a definition of syncopation.
3. Clap the following 4/4 rhythm:

    While tapping the beat with your foot, clap an example using a syncopated pattern.
4. Sing or play the melody of the song "Swanee River." Sing or play this melody with a jazz interpretation. What did you alter or perform differently in order to change the style of your performance?
5. It is fun to improvise. With little musical knowledge, one can make up his own melody at the piano keyboard. Using only the black keys on the piano, start with the black key C sharp and play any series of tones with the rhythmic patterns found in the familiar song "Twinkle, Twinkle, Little Star." Repeat the same melody you made up and vary the rhythmic patterns.
6. Listen to "The Kid from Red Bank" from $E = MC^2$ (Roulette R–52003). In your own words, describe some of the improvisational techniques the pianist uses. For example, does the player use primarily melodic or harmonic configurations?
7. Classical composers have frequently used the theme-and-variations form in their compositions.

Listening to a number of compositions that use this form will help a listener identify the various elements of jazz and how they can be altered or changed in jazz performances.

   a. Ravel uses the theme-and-variations design in his composition *Bolero.* Listen to this piece and discover which musical element is used predominately in the eighteen variations—melody, rhythm, harmony, or tone color (instrumentation).
   b. Rimski-Korsakov uses four variations in his composition *Spanish Caprice.* The theme is in a two-part form, each part being nine measures in length. How does Rimski-Korsakov treat the variations?
   c. Listen to Lucien Cailliet's *Variations on the Theme 'Pop! Goes the Weasel.'* You will have to be somewhat of a musical detective in order to follow Cailliet's musical variations on this well-known melody. In which of the variations do you hear at least two of the jazz elements just described? Name the elements.

8. Jazz performers and composers often base their variations on themes of other composers. Compare the different ways that themes are treated in the following examples:
   a. *The Great Benny Goodman,* "Let's Dance," Columbia Records, CL–820.
   b. *Big Band Beat,* "Strike Up The Band," Richmond Records, B–20034.
   c. *Four Freshmen and Five Trombones,* "You Stepped Out of a Dream," Capitol Records, T–683.
   d. "Scheherajazz," Somerset Records, P–9700.
   e. *Barney Kessel Plays 'Carmen,'* Contemporary Records, 3563.
   f. *Dizzy in Greece,* "Anitra's Dance," Verve Records, MEV–8017 ("Anitra's Dance," Grieg, *Peer Gynt Suite*).

9. Listen to the Modern Jazz Quartet's rendition of the very familiar carol "God Rest Ye Merry Gentlemen" (*The Modern Jazz Quartet At Music Inn,* Atlantic Records, 1247). Describe as many of the jazz ingredients as you can, including specific instrumental sounds.

17. Homer Ulrich, *Music: A Design for Listening,* 2nd ed. (New York: Harcourt, Brace & World, Inc., 1962), p. 449.

To appreciate music the listener must be actively involved. Research studies indicate that in full appreciation of music, understanding and enjoyment go hand in hand. Passive listening to music will not bring intelligent musical enjoyment. Rather, musical enjoyment is fostered through active participation that includes understanding, careful listening, and emotional response. The thrust of all musical learning should be to develop a sensitized awareness of those expressive elements of music that will foster a wide range of musical interests and activities and a variety of musical pleasures. One music educator has some remarks about jazz and musical enjoyment:

The concert hall providing Beethoven and Bach offers a convenient refuge for the American since little confrontation could possibly arise from accepting carte blanche, the accepted. The paradox of the whole situation is that the American does not operate in this manner in his other spheres of living. In this respect he can become highly divergent, challenging, adventurous and even egotistical, when choosing his own experiences; yet, when he moves into the area of the fine arts he can become docile and congenial, partaking in those artistic activities which offer the least amount of exploration.

As the American follows this artistic sense on one track, the educational system of America on another tract adheres to a value system which rewards only one type of intelligence, one which can easily be assessed, tested and graded, thus only stroking lightly the "creative thinker". . . . Thus the divergent thinker is submerged in the competitive process of education and can only find solace in recognizing that the value system, which has inculcated millions of children and adults, has produced an artistic environment which can only cope with the tangible, the measured, and what in the final analysis is the most convenient.

The combination of the American in his competitive arena, the educational system in its stereotype value system, and the university consumed in perpetuating the traditional music of another continent, could only produce an American music educator and general educator who is thwarted intellectually when he approaches jazz as an art form and expressive language. It's not written; it's not tangible; it's too American; it's spontaneous, and if one can't play it or understand it, then the best thing to do is to disinherit it. Possibly even the music educator as well as the

2
How to Listen to Jazz

general educator, when it comes to the arts, has been endowed with a somewhat strict adherence to convenience, a most unfortunate dilemma for jazz.[1]

Listening Techniques

When listening to a composition the primary aim is to focus one's attention on the various musical events as they unfold—not an easy task. Mental concentration of a high order is needed. We are so conditioned to hearing music as a background accompaniment to daily activities—in the dentist's office, at the supermarket—that it is difficult to devote full attention to listening to music.

In daily living we encounter many spatial relationships—high walls and low walls, houses and garages, sidewalks and streets, country and urban vistas—that are immediately visual and easily identified. In listening to music we must forget visual mindedness and learn to concentrate on nonvisual elements.

Another difference is that music moves in time, and time relationships are less obvious in daily living. A painting, for example, can be viewed at leisure, and its parts can be observed in relationship to the whole. Not so with a musical composition. Memory becomes an important factor in listening to music. The mind must remember at one point what has transpired so that one part of a piece of music can be compared or contrasted with another part.

Finally, if we are to learn more about the structure of music, it is important to develop the ability to separate juxtaposed musical sounds and focus attention on a single musical element. For example, when identifying the ostinato bass employed in boogie-woogie playing, we must be able to shut out the right-hand piano sounds if we are to recognize what the left hand is realizing at the keyboard.

What to Listen for in Jazz

Persons who can bring to the listening experience a fund of musical knowledge have an advantage in gaining insight into jazz. But *knowledge about* music and an *understanding of* music are not the same. Simply stated, the first deals primarily with information (vocabulary), while the second relates to direct musical experiences involving concepts and possession of the vocabulary to express understanding of the concepts. The term *concept* suggests a mental image or a complete thought that has been acquired through the senses—hearing, seeing, feeling, and so on.

As you listen to music, you will find that the concepts of melody, rhythm, harmony, texture, design, and tone color are common to all music. However, some concepts of rhythm, for example, are treated differently or at least are more prominent in jazz than in other types of music.

As a preparatory exercise for listening to jazz, you will find it helpful to list under each main musical element words and concepts that you identify with that musical element. For example, (1) under *melody*: high, low, smooth, jagged, scale, skips, key, diatonic, and chromatic; (2) under *texture*: thick, thin, few instruments, many instruments, homophonic, polyphonic; (3) under *form*: repetition, contrast, theme, variations, imitation, section, part, three parts, improvisation; (4) under *harmony*: tension, relaxation, rounds, and chords; (5) under *rhythm*: fast, slow, weak accents, strong accents, beat, tempo, pattern, and meter; (6) under *tone*: piano, soprano, contralto, bass, trumpet, sax, clarinet, and bass drum.

Jazz Ensembles

An initial consideration in listening to jazz ensembles is the size of the instrumental group. Does it sound like a large group of ten to twenty or thirty players or does it sound like a small combo of two to six or eight instrumentalists? If the group is a large band and there is a soloist, the listener has very few real clues to the size of the organization unless the soloist is supported by some other part of the band besides the rhythm section. An example is a saxophone solo backed up by a trombone section consisting of three or four trombones or by the entire brass section including trumpets and trombones. While the ensemble is playing, listen for the "bigness" or "thickness" of the overall sound. Sometimes the total sound may be so full that it is almost overwhelming, such as the ensemble portion of Kenton's "Commencement."[2] Listen for complete sections of instruments—saxophone, trumpet, and trombone sections. The sections are quite easy to determine on most albums by bands like Count Basie.[3] Almost

1. Harry Evans, "On Jazz—From an Educator," *NAJE Educator* (Official magazine of the National Association of Jazz Educators) 2, no. 4 (April–May 1971): 17.

2. Stan Kenton, "Commencement," *The Jazz Story*, vol. 5, Capitol Records, W2141; Buddy Rich, "Westside Story," *Swingin' New Band*, Pacific Jazz Records, PJ-1013.

3. Count Basie, *The Best of Basie*, Roulette Records, R52018; $E=MC^2$, Roulette Records, R52003.

always, both large and small jazz groups have rhythm sections consisting of piano, bass, guitar, and drums. Some rhythm sections do not use all four, rather only piano with bass or bass and drums with piano.

Another problem with listening is that sometimes a small group or combo may confuse the ear by sounding larger than a full band if the playing and recording techniques are purposefully planned to give that illusion of sound. However, in a combo, listen for the individual instruments. Instead of the saxophone section, listen for the saxophone player; do this for other instrumentalists such as the trumpet or trombone player.[4]

Some Musical Concepts in Jazz

Melody

It is important that listeners of expressive jazz music listen for the melodic inventiveness or improvisation on a given melody or the musical interpretation of a given melody. The emotional tone communicated by the jazz performer often reveals the temperament of the player and of society in general at the time of the playing. Usually music is quite accurate in mirroring the temperament of the times—war, peace, and so on.

Listen as the performers create. Is the emotional tone excitement? Is it calm? (Can calm music be exciting?[5]) Performing music is extremely personal to be sure, but so is listening. One person cannot listen for another. Sometimes big bands are very outgoing or hot, like Basie's "Jumpin' at the Woodside" or "Every Tub."[6] However, this is not an exclusive element of large groups. Combos can produce the same feeling— listen to such recordings as Kenny Clarke's "Be a Good Girl."[7] The same outgoing big band can sometimes produce an extremely calm, even introverted, feeling. Such an example can be heard in Basie's "Blue and Sentimental" and "Lil' Darlin' " and in Woody Herman's "Misty Morning."[8]

A person who has little technical knowledge of music and who cannot name individual pitches on the staff still may be able to hear the differences between two melodies by feeling ascending tones as they move in steps and descending tones as they skip in varied moves.

Texture

The term *texture* as it is used in music refers to the different ways of treating a melody. It not only includes the various ways of filling the octave and various ways of using the beat, but it includes the many possibilities of repeating the same melody at different pitch levels, of combining two or more different melodies, or of providing a single melody with accompanying chords or harmonies.

A single melody with neither an accompanying melodic part or harmony is known as a *monophonic* construction. The field hollers of the slaves is a good example of a short melodic motive without any accompanying musical sounds.

Another way of treating a melody is to have two melodies start at the *same time* on *different pitch levels*. Another version starts two melodies at *different times* on the *same pitch level*. The combination of two voices singing or playing the same melody but entering at different times is called a *canon*. A canon repeated without a break is called a *round* (i.e., the melody chases itself around and around). The simultaneous sounding of one melody heard in imitation in another voice or instrument and the use of two or more different melodies of equal importance is known as *polyphonic* construction. Listening to polyphonic, or "horizontal," texture in music is somewhat analogous to watching a three-ring circus. You realize something important is going on in each of the three rings, but it is difficult to concentrate on them simultaneously. However, it all adds to the excitement of the moment.

A third way of treating a melody is to have all of the voices or instruments move together with a single melody, usually in the highest voice part. Harmony in the form of chords in the lower voices acts as an accompaniment to the single melody. This is called *homophonic*, or "vertical," construction. Hymns and spirituals are excellent examples of this type of melodic treatment.

4. Charlie Parker, "Another Hair Do," *Charlie Parker Memorial Album*, vol. 1, Savoy Records, MG–12000; Louis Armstrong, "I Gotta Right to Sing the Blues," *The Essential Louis Armstrong*, Verve Records, V–8569; Cannonball Adderley, "I Can't Get Started With You," *The Jazz Story*, vol. 5, Capitol Records, W2141.

5. Count Basie, "Blue and Sentimental," *The Best of Basie*, Roulette Records, R52081; Gerry Mulligan and Ben Webster, "Chelsea Bridge," *The Greatest Names in Jazz*, Verve Records, PR 2-3.

6. Count Basie, "Jumpin' at the Woodside," "Every Tub," *The Best of Basie*, and "The Kid from Redbank," *Basie E=MC².*

7. Kenny Clarke, "Be a Good Girl," *The Jazz Story*, vol. 5; Dizzy Gillespie and Charlie Parker, "Wee," *Jazz at Massey Hall*, Fantasy Records, 6003.

8. Count Basie, "Blue and Sentimental," *The Best of Basie*, and "Lil' Darlin'," *E=MC²*; Woody Herman "Misty Morning," *The Jazz Story*, vol. 5.

Form

The word *form* in music denotes both shorter parts or sections (repetition, contrast, etc.) and specific overall schematic designs (binary, ternary, rondo, etc.). Perception and understanding of the elements of form present a greater challenge in listening to music than they do in consideration of visual art. In music, the various parts of a composition are presented in time, and a listener can compare them by memory only.

Repetition is the presentation of the same musical material in two or more parts of a composition. Contrast, on the other hand, is the introduction of different musical material. From earliest times, repetition of a melody has played a vital role in prolonging a game, a dance, or a story. A similar reason for repetition is found in the work songs where repetition of the melody depends on the amount of work. Soon contrasting musical ideas were introduced in two- and three-part forms. Here the repetitions tend not only to expand each part, but also to give a feeling of balance and symmetry to the melody as a whole. If you understand the principles of repetition and contrast, you can sharpen your listening focus by anticipating the parts that are repeated and those that are contrasted. Thus, you will have a much better idea of what to listen to and for, and consequently you will enjoy the music more as it unfolds.

The basic units of form in music are often compared to the basic units in written language. The individual musical note is comparable to the single alphabetical letter in written language. The musical motive or figure (two or more tones forming a distinctive rhythmic-melodic pattern) is the equivalent of a language syllable or word. The first appearance of a phrase (usually four measures in length) denotes a language phrase. The extension of the phrase into two phrases or *period* (eight measures in length) denotes a language sentence. Sometimes language sentences are longer. In music, long phrases are called double periods, or phrase groups.

For easy identification, phrases and periods are designated by letters. The first phrase is called A, and as each new phrase appears, it is given a different letter (B, C, D, etc.).

The forms used extensively in jazz are the twelve-bar (measure) blues strain and the sixteen- and thirty-two-bar choruses that are usually designated ABAB or AABA.

The twelve-bar blues strain has two identical phrases of four measures each and a third phrase that is different. In the blues melody given in example 3, measures 1 through 4 are the first phrases, or A part.

Harmony

Closely akin to the need to recognize the melodic line is the necessity of response to the musical element of *harmony* in jazz. Harmony is the simultaneous sounding of two or more tones. Two tones sounding together make an interval. The effect produced by the interval depends upon the ratio between the vibrations created by the two tones. In general, simple ratios tend to be more harmonious and complex ratios more dissonant. For example, for most listeners the sound of three-tone chords with intervals of thirds seems pleasingly consonant and restful, whereas six- or seven-tone chords with intervals of thirds having more complex ratios seem to give listeners feelings of dissonance and tension.

A listener must decide whether the harmonies are too simple, have little variety, and hence are of little interest. In more academic terms, the harmonies or chord progressions should have a sense of forward motion. Sometimes a composition has a pleasing melodic line but is quite dull harmonically. The opposite situation occurs when the composer-arranger or piano soloist is so intent on playing interesting harmonies that the music sounds contrived. This seemed to be prevalent with some large bands in the 1940s and again in the 1960s. Rather than complex harmonies with very little melodic originality, a balance between the two is usually more acceptable.

Rhythm

Rhythm is the very heart of nature and of man. It is the pulse of life and is found in all kinds of physical activity. We unconsciously use rhythm—in walking, dancing, running, skipping, and so forth. However, *rhythm* is a generic term and has many meanings.

In music one basic element of *rhythm* is the repetition of sound, either felt or heard, called the beat, or pulse, of the music. To feel the beat or pulse of the music, listen and tap or clap the regular repetitions generated by the musical sound.

Although beat is a constant force in every composition, the speed of the beats varies greatly, and depends on the feeling, tone, and mood of the music. In some music the beat is fast; in others it is quite slow. The speed of the beat is called the *tempo*. Hence, when we say that the rhythm is slowing down, we mean that the beat is moving at a slower rate.

Occasions occur in which a great rhythmic pulse is felt but no melodic line is realized; the rhythm section merely sets a mood. These sections are usually called *vamps*. Some contemporary players play on melodic instruments but avoid the usual concept of melody. They say that they are playing a mood or an attitude. Listen to Joe Harriott's "Shadows."[9] (Mood and attitude are discussed more fully in chapter 13.) There are many situations in which there is a definite melody,

9. Joe Harriott, "Shadows," *The Jazz Story*, vol. 5; Archie Shepp, "The Chased," *The Definitive Jazz Scene*, vol. 3, Impulse Records, A-99; "The Mac Man," *On This Night*, Impulse Records, A-97.

Example 3

Blues Melody

When the notes in the second line of a song look the same as in the first line or phrase they also sound the same. As you can tell, the second phrase of the song (measures 5 to 8) looks and sounds exactly like the first phrase. This phrase may also be indicated by an "A":

The third phrase (measures 9 to 12) is obviously different. Therefore, it is indicated by the letter "B":

Next examine carefully the AABA song (example 4). Look at the first period (measures 1 to 8). This is the A part. Now compare the second part (measures 9 to 16) with the A part. You will discover that the A part and the second part are identical. Thus far we have AA. Examine measures 17 to 24. You will discover that this part is different from the A part and is therefore called B. Look at the remainder of the song (measures 25 to 32). As you can see, this is the same as the A part, with a slight variation in the ending. This is the most commonly used form in jazz—the three-part form, or AABA thirty-two-bar chorus.

Example 4

AABA Song

but it is subservient to the rhythmic sounds. It is primarily this rhythmic pulse or juxtaposition of patterns that expresses the emotion. The technique is quite common in many rock and jazz/rock recordings.[10]

One of the most important elements of rhythm is duration. The performing musician is concerned with translating the symbols on a page of music into sounds and silences (tone pauses, or "rests"). These sounds and silences may be of any duration. For this reason, clapping the rhythmic pattern does not accurately represent a melody, since the claps are all of equal duration.

Listen to the ticking of a clock. Do some of the ticks seem to be stronger than others? Try tapping on the table with your hand, imitating the regularity of

10. Blood, Sweat & Tears, "Spinning Wheel," *Blood, Sweat and Tears*, Columbia Records, CS9720.

Example 5A

4/4 or flat four

$\frac{4}{4}$ ♩ ♩ ♩ ♩ | ♩ ♩ ♩ ♩ |

Example 5B

2/4 in classical music

$\frac{2}{4}$ ♩ ♩ | ♩ ♩ |

Example 5C

2/4 in jazz

¢ ♩ ♩ ♩ ♩ | ♩ ♩ ♩ ♩ |
   > > > > > > > >

the sound of a clock. Next, tap one beat louder than the following beat. Alternate between loud taps and soft taps. Try tapping one loud beat followed by two soft beats. You should find that in one case the beats occur in groupings of twos and in the other case in groupings of threes. The easiest approach to understanding accent, the basis of meter, is to study the grouping of louds and softs into twos, threes, fours, or more. Meter is the regular (or irregular) grouping of beats according to accent.

In musical notation the time signature located at the beginning of a composition tells a player that the music moves in groupings of threes, fours, or whatever. There are complete styles of jazz that stay primarily in one meter grouping, and the listener should be able to detect these groupings fairly easily. The feeling of 4/4, or flat-four, is used by players of Early New Orleans Dixieland, by most swing players, and by a great many bop and cool players.[11]

When 2/4 meter is designated in jazz music, it denotes something different from 2/4 meter in classical music. In classical music, it means there are two beats to each measure and quarter notes receive one beat. In jazz, however, it means that there are four beats to the measure but that the second and fourth beats are accented. Hence, a jazz player never snaps his fingers or claps his hands on beats one and three but always on beats two and four as shown by the accents in examples 5A, 5B, and 5C. This is the only time when meter indication (time signature) in jazz is different than in other music.

The 2/4 beat in jazz is heard most prominently in ragtime and Chicago Style Dixieland music.[12] When

funky-style jazz music has four beats to the measure, the second and fourth beats are accented. Sometimes, however, funky is played in 3/4 meter. Rock drummers accent the second and fourth beats, feeling that it adds interest and momentum. Very good jazz, by both small combos and large orchestras, is performed in 3/4 meter.[13]

The style of jazz called boogie-woogie is performed in 8/8 meter, eight beats to each measure. (See chapter 8.) In fact, it is the identifying feature of this style, whether it is a piano solo or a large band.[14] Rock players make excellent use of 8/8 meter without actually playing boogie-woogie. They seem to use 4/4 meter in a double-time fashion.[15]

Tone

Another important consideration in listening to music is *tone*. Some listeners prefer instrumental tones to have a soft, pretty sound, while other listeners consider this tone quality to lack intensity, sincerity, and even confidence. These listeners prefer to hear the type of tone made by a very strong trumpet player, for example. Which sound do you find more interesting: a smooth, pretty tone or a rough, aggressive sound? Listening is very personal, almost as personal as performing.

One of the most important points to be considered is the creativeness of individual players. Do their thoughts sound interesting and fresh or are they playing old clichés that should be forgotten? Players have been known to improvise several consecutive choruses on just one tone. This kind of playing lacks all imagination. On the other hand, some players improvise lines

11. Record in this textbook.

12. Record in this textbook.

13. Clark Terry, "Hammer-head Waltz," *The Definitive Jazz Scene*, vol. 1, Impulse Records, A99; Les McCann, "A Little 3/4 for God and Company," *The Truth*, Pacific Jazz Records, PJ–2; Tommy Vig, "Sunrise Sunset," *The Sound of the Seventies*, Milestone Records, 9007.

14. Meade Lux Lewis, "Honky Tonk Train," *Boogie-woogie*, Folkways Records, FJ2810; Will Bradley, "Beat Me Daddy, Eight to the Bar," Columbia Records, 35530; Count Basie, "Boogie-woogie," Columbia Records, 35959; Tommy Dorsey, "Boogie-woogie," Victor Records, 26054; Benny Goodman, "Roll 'Em," Victor Records, 25627.

15. Spirit, "Topanga Windows," *Spirit*, Ode 70 Records, Z18–4404.

so far ahead of their contemporaries that acceptance and acclaim come too late to be of much satisfaction.

The real judge, of course, is the listener who must hear the melodies, perceive the rhythm, detect the tone, and so on. Jazz observers are not particularly impressed by classical correctness. They hear enough excellent piano from Art Tatum to consider him a genius. They are not disturbed at all that Tatum's fingering was atrocious. Jazz listeners hear creativeness from Gillespie's trumpet and are not disturbed by the way he puffs out the cheeks. Present-day jazz observers actually appreciate the primitive approach to playing of many early jazz performers, most of whom had little or no musical schooling. Their lack of schooling, of knowing how to perform "correctly" by European standards, gave the early players a freedom that endears them to most jazz listeners.

One should be reminded that the "test of time" commonly used to judge classical music is not appropriate for jazz. It is true that there are jazz classics (Armstrong's "Savoy Blues," Hawkins' "Body and Soul," Parker's "Ornithology," and many others), but jazz players are much more concerned with immediate communication. In fact, many players do not like to compare their present playing style to works they have done in the past; they like to think that they have improved their style by fresher, more contemporary inventiveness and creativity.

Listening Suggestions

Techniques of perceptive listening improve as one develops an understanding of the musical vocabulary of jazz (and of other music). The jazz Listening Guide provided here (page 16) was developed to give students a systematic aid to use in identifying what to listen to and for. This indentification leads to the development of effective listening habits.

A valuable aid in developing perceptive listening is to listen to a composition with other persons. After the first hearing, freely exchange ideas with the other listeners about what has been heard. After a brief discussion period, replay the record. This experience tends to improve one's ability to concentrate as well as to pick up previously missed nuances.

Read the Listening Guide before listening to be sure that you understand what the various items in the Guide mean. After the first hearing, quickly respond to the items you can identify easily. Do not labor over items about which you are unsure. After the second hearing, go back and fill in all the remaining items on the Guide. Obviously, some items may not apply to every listening experience. Effective listening takes practice by the listener as well as guidance by a teacher.

Passive listening will not aid in developing understanding and enjoyment of jazz. Listeners must train themselves to listen *to* and *for* the content of the music and to respond actively, not only emotionally but intellectually. The next step is for each listener to develop a specific set of references to use in deciding whether he or she enjoys and understands jazz.

Suggested Classroom Activities

1. If you were asked to describe why you prefer a particular type of music, what would you say?

2. In your own words, define the following: melody, harmony, rhythm, design, and timbre, or tone color.

3. Skilled listeners should be able to focus attention on different musical elements as they listen. Listen several times to *Yancey Stomp* by Jimmy Yancey, pianist (Jazz vol. 10, Folkways Records, FJ 2810) and answer the following:
   a. Does the music have an introduction?
   b. Is the left hand at the piano (the bass part) realizing mostly harmony or a repeated melodic figure?
   c. Is the right hand realizing a distinguishable melodic line or short figures that seem almost harmonic in total effect?
   d. Is the meter in duple or triple feeling?

4. Listen to "Silver" from the album *The Modern Jazz Quartet with Laurindo Almeida* (Atlantic Records, 1429) and answer the following:
   a. Is the ensemble a large group or a small combo?
   b. See how many of the following instruments you can identify in the tune: violin, vibraphones, saxophone, oboe, piano, percussion (drums and others), string bass, and amplified guitar.

5. Listen to the three-part form of "Fish This Week" as played by Les McCann (*Les McCann Plays The Truth*, Pacific Jazz Records, PJ–2). Listen for the expanded improvised bridge part: A, A, B, bridge, A.

Listening Guide

Melody

Parts with jazz interpretation
All parts improvised
Parts improvised
Uses blue tones

Tempo

Slow
Fast
Moderate speed
Extremely fast

Meter

2/4
3/4
4/4 (flat-four)
Other

Rhythm

Syncopated patterns very fast

Harmony

Relaxed (not complex)
Uses IV to I
Tense (complex)
Chord progressions

Texture

Vertical (homophonic)
Horizontal (polyphonic)
Both

Tone color

Solo spots played by
piano
cornet (trumpet)
clarinet
trombone
saxophone
guitar
banjo
string bass
percussion
other (name)
other (name)
other (name)

Form

Twelve-bar blues
AABA
ABAB
Other (identify)

Size of group

Small (2 to 8 players)
Large, with sections

Mood or feeling tone

Sweet, calm, smooth
Soulful
Frantic, driving
Rough, aggressive
Happy
Low key, understatement
Other

Era or style

Piano style

Left hand (bass part in 2/4 rhythm)
Left hand (walking bass)
Left hand (chordal)
Other

Other jazz influences

Liturgical
Electronic
Free form
Classical
Rock
Contemporary large band

3
Jazz Heritages

African and European

The beginnings of jazz came about through a blending of the musical cultures of Africa and Europe. From the merging of these heritages came American jazz. That the blending has never ceased is shown not only by the addition of more complex rhythms from Africa in the 1940s, but also by the innovation of present-day third-stream music with its use of European musical forms. Too often, it has been stated that jazz is the music of the black man. This belief contains two quite erroneous implications: first, that only blacks can play jazz, thereby excluding such white musicians as Goodman, Teagarden, Beiderbecke, and Evans, and second, that blacks are successful in no other kind of music. There are far too many excellent musicians to begin to list the talented nonjazz black artists, both composers and performers. However, the point should be made clear that each new style (or era) in jazz was pioneered by an American Negro musician. Any talented player of any race can probably learn to play the different styles. Race has nothing to do with developing a style after its innovation, but the American black was and is the innovator.

Mrs. William Grant Still (Verna Arvey), the wife of an outstanding black classical composer, discussed this question as it related to her husband and George Gershwin:

It was with considerable surprise that I read in a recent book (Music in the Twentieth Century, *by William W. Austin, published by W.W. Norton and Company, 1966) by a Cornell University professor, the statement that "Gershwin's* Rhapsody *helped inspire William Grant Still to make use of Jazz and Negro folk song in his symphonies and operas." Surprise, because it seemed so unrealistic to assume that a Negro composer could have been motivated by a white composer who had made no secret of his own devotion to Negro musicians and their music.*

For Gershwin's indebtedness has been well documented over the years, and it does no disservice to his memory to acknowledge it, since he himself did just that during his lifetime. One of these acknowledgments came when on August 30, 1926 he autographed a copy of his Rhapsody in Blue *to W.C. Handy. "For Mr. Handy" he wrote respectfully (for at the time the beloved Father of the Blues was almost twice his age), "Whose early 'blue' songs are the forefathers of this work. With admiration and best wishes."*

Those people who lived—as did Gershwin—through the exciting Twenties in New York can attest to the presence of both Gershwins (George and Ira) at nearly every place where Negroes were performing, or even enjoying themselves at parties.[1]

Music was by far the most vital and demonstrative form of expression in the life of the Africans. From morning until night, from the cradle to the grave, everything was done to the rhythm of their music. The art form was passed down by word of mouth from one generation to the next. It was a means of preserving tribal traditions, ambitions, and lore. Music performed a vital role in maintaining the unity of the social group. Singing the same songs in the same way at the same time bound individuals together and established a strong group feeling. Whether religious or secular, improvised or traditional, the music of the Africans was a powerful influence in their lives.

In Africa, music was for a whole community, and everyone from youngest to oldest participated. Music was so interwoven with work, play, and social and religious activities that to isolate one phase from its role in the total life of the people is difficult. The Africans themselves did not consider their music an art. Arts are seldom taken seriously in their birthplace. Innovators, Charlie Parker for example, have always suffered from this fact.

Many of the daily activities within a tribe were accompanied by the pulse and beating of a drum. It was a part of religious ceremonies and special occasions such as births, deaths, and weddings. Drums, ranging in size from very small hand drums to great tree drums, sometimes fifteen feet high, were used to frighten wild beasts and to bolster courage in times of emergency. The drum served as one fundamental means of coordinating the movements of the wonderful rhythmic native dances, aided hunting parties, and played an important part in sport and physical exhibitions.

It was this background, brought by African slaves to the United States and nurtured in the woe and hardship of slavery, that provided the seeds of jazz as we know it today. Obviously the slaves did not intentionally invent a new music at this point; the new music arose unconsciously out of the transplantation of the black culture and the blacks' struggle for survival.

One common misconception about the origins of jazz is that jazz rhythms came from Africa. Actually, it is only the *emphasis* on rhythm that can truly be designated African, not the direct influence of any specific rhythmic pattern.[2] There are three important points to keep in mind concerning Africans and rhythmic sounds: (1) religion is very important in the culture of Africans, a daily way of life, not just a Sunday activity; (2) African religion is greatly oriented toward ritual—their sincerest form of expression; and (3) African ritual has always involved a great deal of dancing; hence, rhythmic sounds have always been very important in the lives of the Africans.

We do not imply that European music is not rhythmic. A very short excursion into Bach, for example, reveals that if his inventions are not played rhythmically they are not played well. At the time when the chief exponents of jazz were generically closest to their African ancestry, the rhythms utilized by these jazz performers were of a very simple nature, far removed from the complex pattern combinations actually used by the natives in Africa. The rhythm used by these early jazz players generally consisted of quarter notes evenly spaced in the measure of music without syncopation or accent. At this time the very complex African rhythms should have been most influential upon their performance!

However, emphasis on rhythm is such a natural element in African life that even African languages are very rhythm oriented. Because of their rhythmic culture, Africans were interested in Spanish music. Some researchers even state that the main reason Spanish music is so rhythmical is because Spain was once conquered by the Moors from North Africa. Thus, it is conceivable that slaves in America heard something from their past in this particular branch of European music. In a pamphlet entitled *Afro-American Music* printed by the Music Educators National Conference, William Tallmadge writes of African penetration into Spain:

This penetration occurred during the Mohammedan conquest (758–1492), and accounts for much of the highly individualistic and non-European rhythmic character of Spanish music. Spanish fandangos, tangos, habaneras, etc., were derived from African antecedents. This Spanish music readily amalgamated with the music of the African slaves who were shipped to Latin American countries as early as 1510. Afro-Spanish music influenced the music in North America in two ways: through Spanish possessions in America and through the importation of slaves into America from Spanish colonies. Since New Orleans played such an important part in the early development of jazz, it should be mentioned that Spain controlled that city from 1763 to 1803.

1. Verna Arvey, "Afro-American Music Memo," *Music Journal* 27, no. 9 (November 1969):36.

2. "Royal Drums of the Abatusi," *History of Classic Jazz,* Riverside Records, SDP–11.

It was soon discovered that slaves adjusted themselves to conditions in North America much better if they were first shipped to the West Indies and acclimatized there before being sent on. Latin American influences have, therefore, been a factor in Afro-American music from earliest times. "Jelly Roll" Morton, a jazz pioneer, once stated that Spanish rhythms were a part of jazz. In connection with that statement one might point out that the traditional bass pattern of [one strain of] the "St. Louis Blues" is a tango. Latin American rhythms continue to exert an influence on the progress of jazz, as these rhythmic patterns are employed in many contemporary styles.[3]

There is no doubt that the Moorish conquest considerably changed the music of Spain, Portugal, and Southern France. Therefore, European music brought to the United States had already been influenced by Africa. The Caribbean Islands were French or Spanish possessions before they became British. Many slaves brought to America were first kept on these islands for months and sometimes for years, and thus were heavily exposed to French or Spanish music before ever arriving in the United States.

The call-and-response pattern heard recurrently in jazz can be traced directly to African tribal traditions. In its original form, the call and response was a ritual in which a leader shouted a cry to which the group responded.[4] A common, present-day form is a congregation's response to a minister or other leader. One hears the influence of the call-and-response pattern constantly in jazz. One example is the musical instance called "trading fours," when two improvising instrumentalists play solo parts on alternating four bars. In short, they are responding to each other's musical thoughts.[5] This interplay can be heard on many jazz recordings. Listen to Stanley Turrentine on tenor saxophone and Kenny Burrell on guitar as they use a minor blues tune to go as far as to alternate single measures of improvisation.[6] At one spot in "Casa Loma Stomp" the complete brass and saxophone sections alternate with one measure apiece.[7] Another example is when a soloing instrument "calls" and is responded to by the background melodic and/or percussive figures of the other members of the band or by a specific section of the band. Listen to the entire band responding to Count Basie's piano in "Queer Street."[8] On the swing part of the record in the back of this book, the clarinet solo is answered by the trombone section; later, the saxophone section is answered by the brass section. In Manny Albam's "Blues Company," Oliver Nelson

and Phil Woods on saxophones are answered by trombones.[9] In Benny Goodman's "King Porter Stomp," Goodman's clarinet has the brass section as a background, whereas the saxophone section is the background for Harry James's trumpet solo. Later in the same selection, the brass and saxes alternate measures.[10]

The melodic feature of jazz is inherited directly from European music. The diatonic and chromatic scales used in jazz are the same as those used for centuries by European composers, whereas Africans used a pentatonic scale.

The harmonic sonorities also derive from European sources: polkas, quadrilles, hymns, and marches. This does not dispute the fact that Africans had varying pitches in their drums, reeds, logs; but the sense of harmony absorbed by jazz is strictly that of the European school.

The Afro-Americans who first sang gospel music, work songs, and the like, satisfied the desire to imitate rich European melody and harmony. On the other hand, nothing in European music could compare with their oral sonority and the vitality of their music, so blessed with rhythmic tradition.

The musical forms of Europe became standard in jazz works. The twelve-bar strains such as those found in the blues are directly traceable to very early European music. A great majority of jazz is constructed in a theme-and-variations form. The Africans were not concerned with symmetry of form. In fact, if their music resulted in a symmetrical construction, they considered it crude and unimaginative.

The evolution of African music in the colonies greatly depended on the particular colony to which the slaves were brought. In the Latin Catholic colonies, their musical life was allowed more latitude. Latin planters were not too concerned with the activities of

3.   William Tallmadge, "Afro-American Music," *Music Educators National Conference,* Washington, D.C., 1957. Authors' brackets.

4.   Ethnic Folkways Library, 01482B, vol. 1, Secular.

5.   Santos Brothers, "Beat the Devil," *Jazz for Two Trumpets,* Metro Jazz Records, E1015.

6.   Kenny Burrell, "Chittlins Con Carne," *Three Decades of Jazz,* vol. 1 (1959–1969), Blue Note Records, BST89904.

7.   Glen Gray, "Casa Loma Stomp," *The Jazz Story,* vol. 4, Capitol Records, W2140.

8.   Count Basie, "Queer Street," Columbia Records, 36889.

9.   Manny Albam, "Blues Company," *The Definitive Jazz Scene,* vol. 2, Impulse Records, A–100.

10.   Benny Goodman, "King Porter Stomp," *The Great Benny Goodman,* Columbia Records, CL820.

the slaves as long as the work was done. Thus, the slaves were allowed to play their drums and sing and dance when not working. The British Protestants, on the other hand, tried to convert the slaves to Christianity. The slaves in these colonies were required to conceal their pagan musical inheritance. (It might be interesting to speculate about how the resulting music would have sounded if the slaves from Africa had been taken to some part of Asia. If African and Japanese music, for example, had influenced each other centuries ago, what would be the result? Would it resemble any music we know today?)

The name Congo Square is frequently mentioned in many accounts of jazz. Congo Square was a large field in New Orleans (called Beauregard Square today) where slaves were allowed to gather on Sunday to sing, dance, and play their drums in their native traditional manner. The principal significance of Congo Square to the history of jazz was that it gave this original African music a place to be heard where it "could influence and be influenced by European music."[11] When the famous dances of Congo Square began around 1817, the background of the participants produced a music that was often a cross between French and Spanish, with African rhythms.

About ten years after the Civil War, a segregation movement began. The Creoles were ostracized from white society and joined the ranks of the true Negro. Until segregation, the Creoles had enjoyed the rights and privileges of whites, which included conservatory training for musicians. The amalgamation of the musical talents of conservatory-trained Creoles and the spontaneous oral tradition of blacks resulted in an interchange of musical expression. The music that evolved from this early assimilation was one of the beginnings of jazz. The unfavorable aspects of this segregation movement are still apparent today, as pointed out by Charles Suber:

There is a sociological reason why more black student musicians are not involved in jazz. That reason lies in the images retained by many black educators, school administrators, and community leaders. Jazz means slavery, sporting houses, "natural rhythm" and sin and damnation. Jazz stands for those unpleasant things that could "reduce endowments" or "debase our cultural standards."[12]

An interesting point is that so much of the music teaching in the United States propagates the theory that the music that stems from European culture typifies what is good in the arts; yet the Europeans accepted jazz as an art form long before the Americans. It is often felt

that jazz players are unregimented individualists who play together cohesively with a mutual feeling; these opposing concepts (individuality and unity) represent the freedom of America.

Most jazz historians leave a considerable gap between the activities at Congo Square and the first known jazz band led by Buddy Bolden at the turn of the century. In actuality, there was no gap because it was filled by the Creole music in New Orleans. It was natural that this music was mainly French and Spanish and much more advanced (at least by European standards) than the music of the first jazz bands. Henry Pleasants points to the similarities of jazz and early European music:

What I want to stress, however, is not the differences separating the two idioms, but the similarities. The differences are, indeed, startling and disturbing to those who think of the traditional European criteria as immutable, so startling and disturbing that they have tended to overshadow and obscure the similarities. But it is in the similarities that I see a fertile area for the reconciliation of long standing incompatibility and for a fruitful give-and-take in music education.

This reconciliation is easier the further back we go in European musical history. The most common form of jazz has always been theme and variations, advanced and refined in bebop to something closer to chaconne or passacaglia. The jazz band arrangement or original composition bears an unmistakable resemblance to the concerto grosso of the eighteenth century. Without its distinctive rhythmic and phrasing characteristics, the jazz combo is indistinguishable from the Baroque chamber group.

Let me be precise about this. If I were a teacher today, trying to give my students an insight into seventeenth- and eighteenth-century musical conventions, I would suggest that they study sympathetically the conventions of jazz. How to fill in a bass line in continuo playing, for example; how to improvise from a figured bass. Every jazz pianist and every jazz bass player does it, and the best of them do it superbly. Or how to apply ornaments and embellishments. Every jazz musician does it, and the best of them do it every

11. Marshall Stearns, *The Story of Jazz* (London: Oxford University Press, 1958), p. 38.

12. Charles Suber, "The First Chorus," *Down Beat* 36, no. 9 (May 1969):4.

bit as well as it was done in the seventeenth and eighteenth centuries, and probably better. And the embellishments, I hasten to add, are essentially the same.

If I were a singing teacher trying to assist my pupil to a mastery of seventeenth- and eighteenth-century practices, I would have them listen to Frank Sinatra, Sarah Vaughan, Ella Fitzgerald, and Peggy Lee. If you want to know what appoggiatura and rubato are all about, listen to Sinatra. No one has ever used them better than he. If you want to study the mordent, listen to Bing Crosby. If you want to know about the portamento and slurs and melodic deviation, listen to Sarah Vaughan. None of these singers, I may assume, think in those terms. They may not use those terms, but they do use those devices. And what makes their use of them so instructive is the spontaneity. They use tempo rubato, appoggiatura, mordent, slur, portamento, and so on not because they are told that someone else used them two or three hundred years ago, but because they feel they are appropriate or even essential to the articulation of text and melodic line, which is precisely why they came into use in the first place.[13]

Field Hollers (Cries)

In West Africa there was no art music, by European standards, only functional music used for work, love, war, ceremonies, or merely communication. Slaves were often not allowed to talk to one another in the fields while working, but garbled singing was permitted. They established communication between themselves by field hollers, or cries, that whites could not understand. The outstanding element of the field cry that is constantly utilized in jazz is the bending of a tone.[14] This is simply the over-exaggerated use of a slide or slur. A tone is bent (slurred) upward to a different tone or pitch, downward to another pitch, upward to no specific tone, or downward to no specific tone. Examples of the four typical ways of employing this feature in jazz are as follows:

1. Example 6A demonstrates the bending of a minor third up to a major third.
2. Example 6B uses an old blues cliché to show the bending of a fifth downward to a flatted fifth.

Example 6A
(Side 1, Band 2A)

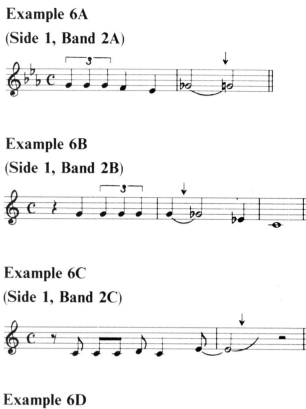

Example 6B
(Side 1, Band 2B)

Example 6C
(Side 1, Band 2C)

Example 6D
(Side 1, Band 2D)

3. Example 6C illustrates the bending of a tone upward to no specific pitch.
4. Example 6D illustrates the bending of a tone downward to no specific tone. As it is demonstrated here it is a "fall off." Every jazz fan has heard ensemble endings with this type of bending.

The adaptation of these effects allowed the musician a freedom of embellishment not available in European music.

13. Henry Pleasants, "Afro-American Epoch—Emergence of a New Idiom," *Music Educators Journal* 57, no. 1 (September 1970): 35–36.

14. "Field Cries or Hollers," Album 8, Library of Congress Recording.

Example 7

GRUNT   GRUNT

Work Songs

Rex Harris has described work songs as "tribal songs which started life in West Africa."[15] In addition he stated that they were used "to ease the monotony of a regular task and to synchronize a word or exclamation with a regularly repeated action."[16] An example of this type of work song is the "Song of the Volga Boatman," probably the most well known of all work songs. In example 7, the grunt indicates the exact time when concerted action is to take place—in this case, pulling on the oars. (Circus workers standing in a circle hammering huge tent stakes are another example of accomplishing a difficult task through rhythmic coordination.)

A good work-song leader was very essential in coordinating efforts of the workers. He not only caused the work to be more efficient, but also helped to make time pass. Huddie Ledbetter (Leadbelly) is reputed to have been one of the best "leadmen" ever, and there are recordings available to prove it.[17]

Though work songs varied according to their use, the main contribution of the work song to jazz was the emphasis on rhythm and meter.

Religious Music

"The impact of Christianity on the Afro-Americans was, of course, the origin of the spiritual; owing to the fact that practically all of the missionary work was done by nonconformist ministers, their evangelical hymns set the style and flavour of the spiritual as we know it today."[18] Around 1800 a religious mass movement in this country known as The Great Awakening occurred. Spirituals and revival hymns with a great amount of emotion were sung at camp meetings. Spirituals, often called hymns with a beat, were the first original songs created by Protestant black slaves on American soil. Spirituals are an excellent example of the blend of African and European cultures and can be easily traced back to 1780. Most seemed to have originated between 1790 and 1883. The slaves added their own rhythmic emphasis to any music taught to them, liturgical or other kind. The better-known spirituals of today are the type that were generally heard in large concert halls. Examples are the familiar "Swing Low, Sweet Chariot" and "Nobody Knows the Trouble I've Seen." The European influence of more emphasis on melody and harmony than on rhythm is obvious in these songs. The greatest number of spirituals performed in the 1800s employed a call-and-response pattern,[19] in which there was great emphasis on rhythm, with hand clapping and foot stomping—an example of the West African influence on European liturgy. The clapping and stomping was in a set pattern of emphasis on the second and fourth beats; as Borneman states, "the accent was shifted from the strong to the weak beat."[20] Piano players executed this rhythmic accentuation with their left hand and brought it to ragtime music.

There are many similarities between popular songs and rhythms and religious music in black church services today. Methodist John Wesley once defended such similarities: "Why should the devil be the only one to make pleasing music?"[21]

The fervent participation in their 'syncopated hymns' is something very remote from the Western conception of reverent quietude as an expression of worship, but hymns without beat are to the Negro religion without God. It is as natural, and no more naive, for them to sing hymns in this style as it was for Renaissance painters to portray Christ in Italian dress and environment.[22]

15. Rex Harris, *Jazz* (Baltimore, Md.: Penguin Books, 1956), p. 34.

16. Ibid., p. 30.

17. *Leadbelly,* Columbia Records, C–30035.

18. Harris, *Jazz,* p. 47.

19. Stearns, *Story of Jazz,* p. 93.

20. Ernest Borneman, "The Roots of Jazz," in *Jazz,* eds. Nat Hentoff and Albert J. McCarthy (New York: Holt, Rinehart & Winston, 1959), p. 17.

21. Andre Francis, *Jazz* (New York: Grove Press, 1960), p. 20.

22. Avril Dankworth, *Jazz, An Introduction to Its Musical Basis* (London: Oxford University Press, 1968), p. 49.

Early black church music can be divided into three categories: (1) Many of the selections were improvised, made up at the moment by the preacher and his congregation; they would be remembered and eventually notated. Many of these were based on the blues chord progression because of its simplicity and the fact that this progression seemed natural and flowing. (2) Some Negro congregations would adopt European church music and add not only their own rhythmic concepts, but also their own variations. (3) In many cases, African ritual music was altered so that it could be utilized in these services on this continent.

"There are gospel songs with hillbilly and cowboy, mambo, waltz, and boogie-woogie rhythms. But most of all, the gospel songs have a strong, full beat."[23] Also it must be remembered that spirituals and gospel songs are not necessarily musical works of yesterday; their thoughts and their very lyrics are often contemporary. In fact, there is a fine set of recordings (four sides) that includes a collection of gospel songs recorded between 1926 and 1968.[24]

Spirituals sometimes contained symbolic references to the railways or rivers that led to freedom or to heaven, and sometimes the songs gave directions for escaping from slavery. Most spirituals and gospel songs refer to biblical characters such as Daniel, Moses, Joshua, Gabriel, and so forth. Many are not only well-known choral and nonjazz instrumental melodies ("Nobody Knows the Trouble I've Seen," "Swing Low, Sweet Chariot," etc.), but also standard dixieland and other jazz pieces ("When the Saints Go Marching In," "A Closer Walk With Thee," etc.).

Gospel songs and spirituals are often considered to be religious forms of the blues. Blues singer T-Bone Walker agreed:

Of course, the blues comes a lot from the church, too. The first time I ever heard a boogie-woogie piano was the first time I went to church. That was the Holy Ghost Church in Dallas, Texas. That boogie-woogie was a kind of blues, I guess. Then the preacher used to preach in a bluesy tone sometimes. . . . Lots of people think I'm going to be a preacher when I quit this business because of the way I sing the blues. They say that it sounds like a sermon.

The visitor to a church in Harlem, or on Chicago's South Side, will not find a great contrast to the ecstatic atmosphere that might be found at a jazz concert or in a jazz club. He will find the identical rhythms, the same beat, and the same swing in the music. Frequently, he will find jazz instruments—saxophones, trombones, drums; he will hear boogie-woogie bass lines and blues structures and see enraptured people who beat time with their hands and sometimes even begin to dance.[25]

In the early Catholic churches, participation in the services by even the most faithful worshippers was limited. In the Latin Catholic colonies, slaves often worshipped a combination of Catholic saints and voodoo deities:

On the English and Protestant side, the question is as diverse as are the numerous sects of the reformed churches. The Protestant churches are less rigid than the Catholic church; one listens to the sermon and then freely sings hymns. It is this freedom which allows one to celebrate God according to one's own conscience which was to encourage a host of Negroes into the Protestant religions. Furthermore, God, among the Protestants, is praised in everyday language and not in the dead language, Latin. This permitted the Negroes to sing to God according to their hearts and according to some of their own traditions. The ancestral rhythm was reborn, transfiguring a religion.[26]

Methodist hymns were the most emotional, but even these were too somber for the slaves, and therefore improvisation gradually began to creep into hymn singing. "The hymn book of the day stressed part-singing which harmonized only by accident."[27] This accidental vocal harmonization indicates that the voice lines were invented independently of each other. In music this is known as polyphonic (horizontal) construction. This approach to the creation of musical line was carried over into dixieland music and was also later employed

23. From the *Jazz Book: From New Orleans to Rock and Free Jazz* by Joachim Berendt, translated by Dan Morgenstern, copyright 1975 Lawrence Hill & Co., Westport, Connecticut.

24. *The Gospel Sound*, Columbia Records, KG 31086/KG 31595.

25. From the *Jazz Book: From New Orleans to Rock and Free Jazz* by Joachim Berendt, translated by Dan Morgenstern, copyright 1975 Lawrence Hill & Co., Westport, Connecticut.

26. Francis, *Jazz*, p. 20.

27. Stearns, *Story of Jazz*, p. 63.

in more contemporary jazz styles. Examples 8A and 8B demonstrate the difference between polyphonic and homophonic (vertical) harmonization. Example 8A is polyphonically constructed and shows the independence of the harmonic line. Example 8B is homophonically constructed and demonstrates the extreme dependency of the harmony part upon the melody.

There appears to be some confusion about the difference between spirituals and gospel songs. Often the two words are used interchangeably. However, gospel songs are usually considered religious songs that recount passages from the scriptures, and spirituals are considered hymns.[28]

In 1867, a choral group from Fisk University in Nashville, Tennessee, left school to do a series of concerts to raise money for their college. This group, called the Fisk Jubilee Singers (*jubilee* is another name for a very spirited, joyful hymn), traveled all over the United States, England, and Europe, carrying spirituals, gospel songs, and work songs to an international audience. Examples of this type of singing today are heard in the records of Mahalia Jackson.[29] Generally speaking, most gospel music is very simple in melody and harmony. The excitement comes from the jazz type of rhythmic pulse. Gospel music as an art form was all but ignored until the recognition, or rather the great triumphs, of Mahalia Jackson.

Miss Jackson never performed in a jazz situation and sang only songs that she believed served her religious feelings. She believed so profoundly in her religious convictions that she felt entirely free to expose her emotions as sincerely as any singer had ever done.

Francis Ward, writing about Miss Jackson in the *Los Angeles Times* said, "the earliest important musical influence in her life was blues singer Bessie Smith whose recording of 'Careless Love' was a favorite of Miss Jackson's and from which she learned much about the phrasing of black folk music. Despite Bessie Smith's influence, Miss Jackson never sang blues or any kind of jazz, only gospel."[30]

For many years Mahalia Jackson's singing was not accepted in middle-class black churches. Her music was a reminder of a life-style that parishioners seemed to want to forget. But record sales grew, and she primed the world for the many gospel singers who eventually followed. Mahalia Jackson went on to become one of the most stirring, most sought-after singers in the world. Miss Jackson died from heart disease in Chicago on January 27, 1972.

When a Gospel group gets up on stage before an audience, two things become important to them. They want to sing well and to express some religious convictions so that they can reach the souls of the listeners. When the soul of an audience is reached, you will very often see the people shouting, crying, screaming, clapping as a genuine response to the music.

28. Francis, *Jazz*, p. 20.

29. Mahalia Jackson, "If We Ever Needed the Lord Before," *Come On Children, Let's Sing*, Columbia Records, CS8225; *Mahalia Jackson*, Columbia Records, CL 644.

30. Francis Ward, "Mahalia Jackson, Renowned Gospel Singer, Dies at 60," *Los Angeles Times*, 28 January 1972.

Example 8A

Example 8B

Mahalia Jackson with Louis Armstrong. Courtesy of Les McCann.

Although many Gospel groups write some of their own material, most of the songs making up the repertoires of these singers are old spirituals and religious songs that date back to slavery.

These songs have been passed down from generation to generation and the people have sung them in church since early childhood. There are about fifteen or twenty "Gospel standards" that are sung by hundreds of choirs, quartets and groups throughout the country.

It is therefore important for a group or singer to create his own sound.[31]

Some black churches today still believe that association with jazz is wicked, and this attitude may account for the lack of black jazz critics. However, because of the sacred works of Ellington and many other fine jazz composers, this attitude has moderated considerably.[32]

In an interview with Leonard Feather, singer Vi Redd explains:

The church was people's only hope in the midst of all the discrimination and oppression, so their ties to it remained very close and they felt obliged to go along with whatever precepts it dictated.

I was brought up in this environment, but not as strictly as some of the other children, perhaps because my father was a musician. Some of the kids I associated with were not even allowed to have a record player in the house. They used to come over to my place to listen to King Cole Trio records. That was their only opportunity to listen to jazz.

31. Charles Hobson, "Gospel," *Sounds and Fury* 1, no. 4 (February 1966):30.

32. Dave Brubeck, *The Light in the Wilderness,* Decca Records, DX3A–7202; Duke Ellington, *Concert of Sacred Music,* RCA Victor Records, LSP–3582; Duke Ellington, *Third Sacred Concert,* RCA Victor Records, APL 1–0785; Lalo Schifrin and Paul Horn, *Jazz Suite on the Mass Texts,* RCA Victor Records, LSP–3414.

Her music [Mahalia Jackson] has the same harmonic structure, the same feeling, in many of those gospel songs. By the same token, Milt Jackson is a product of the sanctified church. Sarah Vaughan, Dinah Washington and a lot of the greatest jazz artists came directly out of a church background; yet the people in the church, in all sincerity, still refuse to accept it when it's known as jazz.[33]

Milt Jackson, a leading jazz vibraphonist, has been asked many times about the origin of his "funky" style. His answer is always that it came from the church. When asked about "soul" in jazz, he replies "What is soul in jazz? It's what comes from inside."[34] Good contemporary jazz players often record music that is clearly church music, such as Stanley Turrentine's record of "I Told Jesus."[35] Even the most casual listening to Ray Charles will reveal the obvious relationship between jazz and black church music:

The man who gave R and B [rhythm and blues] its fresh thrust was a blind, Georgia-born bard named Ray Charles, one of the most hauntingly effective and versatile Negro singers in the history of pop music.

Negroes have always rigorously maintained a distinction between gospel and blues—the sacred and profane—despite the affinity of their sounds. But Charles boldly brought them together, blending foot-stamping orgiastic jubilation shouts with the abrasive, existentialist irony of "devil songs." He even carried over the original gospel tunes and changed the words to fit the emotion. "Lord" became "you," or "baby," and it didn't matter if the bulk of the prayerful text remained the same. Thus Clara Ward's rousing old gospel song, "This Little Light of Mine," became Charles's "This Little Girl of Mine." (A wonderful identification!) Old timers who had once been forced to choose between the two genres were offended. "I know that's wrong," said Bluesman and former Preacher Big Bill Broonzy. "He should be singing in a church."

But Charles's innovation brought waves of gospel talent into the blues field, and at the same time offered blues performers a chance to employ the climactic cadences and mythic ritual of black evangelism. . . . Most important, once Charles broke the barrier between gospel and blues, the way was open for a whole cluster of ingredients to converge around an R and B core and form the potent musical mix now known as soul.[36]

Sam Cooke, who became a top rock singer, was a leading gospel attraction for years.

A current trend in jazz is labeled gospel jazz. Although this recent style encompasses seventy years of development in the art, it is directly traceable to the early religious roots.

Modern liturgical jazz must also be included in the discussion of religious music. Music of this type has been performed in the United States as well as other countries. These services have taken place in churches of various denominations. All types of contemporary music are being performed in celebration of various religious services. These works can now be added to the important repertoire of religious works of past centuries. In 1971, Leonard Bernstein's "Mass" premiered at the opening of the John F. Kennedy Center for the Performing Arts in Washington, D.C. Press coverage was most favorable. Critic David E. Anderson of United Press International called it a "powerful experience." Paul Hume of the *Washington Post* stated that the central message of "Mass" and its crucial challenge is the place and function of religion in a world of violence. Anderson agreed that Bernstein's message was "one of hope."[37]

Currently, there are many recorded compositions that use the jazz elements in strict conformity to the mass.[38] Other performances are based on the historic liturgy of John Wesley and the Methodist Church and underscored by original contemporary music. These performances usually consist of jazz played in all portions of the service except during the actual sermon. These worship hours are not attended by curiosity seekers. This jazz is given serious thought and is well written and performed for these specific services, which are well-received by congregations and considered appropriate and in good taste. Sometimes they are called liturgical jazz services, sometimes jazz masses, sometimes jazz-rock masses.

33. Leonard Feather, "End of the Brainwash Era," *Down Beat* 36, no. 16 (August 1969):71.

34. From the *Jazz Book: From New Orleans to Rock and Free Jazz* by Joachim Berendt, translated by Dan Morgenstern, copyright 1975 Lawrence Hill & Co., Westport, Connecticut.

35. Stanley Turrentine, "I Told Jesus," *Salt Song*, CTI Recordings, 6010.

36. James Baldwin, "No Music Like That Music," from *The Fire Next Time*. Reprinted by permission from *Time* The Weekly News Magazine; © Time Inc., 1968.

37. "Bernstein's 'Mass' Wins Music Critics Acclaim," *Los Angeles Times*, 9 September 1971.

38. Geoffrey Beaumont, *20th Century Folk Mass*, Fiesta Recordings, FLP–25000; Joe Masters, *The Jazz Mass*, Columbia Records, CS9398.

Though Ellington's 1965 concert at Grace Cathedral in San Francisco seemed to include jazz and ecclesiastical elements, it consisted mostly of "Ellingtonia."

Of the many significant works, one that stands out is the "Jazz Suite on a Mass Text" by Lalo Schifrin and Paul Horn. The freest portion of this work is the "Credo," with a most unusual use of voices and Horn improvising on the alto saxophone. Actually, one of the problems in the acceptance of this music is its "free" quality; it seems in opposition to the inhibited, controlled performance of most church music. The beginnings of jazz and present-day liturgical jazz services prove that the supposed antithesis between jazz and liturgy is not valid. In 1970, eighteen-year-old Gerald Gipson of the University of Missouri wrote this about the controversy:

Can a musical language that is so charged with emotions and extra-musical connotations be admitted as a part of the church service?

To pass judgment on this question is difficult; there are as many arguments for as there are against. It must be remembered that jazz is a form of music alien to the church. Churchgoers are used to hymns and unison readings that have been so much a part of worship for years. They hesitate to make changes, partly out of fear and partly out of custom of thought. At times their attitude seems almost lackadaisical. There is fear of being embarrassed by the demonstrativeness of jazz by the person accustomed to the disciplined routine church service. Still jazz has a religious origin. The spirituals of the Negro slaves of yesterday show the authentically religious roots of jazz. . . . Is this so-called embarrassment real on the part of the puritanical when we remember the emotion-packed sermons of the revivals, the public confession of sin, and the public adoration of Christ? . . . Services keyed to the thinking and problems of modern man should be offered as should music geared to the thinking of a modern world. . . . When jazz first made the crossover between the sacred and the secular, it was more of a folk cult than a commercial empire. The unnamed and unhonored jazz musicians of the earliest days never dreamed that jazz would become the idol that it is now. An example of the new thinking in modern music is Duke Ellington, who has performed in numerous jazz liturgies and written a great deal of music for this purpose. Dave Brubeck (The Light in the Wilderness) has also been fundamental in the organization of good jazz liturgical music.

There seems to be a need for an awakening. It is necessary to utilize the wants and desires of a modern people so that our churches will grow stronger instead of weaker.[39]

Reverend Norman J. O'Connor, director of the New York Paulist Fathers' office for radio and television, says of the Schifrin-Horn *Jazz Suite:* "At a moment in our lives when music is finding a new life in the church, this work turns our eyes from the past—where they have lingered too long—to the present and to the future. How could it be that (until now) liturgical music could fail to grow and incorporate the values of our world?"[40]

Charles Weisenberg has also commented on the place of jazz in modern church services:

Jazz has roots in the religious service through its association with the Negro spiritual. The contemporary use of jazz in church is thus not a new adventure. It is important to note that J.S. Bach, whose music is used in many church services, composed in a contemporary style. There is certainly no reason why 20th century contemporary music, whether or not it is jazz, cannot be suitably prepared for church use.[41]

Union of church and jazz should surprise no one. (There is an anonymous saying: "Each Sunday Buddy Bolden went to church and that's where he got his idea of jazz music.") Since the beginnings of jazz were in the church, it is only natural that modern concepts should also be acceptable. The authors of this book have personally been involved in such services and feel that jazz can express solemnity, peacefulness, dedication, vitality, rejoicing, and any other sentiment embraced by the church. One thing that must be remembered is that in order for this type of service to be successful the jazz must enhance the service; it must reinforce the emotions, but not become the main attraction. It is true that it is next to impossible for a person to leave a jazz service untouched as surely happens in many standard services.

39. Gerald L. Gipson, "The Church and Jazz," *Music Journal* 28, no. 4 (1970):38.

40. Dan L. Thrapp, *Los Angeles Times,* 24 April 1966.

41. Charles M. Weisenberg, "On Brubeck and Others," *Frontier* 2, no. 9 (July 1960):24.

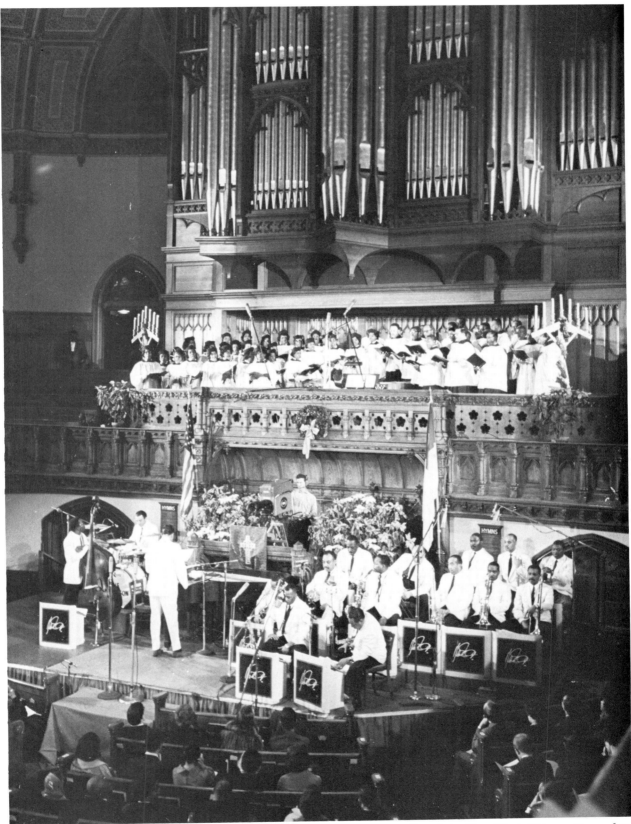

Duke Ellington and His Orchestra at the Fifth Avenue Presbyterian Church in New York City on December 26, 1965. Photo from United Press International.

Marching band in New Orleans. Courtesy of Ray Avery.

Marching Bands

At first, black music in this country was vocal, accompanied by a rhythm of clapping, stamping, and beating on anything available. Then gradually, after the Civil War, the blacks were able to make some instruments and to buy pawned and war surplus instruments. Marching bands began to influence black music.

Military bands, important in all French settlements, also influenced the beginnings of jazz. There were many bands in the New Orleans area. Every secret society or fraternity, for example, had its own band, and there were bands for hire who were not attached to any organization. Most of the early jazz players started their careers in such bands, playing marches, polkas, quadrilles, and so on.

At the turn of the century the most publicized use of the marching bands was for funerals. Bands were used not only in New Orleans, but over the Southeast and as far west as Oklahoma. Such bands, usually composed of five or six players, should be considered a separate type of musical aggregation, in contrast to large modern bands. These small marching bands played an important part in the early development of jazz.

For a funeral procession, the black band would drone a traditional funeral march on the way to the cemetery. After the burial ceremony, the band would march two or three blocks from the cemetery with only a conservative drum beat. Then the band would break into a jazz type of march, such as "Didn't He Ramble" or "When the Saints Go Marching In." The reasoning behind this established plan of the music played at funerals was that the traditional funeral music depicted mourning, while the later use of the more rhythmic music signified the fact that the departed was going to a happier place, which was a cause for rejoicing.

When the band began to play a livelier version of the march, its followers would gradually respond more and more to the music. Their responses were often in the form of clapping, stomping, or any physical rhythmic movement leading toward dancing. In those early days a band often marched directly from the street into a hall and there the music was used for dancing instead of marching, even though the music was the same.[42]

The most common instrumentation used by these bands consisted of a cornet, trombone, clarinet, tuba, banjo, and drums. According to research, the first leader of a jazz marching band was Buddy Bolden. Consequently, he is usually credited with establishing the set instrumentation for these bands. Bolden combined brass-band music with ragtime, quadrilles, and blues in the first stages of jazz. Its small size made the group adaptable for various functions such as advertising campaigns, weddings, serenades, and the like. A group often performed in a horse-drawn wagon. One of the authors played on such wagons while living in the South and discovered the reason for the name "tailgate trombone" when he sat at the end of the wagon in order to have sufficient room for his trombone slide.

Because this music lent itself so well to dancing, much of the early jazz repertoire developed from marches.

The transformation of straightforward marches into jazz may be compared with the process which took place when hymns were changed into spirituals. . . . This jazzing of marches was achieved partly by the trick of shifting the accent from the strong to the weak beat and partly by allowing solo players to "decorate" the melody they were playing—solo improvisation; or several players to indulge in their extemporization simultaneously—collective improvisation.[43]

The regularity of march music could have easily influenced early jazz; today people often "swing" as they march. The integration of the playing of the conservatory-trained Creoles with the self-taught blacks produced well-played marches with the freedom of an oral tradition.

Most important to jazz are the emphasis on rhythm taken from the African music, the harmonies taken from European music, and the melodies added by the improvisations from the American culture. All of these elements fuse to make jazz an American music, rather than the music of a specific ethnic group. However, we emphasize again that the pioneers and innovators of jazz were and are American black musicians.

Additional Reading Resources

Roberts, John Storm. *Black Music of Two Worlds.*
Roach, Hildred. *Black American Music Past and Present.*
Note: Complete information including name of publisher and date of publication is provided in the bibliography.

Suggested Classroom Activities

1. American jazz came about through the blend of the musical cultures of Africa and Europe. Discuss those influences upon early jazz made by Africans and those made by Europeans.

2. Explain why it is incorrect to say that "jazz rhythms came from Africa."

3. Explain the importance of Congo Square and other similar places in the South to the beginnings of jazz.

4. Compare and contrast spiritual songs with gospel songs and with modern liturgical jazz.

5. Describe the following and discuss their contribution to early jazz:
   a. Field hollers
   b. Work songs
   c. Spirituals
   d. Marching bands

6. Give the instrumentation most commonly used in the early marching bands.

7. What is the difference between the construction of homophonic (vertical) harmony and polyphonic (horizontal) harmony?

8. Pretend that you are pounding railroad spikes as you sing the work song "I Got To Roll." Notice the places in the music where the singers give a half-shout or grunt. This song is found on page 544 of Alan Lomax's *The Folk Songs of North America* (Doubleday & Company). This book is a splendid resource for background material on spirituals, work songs, ballads, and blues.

42. Olympia Brass Band of New Orleans, *New Orleans Street Parade,* BASF Recordings, 20678.

43. Harris, *Jazz,* p. 57.

4
The Blues

Prior to any discussions of the blues, listen to the recording of the hymnlike melody on Side 1, Band 3A, which uses the blues harmonic construction.

Now listen to this same hymnlike melody (Side 1, Band 3B) as it is given a jazz interpretation. We will attempt to analyze the blues construction.

The blues is not an era in the chronological development of jazz, nor is it actually a particular style of playing or singing jazz. Because of the great variety of individual styles used by different singers who are referred to as "blues" singers, we contend that there is no single or set manner of interpreting this type of jazz that could be labeled a blues style. General research has pictured the blues as something sung by old people accompanied by guitar; yet in the middle 1920s and 1930s, young, energetic singers in Kansas City were accompanied by complete jazz bands.

In the development of jazz, the blues has been played and sung in every era and can be performed with many interpretations. Any recorded anthology of jazz in general or of blues in particular shows this great variety of styles.[1] Blues can be slow and sad like a dirge, or happy and rollicking. Blues is as important today in jazz as it ever was. Many modern jazz selections still use the basic blues progression with expanded harmonies. Charlie Parker's "Another Hair Do" is a good example of blues in bop; Milt Jackson's "Bags' Groove" is played in both cool and funky styles, showing minor blues to be apropos in a contemporary setting.[2] It is interesting to note that the recording in the back of this book is a blues number that progresses through demonstrations of each era. In fact, the exact

1. *Many Faces of the Blues*, Savoy Records, MG12125; Bessie Smith, *Empty Bed Blues*, Columbia Records, G39450; *The Story of the Blues*, Columbia Records, G30008; *Jazz Odyssey*, vol. 1, *The Sound of New Orleans (1917–1947)*, Columbia Records, C3L 30; *Jazz Odyssey*, vol. 2, *The Sound of Chicago (1923–1940)*, Columbia Records, C3L 32; *Jazz Odyssey*, vol. 3, *The Sound of Harlem*, Columbia Records, C3L 33; Port of Harlem Jazzmen, "Port of Harlem Blues," Albert Ammons, "Boogie Woogie Stomp," Meade Lux Lewis, "Honky Tonky Train Blues," Ed Hall, "Profoundly Blue," Josh White, "Milk Cow Blues," Sidney de Paris, "The Call of the Blues," and Sidney Bechet, "Blue Horizon," *Three Decades of Jazz (1939–1949)*, Blue Note Records, BST 89902.

2. Charlie Parker, "Another Hair Do," *Charlie Parker Memorial*, Savoy Records, MG 12000; Milt Jackson, "Bags' Groove," and Horace Silver, "Senor Blues," and Lou Donaldson, "Blues Walk," *Three Decades of Jazz (1949–1959)*, Blue Note Records, BST 89903; Jimmy Smith, "Back at the Chicken Shack," Kenny Burrell, "Chittlins Con Carne," Lee Morgan, "The Sidewinder," and Stanley Turrentine, "River's Invitation," *Three Decades of Jazz (1959–1969)*, Blue Note Records, BST 89904; McCoy Tyner, "Flapstick Blues," *The Definitive Jazz Scene*, vol. 1, Impulse Records, A–99.

Example 9A

(Side 1, Band 3A)

Example 9B

(Side 1, Band 3B)

same blues tune is used in each case, showing the flexibility of this form. Note that no matter how frantic sounding the music may become (the bop, for example) the same blues is very apropos.

When African and European music first began to merge, the slaves sang very sad songs concerning their extreme suffering. At this time, the name "blues" was not in popular use. The singing was in unison and no chords were determined and no specific form designated. After the Civil War, however, Negroes could perform their music more openly, and, as it united with European music, eight-bar, twelve-bar, and sixteen-bar blues forms all developed. By World War I, the twelve-bar construction had become an accepted form.[3]

Most blues researchers claim that the very early blues were patterned after English ballads and often had eight, ten, or sixteen bars.[4] An example of eight-bar blues is "Trouble in Mind," sometimes called "Troubled in Mind," with the following chord progression: I, V_7, I_7, IV, I, V_7, I, I. Another eight-bar

3. Gunther Schuller, *Early Jazz* (London: Oxford University Press, 1968), p. 37.

4. LeRoi Jones, *Blues People* (New York: William Morrow & Co., 1963), p. 62.

blues is "How Long Blues," using a different chord progression: I, I₇, IV, IV, I, V₇, I, I. Among the sixteen-bar blues one can find long lists of songs such as "Careless Love" (I, V₇, I, I,—I, I, V₇, V₇,—I, I₇, IV, IV,—I, V₇, I, I), "Basin Street Blues" (I, III₇, VI₇, VI₇,—II₇, V₇, I, V₇,—I, III₇, VI₇, VI₇,—II₇, V₇, I, I), and sixteen-bar blues tunes that have the standard twelve-bar progression plus a four-bar tag (I, I, I₇,—IV, IV, I, I,—V₇, V₇, I, I,—and then the tag—II₇, V₇, I, I). Few researchers attempt to notate these early blues, perhaps because there are so many different structures.

Today, the blues is a particular harmonic sequence, a definite musical form in much the same manner that the sonnet is a poetic form. The blues now contains a definite set progression of harmonies and consists of twelve measures. The harmonic progression is as follows: I, I, I, I₇, IV, IV, I, I, V₇, V₇, I, I. Each roman numeral indicates a chord built on a specific tone in the scale. Since about 1960, due to the influence of rock 'n' roll artists, the tenth chord in the progression of harmonies has been changed to IV₇. This alteration is now considered standard.

Each roman numeral as specified in the foregoing harmonic progression designates a chord to be played for one measure, resulting in a twelve-measure strain. Examples 10A, 10B, and 10C are in the key of C.

Example 10A

C diatonic scale

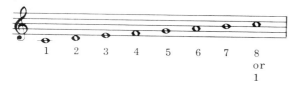

Example 10B

I and IV and V₇ chords spelled out in the key of C

Example 10C

The *basic* chords that are used in the blues in the key of C

Slight variations and embellishments may be used to alter this pattern. If, however, the chord progression is not used as the basic construction, the music being played is *not the blues*. Therefore many melodies that have the word "blues" in the title, and which are often spoken of as being the blues, are not the blues because these melodies lack the blues harmonic construction. The well-known "Bye, Bye Blues," "Limehouse Blues," and "Wabash Blues" are examples. The chord progression for "Bye, Bye Blues" begins with the following harmonies: I, I, ♭VI, ♭VI, I, I, VI, VI. Regardless of the title and the fact that it is often placed in the blues category, its harmonic progressions are not constructed in the blues pattern. One of the most famous melodies with a blues title is "The Saint Louis Blues." But of the three strains found in this music, only two are constructed in the blues pattern.

Another characteristic associated with the blues is the blue tonalities. In our opinion these tonalities resulted from the West Africans' search for comparative tones not included in their pentatonic scale.[5] The easiest way to explain blue tonalities without the use of a piano is to use a diagram such as example 11.

All the tones indicated on the piano keyboard are included in Western diatonic and chromatic music. If the tonal center (C) is arbitrarily used as the basis for discussion, the tones marked with an X are included in the pentatonic scale of the West Africans. As is noted, the West African scale has neither the third or seventh tone nor the flat third or flat seventh. Because of this, in the attempt to imitate either of these tones the pitch was sounded approximately midway between the tone E flat and E natural, and B flat and B natural, causing what is called a blue tonality. Since there are no keys on the piano corresponding to these blue tonalities (or blue notes), pianists must obtain the blues effect by striking these two piano keys at the same time.

"Blue notes" or "blue areas" cannot be designated as concretely as stated in this explanation. Jazz players have always had a tendency to bend and twist notes as an additional means of self-expression. Long ago, lowering of the fifth became a standard device

5. Marshall Stearns, *The Story of Jazz* (New York: New American Library, Mentor Books, 1958), p. 15.

Example 11

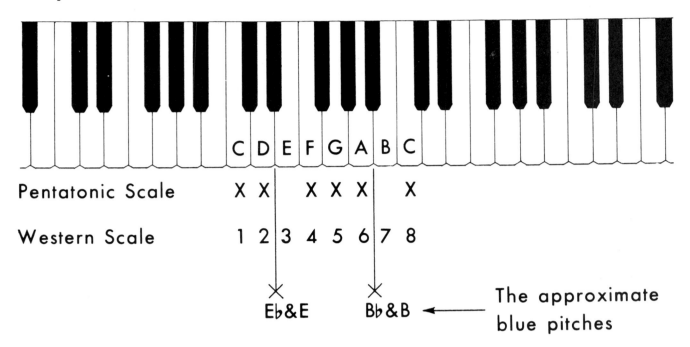

Pentatonic Scale

Western Scale

Eb&E   Bb&B ← The approximate blue pitches

comparable to other blue notes. Therefore, the preceding explanation shows only the consensus regarding how these blue notes originated. One possible reason for why a blues tune does not feel as melancholy when performed at a faster tempo is because there is less time to bend the blue notes around in a dramatic fashion. Some theorists designate a "blues scale" as the Dorian mode (such as the white keys of the piano from D to D) or the Mixolydian mode (the white keys of the piano from G to G). The false logic in this theory is that the blue areas cannot be pinpointed. The Dorian implies a lowered third and lowered seventh; the Mixolydian implies a natural third and a lowered seventh. These blue tonalities are not on definite notes. The problems of analysis result from the rigidity of the well-tempered scale and the fluctuations of the blue tonalities themselves.

Before the field cry, with its bending of notes, it had not occurred to musicians to explore the area of the blue tonalities on instruments. Blue tonalities and bending of notes can be heard on many records by early jazz brass bands.[6] In fact, blue notes are heard in work songs, in spirituals, and in all styles of jazz. Tin Pan Alley (the popular music publishing industry) has used this element excessively. One can also find the use of blue notes in the works of many classical composers.

The meter of the blues lyrics is generally written in iambic pentameter.[7] For example: "I hate to see the ev'nin' sun go down." The first line is generally repeated (a throwback to the African call and response), and is followed by an original third line. The repetition of the first line gives the singer the necessary time to improvise a third line. Very often the lyrics of the blues do not seem to fit the music, but good blues singers "would stress certain syllables and almost eliminate others so that everything falls into place neatly and surely."[8] Each line of the lyrics consists of four measures of music. Because the lyrics seldom use the four measures completely, the remainder of each four-measure segment of the strain is completed by an instrumentalist. These specific areas within the strain are known as *fill-ins* (see examples 12A and 12B). Listen to the saxophone fill-ins for Billie Holiday on "Fine and Mellow," and the trombone performing the same function for Bessie Smith on "Empty Bed Blues."[9]

6. Bunk Johnson, "Didn't He Ramble," *Jazz*, vol. 3, *New Orleans*, Folkways Records, 2804.

7. Leonard Bernstein, "The World of Jazz," in *The Joy of Music* (New York: Simon & Schuster, 1959), p. 109.

8. Rex Harris, *Jazz* (Baltimore: Penguin Books, 1956), p. 39.

9. Billie Holiday, "Fine and Mellow," *Billie Holiday*, Mainstream Records, S/6000; Bessie Smith, "Empty Bed Blues," *Empty Bed Blues*, Columbia Records, G39450.

Example 12A

The usual format showing fill-in areas:

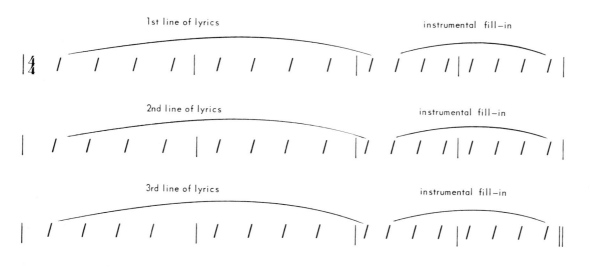

Example 12B

*Iambic pentameter markings.

Fill-ins were the first means that some jazz instrumentalists had to be heard on records. It was in this way that some of the more talented players like Armstrong began to build a broader reputation. (Armstrong can be heard playing fill-ins on some Bessie Smith recordings.) The fill-ins gradually developed in importance and interest to the point where they were called *breaks*. Often their importance was emphasized by the fact that the entire musical organization stopped playing in order to feature the solo instrument filling in the break.

The blues as they are sung use lyrics that are usually concerned with unhappy situations: being out of work, hungry, broke, away from home, or lonely, and with experiencing a broken heart because of an unfaithful lover. Consequently, their melancholy lyrics usually describe the blues emotion: "I'm laughin' to keep from cryin'," "Nobody knows you when you're down and out," "I've got the blues so bad, it's hard to keep from cryin'," and so forth. "By their very etymology the blues are songs of abandon, despair, or lyric sadness. However, content soon goes beyond form, and in the same mold all kinds of sentiments have been cast. Today, given blues are gay, ironic, sarcastic, vengeful. They were slow; they may now be fast (as in boogie-woogie) and even, in modern jazz, very fast."[10] The majority of the public recognizes the blues only by melancholy lyrics, and, as a consequence, many jazz listeners are not aware of the fact that the blues can also be happy swinging tunes. There is such an infinite variety in this one form that some entertainers base their entire repertoire on blues.

Interpretation of the blues by instrumentalists and singers varied all over the United States as early as the latter part of the nineteenth century,[11] a fact that helps to support those who contend that jazz did not originate in any one area of the country.

Washington Irving is credited with first using the term "the blues" in 1807. *Blue* has been associated with melancholia as far back as Elizabethan times. By 1910, the word *blues* was in fairly wide use. Some writers state that the first blues written down was "Dallas Blues" by Hart Wand, a white violinist from Oklahoma City. It was published in 1912. But it is unclear which blues tune was "first." For example, W.C. Handy's "The Memphis Blues" was written in 1909 as a political campaign song. No individual city or state can claim the origin of the blues. W.C. Handy, who was called The Father of the Blues, came from Alabama. His two most famous songs with blues in the title are "The Memphis Blues" and "St. Louis Blues." W.C. Handy proved that money could be made from writing down and publishing blues tunes. Around 1917 blues began to be popular as ragtime began to fade. The first blues recording was Mamie Smith's "Crazy Blues" in 1920; it sold seventy-five thousand copies in the first month and a million copies in the first six months.

A common misconception is that the blues originated with work songs. Actually, work songs were functional, whereas blues were usually quite emotional and had no specific function. The consensus among authorities who write about jazz is that the blues was important to the beginnings of jazz. It is very apparent that this musical form has never lost its importance and is heard as frequently today as in all the previous eras of jazz. Blues performances in general are filled with subtleties. Recent adaptations, such as rhythm and blues in 1945 and rock 'n' roll in 1955, seem fairly devoid of subtleties, but the durability of the form is proved as it continues to survive through all adaptation.

The history of the blues and the story of blues singers are complete studies in themselves, deserving of the fine volumes written about them. Students of this most interesting history will be aided greatly by the historically very important Library of Congress recordings. The aim of this book is merely to point out a very few singers important in this field. The authors believe that all types of blues, from the beginnings to present-day forms, have greatly influenced how jazz players perform, but that certain singers have of course been heard more than others and, as a consequence, have had more influence. "The great blues singers of the twenties and the early thirties bred the jazz men, but they also bred a line of itinerant musicians who sang and played only the blues."[12] Today in retrospect, it is impossible to separate blues from jazz, as performed in the past or in contemporary settings.

After World War I there was a great migration of the black population to large northern cities. As a consequence, ghetto areas arose in cities in many areas of the country. The black population wanted the type of entertainment it was accustomed to, and hence there was a demand in the ghetto areas for blues singers. Because records of Negroes were bought and heard only by Negroes, a collection of what were called "race records" developed. When whites eventually began to hear these records, the result was that fragile 78 rpm records became collector's items selling sometimes for over one hundred dollars each.

There are essentially two periods of blues, the first from the latter part of the nineteenth century to approximately 1930, and the second from about 1930 to the present. The early period is usually divided between performers who sang "country," or "rural," blues and those who sang "city," or "urban," blues. The best known early male blues singers were Big Bill Broonzy, Robert Johnson, Josh White, Blind Lemon Jefferson, Huddie Ledbetter, Son House, and Lightnin' Hopkins, and they were followed by Albert King, T-Bone Walker, B.B. King, and others. The early urban or city blues singers were mostly women—Ma Rainey, Chippie Hill, Mamie Smith, Trixie Smith, and most famous of all, Bessie Smith.

10. Andre Francis, *Jazz* (New York: Grove Press, 1960), p. 17.

11. Marshall Stearns, "Sonny Terry and His Blues," in *The Art of Jazz*, ed. Martin T. Williams (London: Oxford University Press, 1959), p. 9.

12. Ralph J. Gleason, "Records," *Rolling Stones* (May 1971): 45.

Huddie Ledbetter. Courtesy of Orrin Keepnews.

The period from 1930 onward is divided primarily between singers and instrumentalists. The singers include such talented artists as Joe Turner, Jimmy Rushing, Joe Williams, and Jimmy Witherspoon. The problem with listing the best blues instrumentalists is that they were also singers—Louis Armstrong, Jack Teagarden, and Ray Charles, for example. It is an oddity that in the beginnings of jazz, instrumentalists copied vocal techniques, but that later some of the best jazz singers imitated instrumental jazz. Consequently, some of the best jazz singers were also instrumentalists.

City blues seems to be more rhythmic, more crisp than country blues. Most country blues singers accompanied themselves on guitar, whereas urban blues performers often used fairly elaborate accompaniment including jazz musicians like Louis Armstrong.

Huddie Ledbetter, known as Leadbelly, was discovered on a prison farm in Louisiana by John and Alan Lomax. He has been quoted as stating that he was born in 1885 in Louisiana and raised in Texas. He became guide for Blind Lemon Jefferson and learned twelve-string guitar technique from him. Ledbetter spent a considerable amount of time in prison and became known as a valuable lead man for work songs. There are 144 songs in the Library of Congress recorded by Ledbetter between 1933 and 1940 under the supervision of the Lomaxes. Some recordings can be heard today on Folkways records and some on Columbia records. Ledbetter seldom played softly; he felt that blues tunes were meant to be danced to or worked to. His blues and folksongs gained him much popularity and led to many tours and concerts. Huddie Ledbetter died in 1949 in New York. His "Good Night, Irene" became extremely popular even among people who knew nothing about Leadbelly.

Big Bill Broonzy's recordings span a thirty-one year period. Broonzy directly influenced Josh White and many others. He composed about three hundred songs. One of the most famous of his records is "Troubled in Mind" (Folkways Records), which has lyrics in the eight-bar blues construction that have inspired many downtrodden persons to have hope:

Troubled in mind, I'm blue.
But I won't be blue always.
The sun's gonna shine
In my back do' someday.[13]

Ma Rainey, Bessie Smith, and other singers were trained on the minstrel circuits. Sadly, many black minstrels were copies of white minstrels. They were truly imitations of imitations, and their performance was often not as artistic as they were capable of. As Ma Rainey was called The Mother of the Blues, her pupil Bessie Smith was called The Empress of the Blues. Even though Ma Rainey was born in 1886, recordings of her work are still available on Riverside and Folkways records. She recorded about fifty tunes. Reissues of Bessie Smith's work are now available on Columbia records. Technical mastery on these records is very good, and the records are quite important for historical documentation. They are also fine recordings for mere listening pleasure.

Bessie Smith was born in Tennessee in 1894. She made her first recording—"Downhearted Blues"—in 1923, and it sold 800,000 copies to an almost exclusively black public. She became the best known blues singer of the 1920s. Bessie Smith had a large voice and showed a wonderful talent for personal interpretation of lyrics. Even today, when one listens to the recordings available, it is easy to feel the deep emotion produced by her ability to communicate. Her repertoire was quite

Ma Rainey. Courtesy of Orrin Keepnews.

varied, and her personal feelings show on her recordings—sometimes very sad, other times happy and full of humor.

By the end of her first recording year, 1923, Bessie had sold over two million records, and by 1927, four million Bessie Smith records had been sold. She recorded 160 songs and literally saved the Columbia Record Company from bankruptcy at that time. Bessie Smith also made a movie short—quite a breakthrough for a black singer whose market was primarily ethnic. She earned a great deal of money and spent a great

13. "Trouble in Mind," Words and music by Richard M. Jones. © Copyright 1926, 1937 by MCA Music, a Division of MCA, Inc. © Copyright renewed 1953 and assigned to MCA Music, a division of MCA, Inc. © Copyright 1971 by MCA Music, a Division of MCA, Inc., 445 Park Ave., N.Y., N.Y. 10022. Used by permission. All rights reserved.

*Bessie Smith. Courtesy of Columbia Records and the
estate of Carl Van Vechten.*

deal. By 1930, public interest in her began to wane—
some say because she would not adjust to more modern
song material. But in listening to the Bessie Smith
records, one can feel that the blues was very personal
to her, and that she sang these songs with great sincerity.[14] She died, penniless, in 1937 as a result of an
automobile accident. At the time of her death about
ten million of her records had been sold. With her great
gift of communication, Bessie Smith set the standard
for all future singing of the blues.

Bessie Smith was always selective when it came
to choosing her accompanying musicians, among whom
were Clarence Williams, Fletcher Henderson, Louis
Armstrong, Don Redman, Coleman Hawkins, James
P. Johnson, Jack Teagarden, Benny Goodman, Charlie
Green, and Buster Bailey.

Billie Holiday must be considered apart from
others in the jazz field. It is true that many artists defy
categorization, a fact we applaud, but Billie Holiday
crossed musical lines while sticking with her individual
singing style. She sang many blues tunes like "Fine
and Mellow" and could compete most admirably with
this one vehicle. If the blues is a "feeling," she used
the blues on most of her songs. But Holiday was also
deeply into the popular field with beautiful renditions
of songs like "Lover Man" and "Travelin' Light." But
if popular music means selling a great number of records, she never really entered the popular field. There
can never be any doubt, however, that she was a singer
of jazz.

14. Bessie Smith, *Empty Bed Blues*, Columbia Records, G30450;
The Empress, Columbia Records, G30818; *The Bessie Smith Story*,
Columbia Records, Cl 855.

Billie Holiday. Courtesy of Ray Avery.

Early instrumentalists copied singers or at least oral stylings. In the reverse way, Billie Holiday's singing style seemed to stem mainly from her favorite instrumentalist, tenor saxophonist Lester Young.

Besides Young, she was undoubtedly influenced by Bessie Smith and Louis Armstrong. Undoubtedly singers are influenced by their background, but the background does not always lead to a predictable conclusion. Leonard Feather speaks of this unpredictability:

It would be a gigantic oversimplification to pretend that social conditions alone shaped her life, formed her vocal style, led to her death. Ella Fitzgerald had to endure a family background and childhood not greatly different from Billie's. Each was a product of a breaking or broken family; both suffered through years of poverty; both were at the mercy of Jim Crow. In Ella's case these conditions led to a career that started her on an upward curve at the age of 16, to a success story that has never been touched by scandal, and to the achievement of economic security and creature comforts far beyond her most optimistic childhood aspirations. Yet during the same time span, these conditions in Billie's case led to marijuana at 14, a jail term as a prostitute at 15, and heroin addiction from her middle 20s.[15]

One of the most frustrating aspects of Billie Holiday's career must have been that regardless of the fact that musicians *en masse* were her fans, the public was unwilling to accept black and white musicians performing together on the same bandstand. Because of this attitude, some of her best employment situations were short-lived. Musicians enjoyed hearing her sing blues, lovely ballads, novelty tunes, and gripping stories of lynching like "Strange Fruit."

15. Leonard Feather, "Billie Holiday: The Voice of Jazz," *Down Beat* 29, no. 3 (February 1962): 18.

Billie Holiday was born in Baltimore in 1915 but matured on the streets of New York. She recorded with Goodman as early as 1933, but her best recorded efforts were in 1935 with a select group of New York musicians. Most of these records are available now on re-pressings by Columbia Records. She died in 1959, having worked with many bands, including Count Basie's, Artie Shaw's, Paul Whiteman's, and others. She earned a lot of money during her career but died possessing only seventy cents. Saddest of all, she never realized how many people loved her and her singing.

Billie Holiday did not record as many blues tunes as many fans think. Her style and her conceptions often led listeners to feel that she was singing blues when the song was some fairly banal pop tune. Most successful female singers, knowingly or unknowingly, have been influenced by the jazz singing of Billie Holiday.[16]

The popular and talented Ella Fitzgerald has proved that popular singing and jazz singing can be merged with good taste. "A Tisket, A Tasket" was a good swing tune she recorded with Chick Webb in the 1930s. Later, she showed the bop influence by scat singing in that style to "How High the Moon" and "Lady Be Good." One of the authors has recorded with Ella Fitzgerald. Her style, tone, and intonation produce no criticism from anyone except the singer herself.

One of the most notable singers to bridge the gap between blues and popular tunes was Mildred Bailey. Though she had a light, high voice, her jazz interpretation was quite infectious.

B.B. King considers the blues to be a contemporary experience, a living music rather than a folk art. He plays electric guitar, as did T-Bone Walker. King's album *Live and Well* on ABC Records shows the great freedom that was typical of early bluesmen.[17]

Since it is not the aim of this book to discuss, or even to mention, all of the talented blues personalities, the following resources might be suggested. An important two-record set of early music in the United States is Arhoolie's *The Roots of American Music*.[18] Not only are both city and country blues represented, but also examples of Cajun (Clifton Chenier), gospel, and other types of music. Folkways and Riverside record companies have made truly remarkable efforts to preserve the sounds of important pioneers in the music field. Few researchers have delved more deeply into blues than Samuel B. Charters. His book *The Country Blues* is a standard among jazz musicologists.[19] Three other books of merit must be suggested: *Urban Blues* by Charles Keil, *The Meaning of the Blues* by Paul Oliver, and *Blues People* by LeRoi Jones.[20]

Additional Reading Resources

Balliett, Whitney. "Miss Holiday." In *Dinosaurs in the Morning*, pp. 74–80.

Bernstein, Leonard. *The Joy of Music*, pp. 95–111.

Chilton, John. *Billie's Blues.*

Harris, Rex. *Jazz*, pp. 34–42.

Hentoff, Nat, and McCarthy, Albert. *Jazz: New Perspectives in the History of Jazz.*

Holiday, Billie, and Dufty, William. *The Lady Sings the Blues.*

Jones, LeRoi. *Blues People.*

Keil, Charles. *Urban Blues.*

Oliver, Paul. *Bessie Smith* (King of Jazz Series).

————. *The Meaning of the Blues.*

Smith, Charles Edward. "Billie Holiday." In *The Jazz Makers*, pp. 276–295.

Stearns, Marshall. *The Story of Jazz*, pp. 14, 75–81, 196–98.

Ulanov, Barry. *Handbook of Jazz*, chap. 1.

Williams, Martin T. *The Jazz Tradition*, pp. 7–10, 75–93.

Note: Complete information including name of publisher and date of publication is provided in the Bibliography.

Additional Record Resources

The Blues. Folkways Records, FJ 2802.

The Blues, History of Classic Jazz, vol. 3. Riverside Records, SDP–11.

Jazz Singers. Folkways Records, FJ 2804.

Smithsonian Collection of Classic Jazz. Columbia Special Products, P6 11891.

16.   Billie Holiday, *The Golden Years*, Columbia Records, C3L 40; *The Billie Holiday Story*, Decca Records, DXSB 7161; *Lady Day*, Columbia Records, CL 637; *Billie Holiday*, Mainstream Records, S/6000.

17.   B.B. King, *Live and Well*, ABC Records, S–6031; *Best of B.B. King*, ABC Recordings, 767.

18.   *The Roots of American Music*, Arhoolie Records, 2001/2002.

19.   Samuel Charters, *The Country Blues* (New York: Doubleday & Co., 1958).

20.   Charles Keil, *Urban Blues* (Chicago: University of Chicago Press, 1966); Paul Oliver, *The Meaning of the Blues* (New York: Collier Books, 1960); LeRoi Jones, *Blues People* (New York: William Morrow & Co., 1965).

Suggested Classroom Activities

1. Play the hymn "Lord Jesus Christ, With Us Abide,"* or any other hymn that contains the harmonic construction of the blues. Listen carefully and identify the blues chord progressions.

2. Select a blues melody such as the first twelve measures of "St. Louis Blues" and adapt a sonnet or original poem to this melody.

3. Select a sonnet and write a blues melody to the words. See the following suggested example.

4. Sing the C-major scale and note the location of the half steps. Next sing only the tones C, D, F, G, and A. You have just sung a pentatonic scale. Explain the difference between a major diatonic scale and a pentatonic scale.

5. Sing the spiritual "Swing Low, Sweet Chariot" in the key of F-major. What scale does this melody use? Explain your answer.

6. Sing the spiritual "Lord, Lord, Lord." What melodic characteristics in this spiritual suggest a blues melody?

7. Give some titles of blues melodies that do not follow the usual harmonic construction but have the word *blues* in their title.

8. In your own words, describe the "blue tonality." How does a pianist obtain the effect of blue tonality at the keyboard?

9. Listen to "In the House Blues" as sung by Bessie Smith (*The Story of the Blues*, Columbia, G30008) and answer the following:

   a. Is there an introduction?
   b. Do the lyrics follow the iambic pentameter plan, i.e., the first line repeats, while the third line is original?
   c. How many times does she sing the blues song?
   d. What instrument accompanies her? What instruments play the fill-ins?
   e. Finally, when you hear the melody sung, do you hear the singer interpolate the blue notes?

*Melody from Dresden Hymn Book, 1954, arranged by Johann Sebastian Bach, *Anniversary Collection of Bach Chorales*, ed. *Walter E. Buszin*, (Chicago: Hall & McCreary, 1935), p. 6.

When To The Sessions of Sweet Silent Thought

Text by William Shakespeare

Lord, Lord, Lord

Refrain

Spiritual

Lord, Lord, Lord, you've sure been good to me. Lord, Lord, Lord, you've sure been good to me _____

Lord, Lord, Lord, you've sure been good to me; For you've done what the world could not do.

The life span of a musical masterpiece [or style] may encompass a number of generations, but music, being a reflection of society, is subject, like any other art, to social obsolescence. It may endure, metaphorically speaking, in libraries, on records and in the occasional archeological revival, but it will not satisfy a changing society's changing musical requirements.[1]

5
Early New Orleans Dixieland
(1900–1920)

Each new era in jazz came into being as a revolt against the jazz of the preceding era, much as in the case of classical music. We have chosen to designate each era by its most commonly used name, and the dates given for each era are approximate since no style of jazz started or stopped at a given date. For an introduction to Early New Orleans Dixieland jazz listen to Side 1, Band 4 of the recording supplied with this book (see example 15, p. 53 and Appendix A).

Too often, both musicians and lay listeners tend to identify their tastes with specific eras in jazz and to ignore all other styles as being unworthy of their concern. Generally speaking, it is only the jazz *fans* who want *their* style to remain as the one authentic way to play jazz; it is not the musicians themselves who want this. Such clichés as *I don't know much about it but I know what I like* are used to defend this attitude, but most humanities teachers agree that people *like* what they *know*. A deeper understanding of the unfamiliar areas of this art form will develop better discernment and more enjoyment. The intolerant attitude of some musicians who state that the only true jazz is the style in which they and their favorite performers are involved shows an extremely narrow outlook usually based on a minimum of "outside" listening.

At this point, the authors would like to apologize for the "accepted" labels that are used throughout this book. Many, possibly most, musicians do not restrict themselves to one era or style of jazz; their style may even vary within a given improvised chorus. However, the various styles do have certain characteristics that differentiate them, and only by the use of labels can these differences be discussed. Labels are used only to further communication. On the other hand, one of the most exciting aspects of more contemporary jazz is its lack of established explanation, hence, lack of labels.

The era of jazz discussed in this chapter is called Early New Orleans Dixieland jazz not because New Orleans was the only geographical origin of this type of music, but because at the beginning of the twentieth century New Orleans bred more jazz and more important jazz musicians than any other area. However,

1. Henry Pleasants, *Serious Music and All That Jazz*, p. 47. Copyright © 1969 by Henry Pleasants. Reprinted by permission of Simon & Schuster, a Division of Gulf and Western Corporation.

when considering New Orleans as the birthplace of jazz, we must keep two facts in mind: (1) Slaves were brought first to Virginia in 1619, and they brought with them their musical traditions, thereby producing, through the merging of their music with European music, the first faint beginning of jazz; (2) The first instrumental jazz was recorded in New York City about three hundred years later (1917).

The deeper the research probes, the more difficult it becomes to claim one city as the origin of this art form. W.C. Handy said that music that was later called jazz was played in Memphis around 1905, but that the performers did not know until about 1917 that New Orleans had the same kind of music.[2] However, jazz critic Dan Morgenstern wrote; "Jazz: one of the great and wonderful mysteries of our age. New Orleans: the cradle of this mystery. You don't agree? Have you a better myth? Have you Louis Armstrong?"[3] The word *early* is included to differentiate between the dixieland music played from approximately 1890 to 1920 from the jazz developed in Chicago after 1920. The dixieland music performed in New Orleans today, however, often includes elements of all the jazz eras since 1920.

The historical background of New Orleans, an exciting city that keeps alive many of its early customs and traditions, provided a receptive environment for jazz to develop and grow. For the first forty-six years New Orleans was a French possession. It was then ceded to Spain in 1764 and remained a Spanish possession for the next thirty-six years when it once again came under French rule. In 1803 it came to the United States as part of the Louisiana Purchase. This heterogeneous atmosphere was tolerant of all races and was a natural setting for the music of West Africa and Europe to meet and to merge. New Orleans was and is an exciting city with great activity of all sorts, both business and pleasure.

Oddly enough, recognition of jazz players in New Orleans by the New Orleans press has always been quite poor ever since the art form took shape at the turn of the century. The New Orleans musicians "testify that it is easier to get national and international recognition of their talents than it is to get the attention of the *Times-Picayune* and the *States & Items* . . . when their talents are adequately fossilized, their instruments museum pieces, and the musical forms they are creating safely a part of jazz history, they probably will show up on the cover of the *Picayune* Sunday supplement."[4]

It has been stated previously that early jazz combined the techniques of formally trained Creole musicians with the techniques of blacks whose playing was based on oral tradition. There is no better example of playing based on the oral tradition than that heard on any Louis Armstrong record when he sings first and then plays the melody. His phrasing in each instance is identical. This is an example of how the instrument is used as an extension of the voice.

Charles "Buddy" Bolden, who led one of the earliest marching bands, is usually credited with establishing the fixed instrumental combination used in this era.[5] The first jazz instrumentation was logical since the same instruments were also used in the marching bands and in the music halls. In its beginnings, this music was generally a creation of blacks, with the exception of a few whites like the drummer Jack "Papa" Laine who led a band as early as 1891. But soon the music was being created by both blacks and whites. It should be noted, however, that the black musicians did much more to foster these beginnings and to continue its development. Bolden was eighteen years old when the African type of dancing in Congo Square every Sunday came to an end. He was a trumpet player in his brass band and was a member of a "shouting congregation" in his church. Obviously, he was heir to many of the early influences leading toward jazz. His band played ragtime melodies, marches, quadrilles, and a great amount of the blues. Bolden stopped playing entirely in 1907, a fact that points out the diversity of this music at an early date. Unfortunately there are no recordings of Bolden.

Small bands playing dixieland music developed concurrently with ragtime. Dixieland and ragtime influenced each other and were influenced a great deal by the same sources. The same players were often involved in both, and ultimately the two styles merged. In their beginnings, however, early dixieland music

2. From the *Jazz Book: From New Orleans to Rock and Free Jazz* by Joachim Berendt, translated by Dan Morgenstern, copyright 1975 Lawrence Hill & Co., Westport, Connecticut.

3. Dan Morgenstern, "The Meaning of New Orleans," *Down Beat* 36, no. 12 (June 1969): 13.

4. Charles Suhor, "Jazz and the New Orleans Press," *Down Beat* 36, no. 12 (June 1969): 19.

5. Barry Ulanov, *Handbook of Jazz* (New York: Viking Press, 1959), p. 8.

used no piano, while early ragtime was primarily piano music. Eventually, though, there were ragtime bands. All Early New Orleans Dixieland bands did not sound the same. In New Orleans there were at least thirty quite well known bands in just the first decade of the twentieth century. It was only natural that the bands varied according to the personnel of the outfit, just as jazz groups do today.

Another important point is that a given jazz band altered its style according to each job. The music played in some black clubs was considered far too "rough" for the white dances, where the musicians would have to adjust to a more "sweet" style.

In any discussion of New Orleans at about the turn of the century, the name *Storyville* figures prominently. In 1896 a New Orleans alderman, Sidney Story, sponsored a civic ordinance confining the red-light district to a thirty-eight-block section adjoining Canal street. Undoubtedly Mr. Story was humiliated when the area came to be called Storyville. Some of the larger night spots in this section hired small bands, but mainly solo piano players were employed. However, there was much activity for street bands. Before the Navy closed Storyville in 1917, the district made important contributions to the beginnings of jazz. Contrary to what some writers claim, however, Storyville was not as important to the origins of jazz as were the religious services.

There is a certain amount of solo work in dixieland music, but from its very beginnings each of the frontline players (cornet, clarinet, and trombone) had a definite obligation to fulfill in ensemble playing.

Since by usual standards it is the loudest instrument in the orchestra, the cornet (or trumpet) played the melody. The cornet player was allowed to "decorate" the melody according to his own interpretation. He usually did not alter the melody to the point where it became unrecognizable to the layman.

The clarinet player had a dual role. He was expected to play a harmony part, a countermelody above the melodic line carried by the trumpet (a natural task for the clarinet because it can be played at a higher pitch than the trumpet). He was also expected to create momentum because the clarinet can be played with more agility than can the two other melodic instruments.

The role delegated to the trombone was to play the most important note in the chord change. One example is in the tune "Indiana." The first chord is composed of the notes F, A, C, D; the second chord moves to F-sharp, A, C, D. The natural resolution for the trombone player is from F to F-sharp, pointing out to the other players that the chord has changed and that this is the change which has occurred.

The banjo, tuba, and drums played straight rhythm parts as they had in the marching bands. No piano was used in these first dixieland groups because they were often the same group that played in the street marches, where a piano could not be used. For this same reason the tuba rather than the string bass was used.

In example 13, twelve measures are scored in Early New Orleans Dixieland style to point out musically the role assigned to each instrument.

Another identifying feature of the music of this era was that the rhythm section played in a flat four, that is, with no accents, four even beats to a measure (or bar).[6] This is contrary to the belief of many dixieland advocates who believe that all dixieland music utilizes a 2/4 rhythm with accented afterbeats. One need only to listen to recordings of the King Oliver band (typical of this era) for confirmation that these rhythm sections played with no regularly accented beats.[7]

It is sometimes felt that Latin rhythm was an element added to jazz in the 1940s by the orchestras of Dizzy Gillespie, Stan Kenton, and others, or in the 1960s when the bossa nova became popular. Actually, the addition of Latin rhythm can be traced to the beginnings of jazz. One example of Latin rhythm in early jazz is the tango section of "St. Louis Blues" written by W.C. Handy in 1914.

Another important aspect was that the frontline players conceived their parts polyphonically (horizontally), as explained in example 8A. It should be noted that the direct roots of the counterpoint in modern jazz are from the music of the dixieland bands and very early classical music since both used the polyphonic approach in construction.

The customary structure of a dixieland arrangement consists of an ensemble chorus, the solo choruses, and a return to the ensemble.

It is often thought that all dixieland music is composed of improvisational playing. But it can be pointed out that while improvising during ensemble playing, patterns were often established in which a

6. Larry Gushee, "King Oliver's Creole Jazz Band," *The Art of Jazz*, ed. Martin Williams (London: Oxford University Press, 1959), p. 45.

7. King Oliver's Savannah Syncopaters, "Snag It," *Introduction to Jazz*, ed. the Reverend A.L. Kershaw, Decca Records, DL8244.

Example 13

player repeated the same part on the last chorus of the arrangement that he played on the opening chorus. Thus these choruses were played from memory rather than being strict improvisation. In spite of this, this type of music had a feeling of spontaneity.

One of the most interesting aspects of dixieland music is the rhythmic complexity caused by "collective improvisation." Example 14 illustrates the involved syncopation that causes the accents to shift constantly among the three lines being played by the trumpet, clarinet, and trombone.

In this phase of jazz, one musician was designated by his peers to be the "king." He was always a trumpet player. Freddie Keppard succeeded Bolden as king. The last trumpeter to be called king was Joe "King" Oliver. Keppard left New Orleans in 1912, played in Los Angeles in 1914, Coney Island, New York, in 1915, and Philadelphia in 1918. These facts surely dispute the "up-the-river" legend, perpetuated by many jazz writers, that has it that jazz came up the river by steamboat directly to Chicago from New

Example 14

Orleans. Other famous New Orleans players, trombonist Kid Ory, for example, went to Los Angeles before going to Chicago.

The type of jazz played by Joe "King" Oliver was exemplary of that which was performed before and during World War I. It is extremely difficult, however, to obtain recordings that have the exact instrumentation and approach to performance that was popular before 1920 because no instrumental jazz was recorded before 1917. By the time Oliver, for example, went into recording studios, his style had been somewhat influenced by the activity in Chicago. He was, for example,

using two trumpets (Louis Armstrong on a second trumpet) and a piano (Lil' Hardin Armstrong). Nevertheless, his recording output around 1923 (thirty-seven numbers in all) is considered a cornerstone in traditional jazz.

The Early New Orleans Dixieland bands relied more on ensemble than on solo improvisation, certainly less improvisation than Chicago Style Dixieland. Still, every member of a band like Oliver's was a star and capable of good solo improvisation. Yet everyone's solos were considerably shorter than those by Oliver

Joe ("King") Oliver and His Orchestra. Left to right, Baby Dodds, Honore Dutrey, Oliver, Louis Armstrong, Bill Johnson, Johnny Dodds, and Lil' Armstrong. Courtesy of Orrin Keepnews.

himself. Oliver was the leader and hence the featured attraction. Proof of the esteem in which present-day musicians hold Oliver is that whenever the tune "Dippermouth Blues" is played, the trumpet player must always play Oliver's choruses note for note or he is not considered to be even playing the right number. Yet Oliver was actually improvising when he recorded the tune.[8]

Jazz seemed to become more permanent as it became less localized. Oliver moved to Chicago as did many other well-known bands. The Original Dixieland Jazz Band went to Chicago in 1916, then on to New York in 1917. In fact, The Original Dixieland Jazz Band was the first band to record instrumental jazz instead of merely play background for blues singers; this was in 1917. They were also the first group to go

into New York City where they opened at Reisenweber's Cafe (near Columbus Circle) in 1917, and they were the first jazz band to go to Europe (1919). This band consisted of a group of young white musicians who listened very intently to and absorbed what the black bands in the New Orleans area were playing. They copied these bands until their own style began to

8. King Oliver, *King Oliver*, Epic Records, LA16003; "Jazzin' Babies Blues," *Jazz Odyssey*, vol. 1; "New Orleans Stomp," and "Where Did You Stay Last Night," *Jazz Odyssey*, vol. 2; King Oliver, "Working Man's Blues," *Folkways Jazz*, vol. 2; "Snake Dance," and "Dippermouth Blues," and "High Society," *Folkways Jazz*, vol. 3; "Sugarfoot Stomp," *Folkways Jazz*, vol. 5; "Sweet Lovin' Man," *Folkways Jazz*, vol. 6; "Froggie Moore," *History of Classic Jazz*, Riverside Records, SDP–11.

Original Dixieland Jazz Band. Left to right, Tony Spargo, Eddie Edwards, Harry Barth, Larry Shields, Nick La Rocca, and Russell Robinson. Courtesy of Leo Walker.

develop.[9] Some jazz critics infer that their music and that of The New Orleans Rhythm Kings was more toward barnyard sounds and clowning. It should be kept in mind, however, that the imitation of barnyard animals was as much "in" at that time as electronic distortion became in years later. The Original Dixieland Jazz Band even recorded a piece called "Barnyard Blues."[10] No matter what may be a listener's stylistic preferences, it would be impossible to deny the great energy and exuberance of The Original Dixieland Jazz Band.

Although jazz has undergone many changes since its origin, some bands today play jazz almost as it was played at the turn of the century. The Early New Orleans Dixieland style had a great revival in the early 1940s. Prominent in this movement was Lu Watters and his Yerba Buena Jazz Band (based in Oakland, California). This band, like others in the movement, did everything possible to recreate King Oliver's style. The advocates of this style of jazz refer to their music as the "real" or "pure" jazz. This "purist" jazz school is fairly intolerant, as are other jazz schools. But how, and at what point, with all the borrowings that transpire in jazz and other musical styles, could there be

9. Original Dixieland Jazz Band, "At the Darktown Strutters' Ball," *Jazz Odyssey*, vol. 1; *The Original Dixieland Jazz Band*, RCA Victor Records, LPV–547.

10. The Original Dixieland Jazz Band, "Barnyard Blues," *Jazz Odyssey*, vol. 1.

purity? While traveling in England during the summer of 1961, one of the authors found a tremendous emphasis on the "Trad" (traditional) bands in which the musicians imitated the Early New Orleans Dixieland style by using both the instrumentation and interpretation of that time.

Additional Reading Resources

Berendt, Joachim. *The New Jazz Book*, pp. 4–12, 32–35.

Buerkle, Jack V., and Barker, Danny. *Bourbon Street Black*.

Dexter, Dave. *The Jazz Story*, pp. 6–19.

Feather, Leonard. *The Book of Jazz*, pp. 30–38.

Francis, Andre. *Jazz*, pp. 27–34.

Harris, Rex. *Jazz*, pp. 77–93.

Hentoff, Nat, and McCarthy, Albert. *Jazz: New Perspectives on the History of Jazz*, pp. 21–43.

Schuller, Gunther. *Early Jazz: Its Roots and Musical Development*, pp. 63–88.

Stearns, Marshall. *The Story of Jazz*, pp. 33–60.

Note: Complete information including name of publisher and date of publication is provided in the Bibliography.

Additional Record Resources

Encyclopedia of Jazz on Records, vol. 1. Decca Records, DXSF–7140.

Jazz at Preservation Hall, vol. 2. Atlantic Recordings, S–1409.

The Original Dixieland Jazz Band. RCA Victor Records, LPU–547.

Smithsonian Collection of Classic Jazz. Columbia Special Products, P6 11891.

Suggested Classroom Activities

1. Discuss why New Orleans was important in the development of jazz at the beginning of the twentieth century.

2. At first, early dixieland music used no piano. What was the instrumentation of these bands?

3. Discuss the influence of Storyville upon jazz.

4. Discuss the role each instrument assumed in the overall sound of Early New Orleans Dixieland ensembles.

5. What was the overall plan or design of the music?

6. Listen to the recorded example of the original melody played in Early New Orleans Dixieland style (Side 1, Band 4; see example 15 on p. 53, of recorded examples) and answer the following:

   a. Do you hear the steady pulse of the flat four rhythm? Which instruments realize this musical characteristic?

   b. In this dixieland arrangement which instrument is realizing the solo chorus part?

   c. In the return section which instrument is playing the melody?

Example 15
(Side 1, Band 4)

See Appendix A for complete arrangement.

6
Ragtime
(1900–1917)

Some of those who write about jazz do not consider ragtime music to be jazz because it is composed music. But as was pointed out in chapter 1, if jazz has to be improvised to be jazz, then most of the music generally conceded to be jazz would have to be classified as some other style of music. Even without being improvised, ragtime has the "improvisatory feel" that seems so essential to jazz. On the other hand, there are those who consider ragtime to be another name for early jazz.[1] For an introduction to ragtime, listen to Side 1, Band 5 of the recording included with this book.

Ragtime is often said to have originated in Sedalia, Missouri, because of the large number of such players who performed there, even though a great deal of ragtime was played before these performers migrated to Sedalia. When reform government came to Sedalia in 1901, all ragtime activity there ceased. Ragtime, then, predated jazz if Buddy Bolden is considered to be the one who brought the elements of jazz, or at least of dixieland jazz, together.

Ragtime had a direct impact on the development of jazz, but because of its juxtaposition chronologically to Early New Orleans Dixieland, ragtime was really a piano style that developed as a result of special conditions.

Because pianists were not used in the first dixieland bands (evolved from marching bands), the pianists developed a solo style of playing. A piano player was hired in place of a six- or seven-piece band, a circumstance that forced him to develop a technique that provided a full sound. The left hand had to play both the bass notes and the chords, leaving the right hand free for highly syncopated melodic lines. This playing was much more difficult than merely accompanying a vocalist or instrumentalist in which a pianist was responsible only for the bass notes with the left hand and the chords with the right. The extreme difficulty of the technique, in fact, caused many academic piano players to completely oppose the "unusual" style of ragtime. Examples 16A and 16B point up the difficulty of ragtime interpretation.

In example 16A the accompaniment consists of the bass part confined to the first and third beats and the chords played on the second and fourth beats or offbeats. Because of the physical action of the left hand, it became the practice for pianists to accent these offbeats, a technique that led to the new rhythmic style of the following era.

1. Guy Waterman, "Ragtime," in *Jazz,* eds. Nat Hentoff and Albert J. McCarthy (New York: Holt, Rinehart, & Winston, 1959), p.107.

Example 16A

Example 16B

The intricate syncopation demonstrated by these two examples could well have been the reason why this music was called ragtime, meaning "ragged time." This is only one of many versions concerning the origin of the name *ragtime*. As in the case of the name *jazz*, it is impossible to say which explanation is correct.

Ragtime was a refreshing change from the usual songs with often commonplace melodies and predictable rhythmic feeling. Unlike many of the blues tunes and some of the spirituals, the mood of ragtime is happy. The country welcomed this happy music because it had just experienced the long depression of the 1890s. The general public first became aware of ragtime during a series of World's Fairs held in Chicago, Omaha, Buffalo, St. Louis, and other cities where peripatetic piano players from the Midwest and the South found employment along the midways. Ragtime flourished for over twenty years. When the music publishing industry (called Tin Pan Alley) began to sell "rags," the music was too difficult for uninitiated pianists to play, and had to be considerably simplified in order to sell. Ragtime players frequently earned substantial income teaching ragtime style.

The ragtime players began to migrate to Sedalia, Missouri. As said earlier, many critics state that ragtime was born in Sedalia, but actually these players merely drifted into the town because of employment opportunities. One player, Tom "Million" Turpin, owned a series of clubs in Sedalia, and he sponsored many other ragtime players. Turpin's "Harlem Rag" (1897) is reputed to be the first rag ever published

(some say William Krell's "Mississippi Rag," also published in 1897, was first). When reform came to Sedalia in 1901, many ragtime players moved to St. Louis, which then became the ragtime center of the world.

There is a great deal of controversy about who composed what rag. Possibly, some rags were a compilation of ideas "borrowed" from many players, and the player who had the knowledge to notate the rag on music manuscript received credit for the composition.

An interesting aspect of typical ragtime selections is that they were composed to a definite format, which showed a European influence with its concern for balance and form. Each selection included four themes (or melodies), and each theme had equal stress, equal importance, within the composition. Examples are "Tiger Rag" and "Maple Leaf Rag." This fairly rigid form was probably borrowed from the construction of marches. Ragtime players, both black and white, were expected to be good readers, and sheet music was one of the principal means of disseminating ragtime music.

The most prolific composer of ragtime music was Scott Joplin. Joplin published approximately fifty rags (some say he composed about six hundred). The most famous was "Maple Leaf Rag," which sold hundreds of thousands of copies in the first ten years of publication (1899). Joplin was a schooled musician. Many jazz critics are not aware that he wrote a symphony and two operas. One opera, *Treemonisha*, is still performed today.

A monument in honor of Joplin has now been erected in Sedalia, at the site of the old Maple Leaf Club. Some of the citizens of the city have expressed concern about the popularity of ragtime since the movie *The Sting.* They seem worried that Joplin's tunes will be associated only with the film and that the composer and the city itself will be lost to obscurity. One hindsight suggestion is that more recognition could have been given Joplin and his music when he was living there instead of sixty years later.

Two other very fine ragtime composers are certainly deserving of mention: James Scott and Joseph Lamb.

The best known ragtime piano player was Jelly Roll Morton (Ferdinand de Menthe). In his Library of Congress recordings and on his calling card, Jelly Roll claims that he originated jazz in 1902 and also ragtime, swing, and just about everything else in this area of music. He may not have been that important, but he was surely at the top of the ragtime players. Morton had no peer as a soloist,[2] and he also performed successfully with his variety of bands.[3]

As soon as their finances permitted, some ragtime pianists formed their own orchestras (Jelly Roll Morton and His Red Hot Peppers, Jelly Roll Morton's Stomp Kings, Jelly Roll Morton's Jazz Band), and some already established jazz bands added piano players (Lil' Hardin, later to be Lil' Armstrong, joined King Oliver's orchestra). As the ragtime bands had to have piano players as leaders, this trend carried over to bands not so involved with ragtime. This was especially true in the Southwest—for example, Bennie Moten, Count Basie, Jay McShann, and many other piano players were leaders. Morton was an ideal ragtime band leader. He was an excellent piano player, a creative and knowledgeable arranger, a fair singer, and had an extremely attractive and outgoing personality. In fact, Morton was the first jazz musician who reputedly planned very precisely what each musician was to play on his recordings, and thus opened the way for recorded arrangements of jazz. The recordings on which he plays piano and talks with folklorist Alan Lomax are important in the history of jazz to the 1930s.[4] "In Jelly Roll Morton, we recognize for the first time in jazz that the personality of the performing musician is more important than the material contributed by the composer."[5] Since ragtime players were becoming bandleaders, the need for more musical schooling for players became obvious.

When the piano players began to play with other instrumentalists, the two music styles, dixieland and ragtime, began to merge. There are many recorded

Jelly Roll Morton. Courtesy of Ray Avery.

examples of bands playing rag tunes that were primarily meant to be played on a piano. Listen, for example, to Paul Mares's recording of "Maple Leaf Rag," The New Orleans Rhythm Kings' recording of "Tiger Rag," and others.[6]

2.   *Jelly Roll Morton,* Mainstream Records, S/6020.

3.   Jelly Roll Morton, *The King of New Orleans Jazz,* RCA Victor Records, LPM–1649.

4.   Jelly Roll Morton, *The Saga of Jelly Roll Morton,* Riverside Records, 9001–9012.

5.   From the *Jazz Book: From New Orleans to Rock and Free Jazz* by Joachim Berendt, translated by Dan Morgenstern, copyright 1975 Lawrence Hill & Co., Westport, Connecticut.

6.   Paul Mares, "Maple Leaf Rag," *Folkways Jazz,* vol. 6; New Orleans Rhythm Kings, "Tiger Rag," *Folkways Jazz,* vol. 3; Joe King Oliver, "Snake Rag," *Folkways Jazz,* vol. 3; New Orleans Feetwarmers, "Maple Leaf Rag," *Folkways Jazz,* vol. 11; Papa Celestin, "Original Tuxedo Rag," *Jazz Odyssey,* vol. 1.

Two important changes resulted from the merging of dixieland and ragtime: (1) the basic melodic concept of the rags was changed, and (2) the rhythmic accentuation indigenous to the rags was carried over into dixieland jazz. As a consequence, a new repertoire was added to the music of the jazz bands, who began to play the rags but altered the form. The first melody became a verse, the second and third melodies were omitted completely, and the fourth became a repeated chorus and the basis for improvisation.[7]

The rhythm of the bands changed from a flat-four (four equal pulsations in each measure) to a two-four (2/4) rhythm (four beats to a measure with accents on beats two and four). These measured offbeats correspond to the action of the left hand of the ragtime pianists.

As has been explained, jazz bands ignored the original construction of the rags. Piano players were no longer compelled to play alone; consequently the piano was considered a part of the jazz band instrumentation. Another factor is that as tempos were increased the relaxed feeling of the early ragtime gave way to virtuoso displays. In addition, improvisation, not present in early ragtime, began to gain importance in piano music. The culmination of these developments resulted in what is known as "stride" piano, an extension of ragtime.

There were three basic differences between stride piano playing and ragtime. First, stride players were not at all concerned with form. They played popular tunes of the day and any other kind of music that appealed to them. Second, original ragtime was a composed music, whereas stride players were often very proficient improvisers and utilized this element in their performance. Third, the feeling of stride music was intense because, in general, stride pianists played faster and with much more drive than the more relaxed players of ragtime.

James P. Johnson, composer of the famous tune "Charleston" (among many others), is considered to be the father of stride piano. There are many fine recorded examples of his performances.[8] Closely akin to Johnson and usually discussed in superlatives is Willie "The Lion" Smith. We believe, however, that the most entertaining and exciting stride piano player was Thomas "Fats" Waller, a student of Johnson. Waller mugged and clowned incessantly, and if a purist found this disturbing he merely had to concentrate on the piano playing to hear true artistry and a most energetic rhythmic pulse.[9] Waller began to accompany blues singers on recordings in 1922. He was Bessie Smith's accompanist on tour and worked for a short time in Fletcher Henderson's orchestra. In 1927 he formed a solo act. His records sold well, and he even performed in motion pictures.

Art Tatum was possibly the best, surely the most versatile, piano player in the history of jazz. It is impossible (thankfully) to put Tatum in a stylistic category, but stride was certainly one of his favorites. His recordings include some of the best stride piano on record.[10] Some musicians never have the opportunity to record their achievements for posterity. This cannot be said of Tatum. He was hired by Norman Granz for two days of recording in December, 1953, and for two days in April, 1954. The result was a set of thirteen long-playing records (twenty-six sides). They were released to the public in 1974 (Pablo Records) and are truly a historic event for Tatum followers in particular and for jazz fans in general.[11] Another collection of previously unreleased recordings of Tatum received a Grammy Award from the National Academy of Recording Arts and Sciences as the best solo album of 1973.[12] The collection was recorded on a portable home-recording device by a young friend of Tatum. Some songs were recorded in an apartment and others in various after-hours clubs. The title of the album *God Is in the House* was taken from a remark made by Fats Waller when Tatum entered a club where Waller was playing. It reveals the respect that is quite general among musicians.

Oscar Peterson, though also impossible to label stylistically, often ventures into some of the best stride piano on record. He is a most talented and versatile musician.

7. Waterman, "Ragtime," *Jazz*, p. 7.

8. James P. Johnson, "Harlem Strut," *History of Classic Jazz*, vol. 8; "Snowy Morning Blues," *Folkways Jazz*, vol. 9; "Keep off the Grass," *Jazz Odyssey*, vol. 3; "Black Bottom Dance" and "Mr. Freddie Blues," *Piano Roll Hall of Fame*, Sounds Records, LP 1202.

9. Fats Waller, *Ain't Misbehavin'*, RCA Victor Records, LPM–1246; "Mama's Got the Blues," *History of Classic Jazz*, vol. 8; "Handful of Keys," *Folkways Jazz*, vol. 9; "Squeeze Me," *Folkways Jazz*, vol. 11; "Draggin' My Poor Heart Around," *Jazz Odyssey*, vol. 11; "Do It Mr. So-and-So," and "If I Could Be With You," *Piano Roll Hall of Fame*, Sounds Records, LP 1202; "The Flat Foot Floogie," *Jazz Story*, vol. 3.

10. Art Tatum, *The Art of Tatum*, Decca Records, DL 8715; *Piano Discoveries*, vols. 1 and 2; 20th Fox Records, Fox 3032/3.

11. *The Tatum Solo Masterpieces*, Pablo Recordings, 2625 703.

12. Art Tatum, *God Is in the House*, Onyx Recordings, ORI 205.

Fats Waller. Courtesy of Orrin Keepnews.

Both Basie and Ellington often go into very authentic stride piano during improvisation. Stride can also be heard in a most interesting manner in the 5/4 excursions of Johnny Guarnieri.[13]

Ragtime, then, was a style of playing piano solo that coexisted with Early New Orleans Dixieland jazz. It influenced the interpretation of jazz by shifting the rhythm from a flat 4/4 to 2/4 interpretation and by additions to the jazz repertoire, such as "Maple Leaf Rag" and "Tiger Rag."

Ragtime is still played today, and recordings are available from several sources. One source is the recordings of ragtime played today on a "tack" piano. A tack piano is a piano altered to sound much older than it is, so that the ragtime sounds more authentic. This is accomplished in various ways. One way is to put thumb tacks in all the felts of the piano hammers. Other ways include laying a light chain across the strings or putting newspaper, aluminum foil, or something similar over the strings.[14]

Another good ragtime source is the re-pressing of old master recordings by such players as Morton, Joplin, and others.[15] Many good ragtime and stride players made piano rolls that can be purchased, and recordings made from rolls are quite satisfactory.[16]

13.   Johnny Guarnieri, *Breakthrough in 5/4*, Bet Records, BLPS–1000.

14.   Phil Moody, *Razz-Ma-Tazz*, Urania Records, UR 9009; Joshua Rifkin, *Scott Joplin Ragtime*, Nonesuch Records, H–71248.

15.   Jelly Roll Morton, "Granpa's Spells," *Piano Roll Hall of Fame*, Sounds Records, LP1202; "Perfect Rag," *History of Classic Jazz*, vol. 2; "Big Fat Ham," and "Black Bottom Stomp," *Folkways Jazz*, vol. 5; "Tom Cat Blues" and "Wolverine Blues," *Folkways Jazz*, vol. 9; "Kansas City Stomps," *Folkways Jazz*, vol. 11; "London Blues," *Jazz Odyssey*, vol. 1; "Someday Sweetheart," *Jazz Odyssey*, vol. 2; Scott Joplin, "The Cascades," *History of Classic Jazz*, vol. 2; "Original Rags," *Folkways Jazz*, vol. 11; *History of Classic Jazz*, vol. 2; *The Jazz Story*, vol. 2; *Reunion in Ragtime*, Stereoddities Records, S/1900.

16.   *Piano Roll Hall of Fame, Piano Roll Ragtime*, Sounds Records, 1201; Jelly Roll Morton, *Rare Piano Rolls*, Biograph Records, 1004Q; Fats Waller, *Rare Piano Rolls*, vols. 1 and 2, Biograph Records, 1002Q, 1005Q.

Art Tatum. Courtesy of Ray Avery.

Another important source is the recordings of old-timers, such as the two-record set called *The Eighty-Six Years of Eubie Blake,* played by Eubie Blake, who is now in his nineties.[17]

Interest in authentic ragtime began to wane because some players played the style so fast and aggressively that the original relaxed feeling dissipated, and as a result stride playing became more popular. Also, the dixieland players had destroyed the important ragtime form. Since 1920, however, revivals of this style continue to bring talented composers and players to public notice.

The public was more aware of ragtime during 1973 than during any time since 1920 due to a very popular motion picture called *The Sting.* Throughout the movie Scott Joplin's rags set the mood for the period in which the movie was set, and the composer's name once again became a household word. Marvin Hamlisch, the musician who adapted the Joplin rags for the movie, received an "Oscar" award for the best

movie score of the year. As he accepted the award, Hamlisch acknowledged his absolute indebtedness and gratitude to Scott Joplin and his genius. Joplin was given screen credits as well. It is sad to know that Joplin died frustrated and penniless.

It is interesting to note that while *The Sting* was set in 1936, ragtime had not been popular since 1920, and that though ragtime had not been played at all in 1936, the music was still most apropos for the movie. It is also interesting to note that a quiet revival of ragtime had preceded the movie. It was common during 1971 and 1972 to hear students in college practice rooms working on the intricacies of "Maple Leaf Rag." After the release of the film, students turned their efforts to "The Entertainer," a piece used extensively in the movie. The authors feel that the revival preceded

17. Eubie Blake, *The Eighty-Six Years of Eubie Blake,* Columbia Records, C2S–847.

the movie and that the makers of the movie used the music because of the revival. The important thing, however, is that ragtime is once again popular, to the delight of its present-day practitioners.

At the beginning of this chapter it was stated that some authorities do not consider ragtime to be jazz. To illustrate: In 1974 the Academy of Recording Arts and Sciences gave an award to a ragtime record without placing it specifically in any of their award categories. "The Red Back Book" won a "Grammy" for being the best chamber music record of 1973. Its competition included string quartets, classical piano duos, woodwind trios, and so forth.

The musical example on Side 1, Band 5 on the record accompanying this book is an example of the original theme (see example 2A) and is used for illustrative purposes throughout the book. In this example the theme is the basis of an interpretation showing ragtime style.

Additional Reading Resources

Blesh, Rudi. *Classic Piano Rags.*

Blesh, Rudi, and Janis, Harriet. *They All Played Ragtime.*

Gammond, Peter. *Scott Joplin and the Ragtime Era.*

Harris, Rex. *Jazz,* pp. 60–72.

Hentoff, Nat, and McCarthy, Albert. *Jazz.*

Hodeir, Andre. *Jazz: Its Evolution and Essence.*

Shapiro, Nat, and Hentoff, Nat, eds. *The Jazz Makers,* pp. 3–17.

Stearns, Marshall. *The Story of Jazz.*

Ulanov, Barry. *Handbook of Jazz.*

Note: Complete information including name of publisher and date of publication is provided in the Bibliography.

Additional Record Resources

Classical Jazz Piano Styles. RCA Victor Records, LPV–543.

Johnson, James P. *Father of Stride Piano.* Columbia Records, CL 1780.

———. *1917–1921, Rare Piano Rolls,* vol. 1. Biograph Records, 1003Q.

Joplin, Scott. *Joplin.* Biograph Records, 1013/4Q.

Morton, Jelly Roll. *The Immortal Jelly Roll Morton.* Milestone Records, MLP 2003.

———. *New Orleans Memories.* Atlantic Records, 2–308.

———. *Stomps and Joys.* RCA Victor Records, LPV–508.

New England Conservatory Ragtime Ensemble. "The Red Back Book," by Gunther Schuller and The New England Conservatory Ragtime Ensemble (playing Scott Joplin music). Angel Records, S–36060.

Smithsonian Collection of Classical Jazz. Columbia Special Products, P6 11891.

Waller, Fats. *African Ripples.* RCA Victor Records, LPV–562.

———. *1934–1935.* RCA Victor Records, LPV–516.

Suggested Classroom Activities

1. Compare the musical role of a ragtime pianist with that of a pianist in an instrumental ensemble.

2. How did the techniques of the pianist's left-hand playing alternately bass parts and chords influence the flat-four rhythm played in early dixieland music?

3. Listen to "Grandpa's Spells" as played by Jelly Roll Morton (*Piano Roll*, Sounds, LP 1202) and discover the offbeat accents in the left hand. Is this left-hand technique continuous or does it change at times? If there are changes, what are they?

4. Now listen to "Kansas City Stomp" by Jelly Roll Morton (*The King of New Orleans Jazz*, Dixieland Jazz, RCA Victor, LPM–1649) and compare the ragtime rhythm Morton used in his piano playing with that used in his instrumental rendition of "Kansas City Stomp."

5. Usually, how many different themes or melodies are there in ragtime compositions?

6. As a result of the merging of rags and dixieland, what happened to dixieland's rhythm and rag's melodic design?

7. What is stride piano?

Historians claim that with the closing of Storyville in 1917, a district in New Orleans where a great number of musicians were employed, the heart of the jazz scene shifted to Chicago. Night life in New Orleans did lose some of its attraction when Storyville was closed down by the Navy, and as a consequence many musicians left for cities that offered good jobs. By 1918 many musicians had left New Orleans, and when Congress passed the Volstead Act, prohibiting the use of alcoholic liquors, in 1919, employment for jazz musicians in New Orleans came to a real halt. Quite a few jazz players drifted to Chicago. In the 1920s Chicago was a prosperous city with many opportunities for employment because of the railroads, stockyards, and mills. Many workers in Chicago had migrated from the South and wanted the type of entertainment they had left behind. Thus, there was a demand for jazz in Chicago during the Roaring Twenties. For example, King Oliver came to Chicago in 1918 and went to work immediately at the Royal Gardens with Johnson's Creoles from 8 P.M. to 1 A.M., and then every night went to the Dreamland Cafe and worked until 6 A.M. As an introduction to Chicago Style Dixieland, listen to Side 1, Band 6 of the record included with this book (see example 18, p. 69 and Appendix A).

In 1920, the leading entertainer was Al Jolson, while Bessie Smith was a big success in the Atlanta, Georgia, area. In addition, in September of the same year, the first radio broadcast took place. Radio soon became a part of many households and thereby did much to popularize jazz in general and some jazz artists in particular. In the 1920s, recordings were as important as they are today.

Jazz of quality was played in several cities in the 1920s, but documentation is absent in some areas because most of the recording was done in New York (blues singers) or on the outskirts of Chicago.

In Los Angeles in 1921, New Orleans trombonist Kid Ory recorded what most historians feel were the first instrumental jazz records by a black band. In 1923, Ory scored another first with his radio broadcasts. Kid Ory trombone solos may sound very rough and dated today, but in his time his playing was so modern that he is credited with being greatly responsible for freeing the trombone from playing glorified tuba parts and allowing the instrument such choices as long flowing lines and even improvisation with the aid of a plunger mute.[1] Kid Ory was also a good jazz composer. His most famous work became a Dixieland standard, "Muskrat Ramble."

7
Chicago Style Dixieland
(the 1920s)

---

1. Kid Ory, "Weary Blues," *History of Classic Jazz*, vol. 10.

In New York around 1924, Fletcher Henderson was organizing recording sessions and accompanying blues singers. Chicago Style Dixieland seeped into New York too. Trumpeter Red Nichols, trombonist Miff Mole, and saxophone-clarinet player Jimmy Dorsey all recorded some records that have become jazz classics.[2]

Elsewhere, in Detroit around 1927, a band named McKinney's Cotton Pickers featured a fine young saxophonist-arranger, Don Redman. Jean Goldkette had a fairly commercial type of orchestra in spite of the fact that his personnel included such jazz greats as Bix Beiderbecke, Frankie Trumbauer, and Pee Wee Russell. And in Los Angeles, a former New Orleans Rhythm Kings drummer, Ben Pollack, organized a Chicago Style Dixieland band. Pollack used mainly Chicago musicians like Benny Goodman plus a Texas clique like the Teagardens.

The jazz activity in Kansas City in the twenties is discussed in chapter 9 because it was more truly swing jazz.

To appreciate Chicago Style Dixieland, one must picture the times. It was the Roaring Twenties, what F. Scott Fitzgerald called "the Jazz Age." There were straw hats and arm bands, both Model T and Model A Fords as well as Stutz Bearcat cars, raccoon coats, and speakeasies. In spite of the fact that Chicago was entirely in the hands of gangsters, these were happy times for the general public. Everything seemed to be based on having fun. In fact, musicians today call dixieland music "happy music." World War I was over, and the big stock market crash of 1929 was not even envisaged. Life seemed to be a party. Even new dances such as the Charleston and Black Bottom were invented to suit the new energetic music.

Chicago of the gangster period, the Golden Era, saw the first Vitaphone "talkie" movie from Warner Brothers opening in November 1926. Thirteen months later, the Negro weekly the Chicago Defender *commented on a new-fangled "Amplivox" in a South Side restaurant. It was a machine that reproduced Louis Armstrong's scatting vocal of "Heebie Jeebies." Few musicians recognized the potential popularity of the primitive juke box. And even fewer anticipated the eventual sale of $600 million in records annually, and the millions in fees and royalties payable to the musicians and singers for their services on records.*[3]

The technical differences between Chicago Style Dixieland, which developed in the 1920s, and Early New Orleans Dixieland were as follows:

1. A saxophone (usually a tenor saxophone) was added.
2. The guitar replaced the banjo.
3. Fairly elaborate (by comparison) introductions and endings were common.
4. Ease and relaxation in playing style were sacrificed for tension and drive.
5. Individual solos became more important.
6. Rhythm changed from 4/4 to 2/4.

Listen to the record in the back of the text to hear these items and to compare the two different ways of performing dixieland jazz.

Both dixieland styles used cornet, trombone, clarinet, and drums. The piano was now used in both styles, and the string bass had replaced the tuba. The last two changes occurred because the bands that played for dancing no longer played for marching. The players of the Chicago era preferred the guitar to the banjo. Banjo players made the shift to guitar quite easily, mainly because the type of guitars first played in bands were four-stringed instruments and tuned like banjos. The addition of the tenor saxophone gave more body to ensemble playing and added additional solo color. When one more player is added to an ensemble of twenty or so, the change could go unnoticed. But in early dixieland the front line was only three players; to add another musician to these three made a decided difference. The Original Dixieland Jazz Band added a baritone saxophone and an alto sax in 1920. The role of the saxophone in ensemble playing was comparable to that of the clarinet, except that its harmony line (or countermelody) was directly under the melodic line of the cornet.

As mentioned before, the rhythmic feel in Chicago Style Dixieland changed from the four even beats to a measure of Early New Orleans Dixieland to accent on the second and fourth beats (or the offbeats) of a measure. Once again, this is called 2/4 in jazz. The reason for the change was that the bands, no longer used for marching, could hire piano players, and these piano players had been playing ragtime with its

2. Red Nichols, "Ida," *The Jazz Story*, vol. 2; Miff Mole, "Original Dixieland One Step," *Folkways Jazz*, vol. 7.

3. Dave Dexter, *The Jazz Story: From the Nineties to the Sixties*, © 1964. By permission of Prentice-Hall, Inc., Englewood Cliffs, N.J.

Example 17A

**Early New Orleans Dixieland
(no accents—flat four or 4/4)**

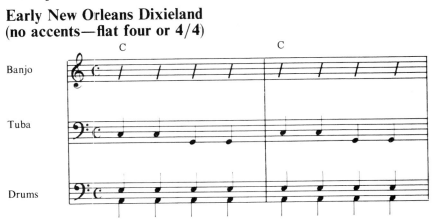

Example 17B

**Chicago Style Dixieland
(accented 2nd and 4th beats—2/4)**

accented offbeats. The jazz drummer was now influenced by the addition of the piano, and he began to accent the second and fourth beats. Listen to young drummer Gene Krupa toward the end of the Chicagoans' record of "Nobody's Sweetheart." Krupa, playing in the Chicago style at that time, plays rim shots on the second and fourth beats; this is as loudly as he can accent these beats without putting a hole in his drum.[4] The bass player followed the left hand of the piano and played only on beats one and three. The guitar player played on two and four or, at least,

accented two and four to adjust to the piano. Examples 17A and 17B demonstrate the difference between the approaches of the rhythm sections of both styles.

These examples show why jazz-oriented people always clap their hands or snap their fingers on beats two and four instead of on one and three.

During the 1920s Louis Armstrong and Earl "Fatha" Hines began a long association, a fact that proves that Armstrong influenced not only all wind

4. Chicagoans, "Nobody's Sweetheart," *Folkways Jazz*, vol. 6.

Earl Hines. Courtesy of Bob Asen, Metronome Magazine.

players but also piano players.[5] Hines developed a way of playing called "trumpet-style" piano because he wanted to play the type of melodic playing so natural to his friend Armstrong instead of playing ragtime or boogie-woogie.

Armstrong was considerably involved in Chicago jazz during the 1920s, and his recordings with the Hot Five and Hot Seven are truly jazz classics.[6] But Armstrong is a good example of a musician who cannot and should not be categorized quite so narrowly. He had

been a member of King Oliver's band earlier, and then later had a famous swing band. His last band was a dixieland group, one of the most enjoyable in the history of jazz.[7]

5. *Louis Armstrong and Earl Hines*, Columbia Records, CL 853.

6. *Louis Armstrong and His Hot Five*, Columbia Records, CL 851.

7. *Louis Armstrong Plays W.C. Handy*, Columbia Records, CL 591.

The period of the 1920s brought many professionally trained instrumentalists into jazz. Until this time, jazz had been a predominantly black art form. The only formally trained black musicians, with the exception of a few piano players, were the Creole performers. The advent of Chicago Style Dixieland brought large numbers of white players with formal musical training into the jazz field.

As is always the case with every new style of jazz, Chicago Style Dixieland brought into jazz many youngsters who were avid fans of the jazz groups who had moved into Chicago. There was a high school clique called the "Austin High Gang." The group formed an important nucleus in the development of this style. Among these young players were Pee Wee Russell, Dave Tough, Bud Freeman, Gene Krupa, Eddie Condon, Mezz Mezzrow, and their friends Benny Goodman, Bix Beiderbecke, Muggsy Spanier, and Bunny Berigan—a group of talented young players for the jazz roster. A jazz historian could never find more enthusiasm than these young Chicago players had for their brand of music. However, by comparison with other styles of jazz, the recordings of these musicians simply do not exemplify either their energetic feeling or musicianly technique.

As Benny Goodman grew up in the hurried pace of Chicago in the twenties, he patterned his early efforts after Jimmy Noone of New Orleans and Frank Teschemacher of Chicago's Austin High Gang, but he soon surpassed his models and went on to become the "King" of the Swing Era.

One of the best and most popular groups in the Chicago era was named the New Orleans Rhythm Kings, even though they never played in New Orleans.[8] This group influenced and inspired many young musicians in the vicinity of Chicago. It should be noted that combos such as this one and the personnel from Austin High School played in downtown Chicago, while Armstrong and Oliver reigned on the south side of town. Whereas the Original Dixieland Jazz Band denied (falsely) being influenced by black musicians, the New Orleans Rhythm Kings stated that they did whatever they could to sound like Oliver and others. It also appears that the New Orleans Rhythm Kings were a link between the New Orleans players and the roster of players entering jazz in the Chicago days. Therefore they were actually more important as an influence than as individual players; in other words, those players they influenced often surpassed them.[9]

Until Beiderbecke came to Chicago, the best white trumpet player was Francis Spanier, a youngster who followed Armstrong every hour possible. Armstrong nicknamed him "Muggsy." His recordings are some of the best examples of the way these young players attempted to play. The music has great vitality and creativeness, and yet it was meant to be and truly is "fun" listening.[10]

Leon "Bix" Beiderbecke was born in 1903 and lived for only twenty-eight years; still, his name on a record makes it a collector's item. It is said that his style was fairly well formed from listening to records of The Original Dixieland Jazz Band and others before he had heard Armstrong. In Chicago, he listened to Oliver, Armstrong, and The New Orleans Rhythm Kings. Some historians state that Beiderbecke developed his style from listening to Emmet Hardy. Hardy played on the riverboats that stopped at Davenport, Iowa, Beiderbecke's hometown. Beiderbecke's first employment was with a group called The Wolverines, whose first recordings were made in 1924.[11] Beiderbecke worked for a while with his close friend saxophonist Frankie "Tram" Trumbauer. Trumbauer soon became dedicated to looking after Beiderbecke's welfare, guiding him to the big bands of Jean Goldkette and Paul Whiteman where top salaries were to be had. Some of Beiderbecke's best records were done with small combos "outside" his regular job with Whiteman. Especially notable are those with Trumbauer.[12] Beiderbecke's piano compositions show Debussy's influence, the best known of which is "In a Mist." On the cornet, Beiderbecke never seemed to let his style become as dramatic or sensual as Armstrong's. Instead, his cornet music is usually described as poetic, fluid, moving, and sensitive—if words can ever truly describe music.[13] Many writers refer to Beiderbecke as the first "cool" artist. It is true that even though he could move an ensemble almost by himself, he usually did not play with the frenzy of most of the Chicago Style trumpets.

8. New Orleans Rhythm Kings, "Sweet Lovin' Man," *Folkways Jazz*, vol. 6; "Livery Stable Blues," *History of Classic Jazz*, vol. 4; Dave Dexter, *The Jazz Story*, p. 34.

9. New Orleans Rhythm Kings, "Tin Roof Blues," *Introduction to Jazz*, Della Records, DL 8244.

10. Muggsy Spanier, "Muskrat Ramble," *History of Classic Jazz*, vol. 9.

11. Wolverine Orchestra, "Jazz Me Blues," *Folkways Jazz*, vol. 6; The Wolverines, "Royal Garden Blues," *History of Classic Jazz*, vol. 7; *Bix Beiderbecke and the Wolverines*, Riverside Records, RLP 12–133.

12. *The Bix Beiderbecke Story*, vols. 1 to 3, Columbia Records, CL 844–6.

13. Bix Beiderbecke, "Somebody Stole My Gal" and "Margie," *Folkways Jazz*, vol. 6.

Left to right, Howdy Quicksell, Tommy Gargano, Paul Mertz, Don Murray, Bix Beiderbecke, and Tommy Dorsey. Courtesy of Leo Walker.

This situation could be compared to that of Miles Davis during the Bop Era when Dizzy Gillespie's virtuosic style was in vogue.

To this day Chicago Style Dixieland music has never lost its appeal, due primarily to its rhythmic concept. When dixieland is played today, it is almost always Chicago Style. Many musicians are not even aware of the fact that there is more than one style of dixieland. There are clubs and societies dedicated to the preservation of dixieland music. However, this music is seldom played exactly as it was, even in the 1920s. The musicians have lived through other jazz eras, all of which have become part of their musical personality. Of course, jazz musicians have always been more concerned about playing with good expression than about playing "authentically." Many seventeen- and eighteen-year-old musicians accept this style as the best way to express themselves and play Chicago Style Dixieland very well.[14] Today, this tradition is carried on most admirably by such groups as The World's Greatest Jazz Band and The Dukes of Dixieland and by individuals like Bobby Hackett.[15] The style was even perpetuated by large orchestras such as the Dorsey Brothers' orchestra and Bob Crosby's orchestra. Bob Crosby built a reputation on a big-band version of this small-band style.[16] In larger orchestras, complete sections play written parts based on lines originally invented for one instrument. This is an example of one style of jazz influencing the style that followed.

Recording companies have not reproduced Chicago Style Dixieland records with nearly the same enthusiasm that they have Early New Orleans Dixieland, blues singers, and swing bands. Of the records that are available, there is more to be said for the soloists than for the ensemble passages.[17] This seems incongruous when one hears the excellence of ensembles on exceptional records like those of Muggsy Spanier.

Some writers feel that the "jazz age" ended about 1927. Although jazz did continue, the large bands began to absorb the better jazz players. For example, Beiderbecke joined the famous Paul Whiteman Orchestra. By the end of the 1920s, the heart of the jazz scene had moved from Chicago to New York.

Additional Reading Resources

Berton, Ralph. *Remembering Bix: A Memoir of the Jazz Age.*

Dexter, Dave. *The Jazz Story*, pp. 30–55.

Harris, Rex. *Jazz*, pp. 189–96.

Henthoff, Nat, and McCarthy, Albert, eds. *Jazz*, pp. 139–69.

Schuller, Gunther. *Early Jazz: Its Roots and Musical Development*, pp. 175–94.

Sudhalter, Richard M., and Evans, Philip R. *Bix: Man and Legend.*

Williams, Martin T., ed. *The Art of Jazz*, pp. 59–73.

Note: Complete information including name of publisher and date of publication is provided in the Bibliography.

Additional Record Resources

Louis Armstrong. RCA Victor Records, VPM–6044.

Bix Beiderbecke and the Chicago Cornets (4 sides). Milestone Records, M–47019.

The Bix Beiderbecke Legend. RCA Victor Records, LPM–2323.

Chicagoans (1928–1930). Decca Records, 79231.

Chicago Ramblers. *Jazz of the 20's*. Merry Makers Records, 103.

Dukes of Dixieland. *At the Jazz Band Ball*. RCA Victor Records, LSP–2097.

Encyclopedia of Jazz on Records, vols. 1 and 2.

Folkways Jazz, vols. 5, 6, and 7. Folkways Records, FJ 2805, 6, 7.

Hackett, Bobby. *The Hackett Horn*. Epic Records, EE 22004.

History of Classic Jazz, vols. 4, 6, 7, and 9.

Jazz Odyssey, vol. 2.

Jazz Story, vols. 1 and 2.

Ruedebusch, Dick. *Mister Trumpet*. Jubilee Records, 5015.

——. *Meet Mr. Trumpet*. Jubilee Records, 5008.

14. The Windjammers, *Jammin' with the Windjammers*, Argo Records, LP–4047.

15. *The World's Greatest Jazz Band*, Atlantic Records, 1570; *The Dukes of Dixieland*, Audio Fidelity Records, 5962, 5976; Harmony Music Records, 11149; Bobby Hackett, "Struttin' with Some Barbecue," *The Jazz Story*, vol. 2.

16. Bob Crosby, *Stomp It Off, Let's Go*, Mono Records, AH 29; *Greatest Hits*, Decca Records, 74856; "Maryland My Maryland," *The Jazz Story*, vol. 4; *Mardi Gras Parade*, Monmouth-Evergreen Records, 7026.

17. *The Best of Dixieland*, RCA Victor Records, LSP–2982.

Suggested Classroom Activities

1. Who recorded the first instrumental jazz records by a black band?

2. Describe Chicago during the Roaring Twenties.

3. Musically, in what ways did the Chicago Style Dixieland music differ from the Early New Orleans Dixieland style?

4. In what way did ragtime piano playing influence the rhythm of Chicago Style Dixieland music?

5. In this era what instruments were added and what instruments replaced other instruments used in Early New Orleans Dixieland ensembles? Why did these changes take place?

6. Gradually, short solo spots crept into jazz ensembles. Listen to "Maple Leaf Rag" by Paul Mares and his Friars' Society Orchestra (Folkways Records, FJ2806, vol. 6, Chicago no. 2). Identify the instruments that are heard in brief solo spots. Does the piano have an opportunity to play solo? Is there a string bass?

7. Listen to Bix Beiderbecke and His Gang play "Margie" (Folkways Records, FJ2806, vol. 6, Chicago no. 2). In the opening statement of the melody, which instrument is featured? Is this a good example of the 2/4 rag rhythm? Notice that a bass sax is used in place of a tenor sax.

Example 18
(Side 1, Band 6)

For complete arrangement see Appendix A.

8
Boogie-Woogie
(the 1920s and 1930s)

Boogie-woogie is considered another stage in the evolution of jazz, and like ragtime it was a piano style important in the development of jazz. The term boogie-woogie itself is very descriptive. Possibly it derives from the sound heard when eight beats to the bar are performed; however, Rousas Rushdoony refers to the term as it concerns ancient rites in Morocco.[1] This style of piano playing came into prominence because of an economic crisis—the Great Depression of the early 1930s. Jazz again faced a situation in which a full style of piano playing was needed as a substitute for hiring a band. For an introduction to boogie-woogie, listen to Side 2, Band 1 of the recorded examples.

The most identifying feature of boogie-woogie is the eight beats to a measure that are played as an *ostinato*. *Ostinato* (an Italian word) is the technical term for a melodic figure that recurs throughout the music. In Purcell's composition "Dido's Lament" (example 19) an *ostinato* phrase is present in the bass line.

In boogie-woogie piano playing, this *ostinato phrase* is always in the bass. It is very possible, however, to hear boogie-woogie played by a big band when the *ostinato* is not present; there will still be eight beats to the bar. Jazz had been played in the 4/4 rhythm of Early New Orleans Dixieland and in the 2/4 rhythm of ragtime and Chicago Style Dixieland. Boogie-woogie, though, employs eight beats to the bar in the *ostinato* bass.

There are two distinct methods of boogie-woogie playing. In both, the right hand is kept free for melodic interpretation or improvisation. The difference between the two methods occurs in the use of the left hand. In one, the left hand plays full, moving chords; in the other, a "walking" bass line outlines the chords in a melodic fashion. Examples 20A and 20B demonstrate the use of full chords. There are various means of outlining the chords with a melodic bass line. Examples 20C, 20D, and 20E illustrate three of the most common.

Although the right hand can play an interesting melodic line, the main feature of this style is rhythmic virtuosity. The left hand and the right hand operate so independently that boogie-woogie often sounds like it is being performed by two pianists instead of by one. The style is extremely taxing physically, since it is usually played loudly with tensed muscles—a most tiring means of performing. The riff emphasis, typical of Kansas City (to be discussed in chapter 9) is often

---

1. Rousas J. Rushdoony, *The Politics of Pornography* (Sandtron City, Sandtron, South Africa: Valiant Publishers, 1975) p. 98.

Example 19

Dido's Lament

from Dido and Aeneas
HENRY PURCELL

heard in the right hand of boogie-woogie players as the left hand busies itself with the *ostinato.* Boogie-woogie is generally, but not always, played in the blues form.

Boogie-woogie was usually played by untrained pianists. Ragtime had incorporated European influences, but it appears as though boogie-woogie piano players worked out their style without any thought of European concert tradition. Many could not read music; they simply listened and developed this full style of playing. Most of the time boogie-woogie players are only comfortable playing this one style of jazz. However, Pete Johnson, who was surely the number one boogie-woogie pianist in Kansas City, was also a fine stride player. He really showed his versatility when he accompanied blues singer Joe Turner hour after hour.[2]

While it is true that boogie-woogie reached its peak of popularity during the depression of the early 1930s, the style surely was not invented then. The first time that the word *boogie* appears to have been used on a record was in 1928 by Chicago's Pine Top Smith as he recorded "Pine Top's Boogie."[3] Huddie Ledbetter claimed that he first heard this type of playing in 1899; Bunk Johnson (early New Orleans trumpeter) said 1904; Jelly Roll Morton said 1904; W.C. Handy said 1909. This music has also been called "Western rolling," "fast Western," and "Texas style," indicating that its origin was in the western part of the country, although Florida has also been named as a birthplace. Boogie-woogie has also been called "8 over 4." Example 21 shows the logic of this label. There are four quarter notes through the bar of 4/4 normally, but boogie-woogie superimposes eight beats in this same measure because eight eighth notes take up the same amount of time as four quarter notes.

There were three fairly defined generations of boogie-woogie players. The earlier pianists were active primarily in the 1920s: Jimmy Yancey, Cow Cow Davenport, and Pine Top Smith.[4] The middle group was

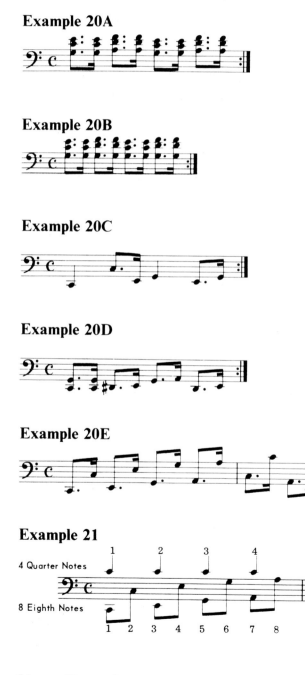

Example 20A

Example 20B

Example 20C

Example 20D

Example 20E

Example 21

4 Quarter Notes

8 Eighth Notes

2. Joe Turner and Pete Johnson, "Roll 'Em Pete," Columbia Records 35959; "Johnson and Turner Blues," *Jazz of Two Decades,* EmArcy Records, DEM–2.

3. Pine Top Smith, "Pine Top's Boogie," *Encyclopedia of Jazz on Records,* vol. 1.

4. Jimmy Yancey, "The Fives," *History of Classic Jazz,* vol. 5; "Yancey Stomp," *Folkways Jazz,* vol. 10.

Meade Lux Lewis. Courtesy of Bob Asen, Metronome Magazine.

popular during the early 1930s: Meade Lux Lewis, Albert Ammons, Joe Sullivan, Clarence Lofton, and Pete Johnson.[5] The last group included such players as Freddie Slack, Cleo Brown, and Bob Zurke.

Max Harrison states that this style of piano playing developed from a guitar technique used in mining, logging, and turpentine camps.[6] When three guitar players performed together, one picked out an improvised melody, the second played rhythmic chords, and

5. Meade Lux Lewis, "Special No. 1," *Folkways Jazz,* vol. 9; "Honky Tonk Train," *Folkways Jazz,* vol. 10; "Far Ago Blues," *History of Classic Jazz,* vol. 5; Albert Ammons, "St. Louis Blues," *Folkways Jazz,* vol. 10; Joe Sullivan, "Little Rock Getaway," *Folkways Jazz,* vol. 9; Clarence Lofton, "Brown Skin Gal," *Folkways Jazz,* vol. 10; "Blue Boogie," *History of Classic Jazz,* vol. 5; Pete Johnson, "Let 'Em Jump," *Folkways Jazz,* vol. 10; "Lone Star Blues," *History of Classic Jazz,* vol. 5.

6. Max Harrison, "Boogie Woogie," in *Jazz,* eds. Nat Hentoff and Albert McCarthy (New York: Holt Rinehart & Winston, 1959), p. 107.

the third played a bass line. In order to imitate three guitars at one time, piano players had to develop a very full style by having the right hand play the melodic improvisation and the left hand substitute for the other two guitars. In examples 20A and 20B, the bass line originally played by the third guitar is omitted; however, this is not apparent because the moving chords cause the music to sound very full and complete. In examples 20C, 20D, and 20E, the left hand plays the bass line while actually outlining the chords. The notes in example 22A are outlined in 22B.

Although boogie-woogie is considered a definite piano style, it has been successfully adapted by large bands such as Will Bradley's, Lionel Hampton's, Tommy Dorsey's, Count Basie's, Harry James's, Glenn Miller's, and others.[7] The eight beats to the bar created by the *ostinato* bass is considered its most important feature. This rhythmic component exemplifies the fact that jazz players are always searching for new means of expression. However, having been created within a fairly limited set of circumstances (the guitar origin), regardless of the rhythmic interest, the range of expression of this style is not very wide. Boogie-woogie has never really disappeared, but it is not prominent today, except for an occasional revival. One revival occurred as late as 1938.

This music has never progressed. If it were to progress (change) rhythmically, it would no longer be considered boogie-woogie. It could progress harmonically, but because of the very mechanics of performing this style, most players are only comfortable with quite simple harmonies. In fact, since the beginnings of this style, the standard chord sequence has always been the blues chord progression; this is still true today.

The boogie-woogie revival around 1938 was so popular that almost all performing groups had at least one number in their repertoire. Some boogie-woogie pianists toured and even played in such notable concert halls as Carnegie Hall. Pete Johnson, Meade Lux Lewis, and Albert Ammons perform a boogie-woogie trio on the *Spirituals to Swing* album, which was recorded live at Carnegie Hall.[8] It seems that when three of these stylistic players perform at the same time, they almost try to outshout each other. In their exuberance they even lose the eight-to-the-bar feeling. The revival was a boon to these players and certainly raises a pertinent question: why, whenever a style or a group of artists *enjoy and benefit* from great popularity, do so many critics and unrealistic students of jazz claim "exploitation"?

The theme (example 2A) is now used as a basis for improvisation in the boogie-woogie style. Example 23 shows the bass pattern used by the pianist on Side 2, Band 1.

Additional Reading Resources

Hentoff, Nat, and McCarthy, Albert, eds. *Jazz,*
    pp. 107–35.
Williams, Martin T. ed. *The Art of Jazz,*
    pp. 95–108.
Note: Complete information including name of publisher and date of publication is included in the Bibliography.

7. Will Bradley, "Beat Me Daddy, Eight to the Bar," Columbia Records, 35530; Lionel Hampton, "Hamp's Boogie Woogie," Decca Records, 71828; Tommy Dorsey, "Boogie Woogie," RCA Victor Records, 26054; Count Basie, "Boogie Woogie," *The Best of Basie,* Roulette Records, R52081; Harry James, "Boo Woo," Columbia Records, 35958; Glenn Miller, "Bugle Woogie," *The Glenn Miller Chesterfield Shows,* RCA Victor Records, LSP–3981 (e).

8. Pete Johnson, Albert Ammons, and Meade Lux Lewis, "Cavalcade of Boogie," *Spirituals to Swing,* Vanguard Records, VRS–8523/4.

Example 22A

Example 22B

Example 23
(Side 2, Band 1)

Additional Record Resources

Boogie Woogie, Folkways Records, FJ2810.

Boogie Woogie, History of Classic Jazz, vol. 5. Riverside Records, SDP–11.

Boogie Woogie Rarities. Milestone Records, MLP 2009.

Suggested Classroom Activities

1. Define the term *boogie-woogie* as applied to piano technique.

2. In this style of piano technique, how many beats are in each measure?

3. Describe two methods of boogie-woogie playing in the bass part or left-hand piano part.

4. Listen to "Yancey Stomp" by pianist Jimmy Yancey (*Jazz*, vol. 10, Folkways Records, Album no. FJ2810).

9
Swing
(1932–42)

Swing is the name given to the era following boogie-woogie in the development of jazz. In general, *swing* refers to large dance bands that played written arrangements, occasionally using improvised solos. Some jazz terms can become quite confusing; *swing* is one of them. Most noteworthy jazz has a rhythmic drive called swing. Still, the era of jazz in the thirties and early forties is called the Swing Era. The confusion comes from the fact that some of the most popular swing music did not swing, but involved jazz players doing a jazz interpretation of pretty ballads. One of the unusual aspects of swing jazz is that though most people remember the up-tempo tunes, the swing bands actually played more ballads than anything else. But it should be remembered that those ballads were played by players who were very jazz-oriented. Listen for example to Benny Goodman, the King of Swing, play his theme, a very pretty ballad called "Good-bye"; jazz trumpeter Harry James plays an obligato in the background.[1]

Some listeners today feel that all of the swing bands sound alike. During the Swing Era, there were literally hundreds of name and semi-name attractions, and so one of the biggest concerns for the leaders was identification. They wanted the fans to be able to distinguish their band from all other bands after hearing just a few measures of music. Therefore, most bands attempted to have an identifying trademark. For example, Tommy Dorsey probably played with a more beautiful tone and control on the trombone than anyone else; so he played solos on just about every arrangement and the fans recognized his sound.[2] Glenn Miller used a clarinet playing lead over his saxophone section, a most identifying feature.[3] As an introduction to swing, listen to Side 2, Band 2 of the recorded examples (see example 27, p. 90 and Appendix A).

Fletcher Henderson proved most influential in the Swing Era, and he is credited with having created, along with Don Redman, the pattern for swing arrangements.[4] That this pattern was successful is demonstrated by the fact that it was copied by almost every popular dance band of the era. Henderson is said to have established the independent use of the trumpet section, trombone section, saxophone section, rhythm section, together with the use of soloists. This exact

1. Benny Goodman, "Good-bye," *The Great Band Era*, RCA Victor Records, RD4–25 (RRIS–5473).

2. Tommy Dorsey, "I'm Gettin' Sentimental Over You," *The Great Band Era*.

3. Glenn Miller, "Moonlight Serenade," *The Great Band Era*.

4. Nat Shapiro and Nat Hentoff, eds., *The Jazz Makers* (New York: Grove Press, 1957), p. 118.

Fletcher Henderson and His Orchestra. Henderson is on the extreme right. Courtesy of Ray Avery.

same format is used today by most of the thousands of college and high school jazz bands around the country. The attitude (also fostered by music publishers) seems to be that this is the only avenue possible for today's jazz.

In New York in 1924, Fletcher Henderson had Louis Armstrong, Coleman Hawkins, and Don Redman among his very exclusive personnel. In 1924 in Kansas City, Benny Moten put together his first saxophone section as such; the idea was simply to create more sonority. Moten added more brass as early as 1931, using three trumpets and two trombones. Henderson had done the same thing in 1929. Some say that the first jazz orchestra to play written arrangements in New York City was the Billy Paige Band with Don Redman as arranger and lead alto sax, in 1922. Redman then joined Fletcher Henderson, stayed with him until 1927, joined McKinney's Cotton Pickers in 1931,

and eventually organized his own band. Henderson, Redman, and others took the parts that were generally conceived to be for one trumpet, for example, and harmonized them to be played by three trumpets (see examples 24A and 24B).

The general procedure in the creation of a swing jazz arrangement is to write a score (see example 25) in which specific notes are planned for each instrument to play in every measure. In jazz, the music arranger indicates measures for solo improvisation. After the arranger has decided what musical notations will result in the desired sounds, he gives the score to a music copyist who extracts from the score the individual parts for the various instruments. This then becomes a blueprint for each instrumentalist, and it shows him exactly what he is to play while the other instrumentalists play their parts.

Example 24A

Example 24B

Short repeated refrains or phrases are quite typical in African music. In jazz, the phrases are called *riffs*. Sometimes riffs are used in an *ostinato* fashion as catalysts that hold the music together. Repeated riffs, which cause great momentum and impetus, were used extensively by Kansas City musicians such as Benny Moten (later Count Basie's band) in the 1920s and by New York musicians such as Fletcher Henderson who was scoring arrangements behind blues singers Bessie Smith, Ma Rainey, and others. The use of riffs became standard in the more jazz-oriented large bands. Sometimes they were used to back up a soloist; sometimes entire selections were made up of riffs. Listen to the swing excerpt on the record supplied with the text (Side 2, Band 2), in which the brass section plays the riff shown in example 26A behind the saxophones. The trombones play the riff shown in example 26B under the clarinet solo.

Fletcher Henderson, a schooled piano player from Georgia, came to New York City in 1920 originally to do postgraduate study at Columbia University as a chemistry major. Duke Ellington, from Washington, D.C., had a scholarship to the Pratt Institute of Art. Both Ellington and Henderson became so involved in music that their other goals were forsaken. Henderson was a pianist, but his most important talent was his arranging. He wrote most of the library of music that launched the career of the Benny Goodman orchestra. The personnel of Henderson's own orchestra was most impressive. At one time or another almost all of the important black musicians of the day played in his band: Louis Armstrong, Roy Eldridge, Don Redman, Coleman Hawkins, Lester Young, and so on. Many members from the Henderson band went on either to have bands of their own or to become featured solo attractions.[5]

There always seem to be many (too many) controversies concerning jazz. Fletcher Henderson became deeply involved in one of the great controversies: the split between the advocates of small dixieland bands and those favoring the larger bands heading in the direction of swing. Many thought that the rise of the big bands meant the fall of jazz completely. There will always be controversy over how large a band can be before it becomes top-heavy and its rhythmic momentum stops. Top-heavy means that too many musicians are playing over the rhythm section.

At first, Henderson toyed with sort of an enlarged dixieland group. But with the addition of Don Redman, who had studied at the Boston and Detroit Music Conservatories, tighter harmonic control became a major interest. Henderson thought that too much improvisation was almost dreary, unless the improvisers were really exceptional. He also thought that the polyphony established in the dixieland styles was too risky, that there should be more control.

During the 1920s when Chicago Style Dixieland was the most popular jazz expression, New York and Kansas City were the most important geographic areas for developments leading toward the swing style of jazz. In the mid-1920s, Ellington was becoming a name attraction, King Oliver was playing in the Savoy Ballroom in New York's Harlem, and Fletcher Henderson was at the Roseland Ballroom in Times Square. In New York were located network radio programs, booking offices, and recording studios, so that musicians began to migrate to that city from all over the country. One of the most swinging bands to invade New York was William McKinney's Cotton Pickers. This band, with many ex-Henderson personnel, recorded more than fifty tunes between 1928 and 1933.[6] The band of Chick Webb was one of the fresh new bands that kept

5. Fletcher Henderson, *A Study in Frustration,* Columbia Records, C4L–19; *Fletcher Henderson,* vols. 1 and 2, Decca Records, 79227–8.

6. William McKinney, "Four or Five Times," *Folkways Jazz,* vol. 8.

Example 25

Example 26A

Example 26B

appearing in New York around 1929 or 1930.[7] However, Fletcher Henderson and Duke Ellington were the best-known performers developing toward swing in New York City in the 1920s.[8]

Generally, the New York bands had heavily structured arrangements. But there was really no New York school as there had been a New Orleans school, a Chicago school, and even a Kansas City school. There were many important performers in New York in the 1920s, but their styles did not seem to coincide very well. However, the direction of most was at least toward swing.

There was great activity in Kansas City from the early 1920s to about 1938. A political organization known as the Pendergast Machine did much more than encourage the nightclub atmosphere, and so there was an abundance of employment opportunities for jazz musicians. The influx showed that Kansas City had become an important jazz mecca: there was Bill Basie from Red Bank, New Jersey, Ben Webster from Tulsa, Lester Young from Mississippi, and Andy Kirk from Dallas.

The Benny Moten band was considered to be the top band in the Kansas City area from about 1926 to 1935,[9] but the competition was extremely keen from the bands of Andy Kirk (piano and arrangements by the talented Mary Lou Williams), Walter Page, Alphonso Trent, and others. The Kansas City bands were looser in musical setting and relied heavily on blues-based riffs.

Count Basie was in New York in the early 1920s when he joined a road show that became stranded in Kansas City. Basie then joined the Benny Moten band and eventually became the leader after Moten died.

However, Basie had started his own band before Moten's death, and most of Moten's better players had gone with Basie. It is therefore natural that some historians state that Basie took over Moten's band—especially since all of these events happened around the time of Moten's death. When Moten died and Basie became the leading figure in the Kansas City style of swing, Basie's players used to good advantage all of the musical advancements developed in the Kansas City territory. For example, Basie anticipated bop by freeing the piano from merely keeping time, and his drummer, Jo Jones, added interesting accents to his very moving style. The Basie organization still swings as hard as any band today.[10]

The depression came in 1929. A few musicians like Armstrong and Ellington left for Europe. Some hotel-type bands like Lombardo's survived. Many of the better jazz players like Benny Goodman were able

7. Chick Webb, "Let's Get Together," *Jazz Odyssey*, vol. 3; *King of Savoy*, Decca Records, DL 9223.

8. Fletcher Henderson, "Copenhagen," and "Money Blues," and "Jackass Blues," and "Down South Camp Meetin'," *Folkways Jazz*, vol. 8; "Nagasaki," and "It's the Talk of the Town," *Jazz Story*, vol. 3; "Hop Off," *History of Classic Jazz*, vol. 8; Duke Ellington, *The Ellington Era*, Columbia Records, C3L 25; *Historically Speaking—The Duke*, Bethlehem Records, BCP 60; "Hot and Bothered," *Folkways Jazz*, vol 8; "Sophisticated Lady," *Jazz Story*, vol. 3; "Happy-Go-Lucky Local," *Jazz Story*, vol. 4; "Rainy Night," *History of Classic Jazz*, vol. 8.

9. Benny Moten, "Kansas City Breakdown," and "Moten's Swing," *Folkways Jazz*, vol. 8.

10. Count Basie, *The Best of Basie*, Columbia Records, C3L-33; E=MC², *Basie*, Roulette Records, ST 52003.

Count Basie and His Rhythm Section: Walter Page, bass; Freddy Green, guitar; Jo Jones, drums. Courtesy of Bob Asen, Metronome Magazine.

to find employment in staff radio jobs. But in general, the entire business suddenly failed. Music was a luxury that most of the public simply had to do without.

Many jazz authorities state that the Swing Era was launched in 1934 when Benny Goodman left the radio studios and formed his own band, using arrangements scored mainly by Fletcher Henderson. However, swing was certainly well on its way before 1934. In 1932, Glen Gray and his Casa Loma Orchestra was playing weekly radio shows for Camel cigarettes. This band was a large band featuring precise arrangements laden with riffs often played with a call-and-response format between the brass and saxes. There were reputable jazz players in the band. But before 1932, as stated earlier, the Fletcher Henderson band was already well established as was Duke Ellington's, and there were good swinging large bands in the Kansas City area. The fact that large jazz bands developed in

two such diverse areas as New York City and Kansas City is another of the phenomena, such as the diverse origins of the music itself, that surround jazz.

The public was trying to forget the stock market crash and the ensuing depression, and one logical manifestation was the great upsurge in dancing. It was at this time that the jazz players of the Swing Era were so well accepted and performed their music for dancing. The speakeasies of the twenties were fairly small and could not house large bands. But with the repeal of the Volstead Act in 1933, social life so changed that large ballrooms were needed for the thousands who wanted to dance every night. Large bands seemed to be the answer to the dance halls. The country was covered with large ballrooms. Bands often played in towns so small that there would be only one house with an indoor bathroom. Yet there would be a ballroom large enough to hold the six or seven thousand people who would come from miles around to hear their favorite swing bands.

The bands of the Swing Era produced a fuller sound than that of the dixieland bands mainly because they utilized two or three times as many players. Because of the number of instrumentalists, the music was organized in a homophonic construction, as in example 25, making the musical sounds more organized in their effect. At times the music of the large bands even sounded less complex than the polyphonically conceived dixieland music. The big blocks of chords used by the swing bands are the obvious clues to the homophonic construction of this type of jazz. Most of the orchestras of the Swing Era returned to the use of a flat-four rhythm to give their music a rhythm distinct from that which immediately preceded it. During the 1920s, the widely imitated Chicago Style Dixieland was played in 2/4, but the Kansas City musicians at this same time played mainly in 4/4; swing jazz was usually in 4/4.

The Original Dixieland Jazz Band had played in New York in 1917, but even more of the public was made aware of the possibilities of jazz elements when Paul Whiteman introduced George Gershwin's "Rhapsody in Blue" in Aeolian Hall in 1924. This work can hardly be considered jazz as it is defined in this text, but it did point out some of the idioms of this music to the public and help focus attention in the general direction of jazz. "Rhapsody in Blue" could conceivably be construed as the first third-stream music effort. (This direction is discussed in chapter 13.)

Obviously Paul Whiteman's title, The King of Jazz, was a misnomer and merely a publicity name, but Whiteman was a very influential man and a great supporter of jazz players. He hired many name jazz musicians and paid the top salary of the day. Jazz players and critics are too quick to degrade Whiteman's position when they fail to consider that the jazz players joined Whiteman's orchestra of their own free will, often when they were not busy enough to keep financially stable.

Whiteman had great admiration for these players. Consider, for example, that Beiderbecke was away from the orchestra for nearly a year trying to recover from alcoholism and related problems. During that time, Whiteman retained him on full salary and, it is also reported, paid Beiderbecke's medical bills. During some of the time, Beiderbecke played individual one-night engagements with competing orchestras.

A look at some of the personnel from the Whiteman roster establishes his regard for and financial support of the jazz players of the day: Bix Beiderbecke, Frankie Trumbauer, Red Norvo, Tommy and Jimmy Dorsey, Jack and Charlie Teagarden, Eddie Lang, Joe Venuti, and others. Most of the recordings of the Whiteman orchestra show very little influence of jazz as it is considered in this text. However, there are certainly noteworthy recordings of jazz players while members of Whiteman's band. For example, Whiteman established a group within his larger organization called The Swing Wing. Jack Teagarden and others were featured in this "band within a band."[11] Among jazz trombonists Jack Teagarden is *the* outstanding performer. He died in 1964, having recorded about 1,000 sides during his lifetime. His long musical lines, flexible technique, and beautiful tone will probably never be repeated.

The influence of the recording companies began to be felt during the Swing Era. The sale of records was a determining factor in the success of a musical organization. The arrangements and improvised solos were confined to fewer measures in order to adjust to the length of three-minute records. This restriction reduced individual solo expression to a minimum. If a player is forced to express himself within a few measures of music, his style of expression must necessarily be different than if he had a longer span of time in which to develop his musical ideas. This does not mean that one improviser is necessarily better than another. The limitations involved in making records that were only three minutes in length greatly affected the choice of material played by jazz bands as well as how they handled it. When technology improved to the point to where more music could be put on a ten-inch record, the powerful jukebox operators still insisted on three minutes only. Not until 1948 when 33⅓ rpm records began to be produced did this situation change, opening the door for much broader musical expositions, much more freedom of expression.

There were great technical problems in the early days of the recording industry. The musicians had to play into a large horn and, as a consequence, were placed around the room according to how hard or easy it was to pick up their sound on recording. For example, softer reed instruments were placed close to the horn, and open brass instruments were placed quite a distance away. In fact, brass players were asked to play muted as much as possible. Often no bass drum was allowed. Musicians generally not only played more

11. Jack Teagarden (Paul Whiteman's Orchestra), "Aunt Hagar's Blues," Decca Records, 2145.

cautiously than they would have in a ballroom or night club, but also usually stood in places in relation to each other that were unfamiliar and uncomfortable to them. It is remarkable that they were able to produce records at all, let alone the important documentations that we have on discs.

Seriously researched discographies have become the most authoritative sources for hard evidence regarding which musician played where. Even more important, this documentation makes it easier to assess a musician's playing by supplying evidence from the records he made. These sources are more reliable than the opinions of old friends or avid fans.

To show how the depression affected the recording industry (which in turn affected the entire music industry), Ross Russell gave the following statistics:

From an all-time high of 104 million units reached in 1927, the sale of phonograph records fell to the astonishing low of 6 million when the returns were in for 1932, a ratio of about 17 to 1. Figures for the same year show that the sale of phonographs, the backbone of the Victor Talking Machines Company's business, dropped from 987,000 units to 40,000, a ratio of 21 to 1.[12]

It seems apropos at this point to make a few statistical observations regarding the record industry as it stands at the end of the 1970s. While some record companies release over a hundred new albums a year, the company that showed the most profit released only ten albums. This brings up the question of quality versus quantity. In 1978, 102 albums "went platinum" (meaning that each sold over a million *units*; an album that has "gone gold" has sold a million *dollars* worth of units); five years earlier that figure was 37; five years before that the number was so small that the designation had not even been coined. A word of caution concerning statistics about record sales: the figure noted is often the number of records shipped *on consignment*; no mention is ever made of the amount of records returned to the company unsold.

The recording industry realizes more money from the public than do either movies or spectator sports, and rock records are responsible for most of this phenomenal growth. This should prove that rock 'n' roll is more than a fad. At this writing, the fusion of jazz and rock threatens to far outdo any stylistic progenitors. Disco is also proving quite irresistible to much of the public. Many companies are now joining the disco craze because disco records are quite reasonable to manufacture. The disco trend is expected to last three or four years.

A few years ago, the biggest percentage of records was purchased by thirteen-year-old girls; now, 37 percent of all records and tapes are purchased by persons aged twenty-five to forty-four. Analyses have been made projecting that, as far ahead as 1985 at least, this present situation will hold fast.

There appears to be less profit from each album. On the average, a company invests $250,000 to place an album on the market. The royalty rates to various artists have at least doubled since their original contracts, averaging 5–15 percent. An album by a top-selling artist can easily cost a company over $1 million dollars including promotion. More than two-thirds of all records made today are absolute financial failures; in order to keep from losing money, the company must sell between 200,000 and 300,000 copies. Six major companies now control 85 percent of the market. In 1978, however, a little known company named Polygram became the first record company to gross over $1 billion dollars in a single year.

One more important consideration is that of distribution. Small record companies are at such a disadvantage in comparison to the giants of the industry in this respect that many small manufacturers have arranged to have a large company handle their distribution. An example of this would be the fact that, at this writing, CBS distributes sixteen labels other than its own.

In contrast to the approximately 2,800 record companies at this writing, in 1933 there were only 3: The American Record Company, which owned Columbia, Brunswick, and Vocalion; Victor Records and its subsidiary, Bluebird; and Decca Records. There was a need for jazz recordings, and therefore Commodore and Blue Note were started in 1938 and 1939, respectively.

By the late 1930s prosperity was returning, and records and radio were extremely instrumental in publicizing jazz. As a consequence, for the first time a segment of jazz was the most-listened-to music in the world, and more excellent musicians were working in this field than during any previous period. During 1937, 18,000 musicians were on the road, and the number continued to increase. Rather suddenly, after having

12. Ross Russell, *Jazz Style in Kansas City and the Southwest* (Berkeley, Calif.: University of California Press, 1971), p. 109. Reprinted by permission of The Regents of the University of California.

Benny Goodman and His Orchestra. Trumpets (left to right): Harry James, Ziggy Elman, Chris Griffin, Johnny Davis; trombones: Murray McEachern, Red Ballard; saxophones: Vido Musso, Hymie Schertzer, Art Rollini, George Koenig; piano: Jess Stacy; bass: Harry Goodman; guitar: Allan Reuss; drums: Gene Krupa. Courtesy of Leo Walker.

been frequently considered to be a fairly tawdry occupation, with the rise of swing, jazz became a respectable, remunerative profession. The jazz concerts given for the first time in Carnegie Hall in 1938 were mile stones in the acceptance of jazz.[13]

Benny Goodman was considered the King of Swing. He was so capable on the clarinet that he became the clarinet image of the world. It was understood that if a clarinet player did not play the instrument in the Goodman manner he was not playing clarinet correctly. This put great pressure on good clarinet players who wanted to play in their own style instead of copying Goodman. By the time Goodman became a success, large black orchestras had already established the format for this size of organization. These were the orchestras of Moten, Kirk, and Trent from the Midwest and those of Henderson, Ellington, McKinney, and Jimmy Lunceford from the East. Goodman's success was not assured at all until he opened at the Palomar Ballroom in Los Angeles in 1935 after a very discouraging tour across the country.

13. *From Spirituals to Swing*, Vanguard Records, VRS–8523/4.

But from that moment on, there was no doubt that this next style of jazz was extremely well received by the public.[14] Dave Dexter wrote glowingly of Goodman:

> . . . Goodman often did generous things, and his courage in mixing Negroes with what was essentially an all-white orchestra and touring the Southern states can never be underestimated. He achieved as much in smashing segregation in the arts as anybody in history.
>
> Through the years, Goodman's clarinet remained the model for all beginners. Shaw could play "prettier" notes at times, Barney Bigard added an elusive coloring to Ellington's ensemble and big Irving Prestopnik [Fazola] wove glorious improvisations above the Dixieland blowings of the Bob Crosbyites, but Goodman had a sound all his own, a technique no other could top and a swinging, rhythmic approach that was irresistible.[15]

The Dorsey Brothers started with a large band version of dixieland.[16] The male singer was Bob Crosby. When Bob Crosby developed his own band with the help of ex-Pollack saxophonist Gil Rodin, it was only natural that Crosby's band would be dixieland oriented because that was the style that Crosby had been weaned on in the early Dorsey Brothers' Orchestra.

Occasionally there were cooperative bands in which all of the members shared in the profits and woes. Glen Gray and the Casa Loma Orchestra operated in this manner.[17] In the beginning the Woody Herman Herds were cooperative, but later the band ended this means of operating. Herman's band went through several distinct changes. At first it was a mixture of an overgrown dixieland band and a Kansas City blues type of swing band. Later it progressed more toward the Goodman approach to swing. Later still, his band became "progressive" (described in chapter 10). Herman still heads one of the most exciting big bands today.[18]

The public decided that the most popular of all the swing bands was the Glenn Miller band. Miller had been involved with jazz in its truest sense since childhood. He had worked with Red Nichols, Ben Pollack, and others in earlier styles. He had organized and worked with the Dorsey Brothers, Ray Noble, and others heading toward swing. Miller was a brilliant arranger, an outstanding businessman, and a fine trombone player. When he started his band, he went deeply in debt; but within two years, he was a millionaire. One of the authors found him to be an exemplary employer. The band worked only the best jobs in the country, had a commercial radio program three nights a week, recorded constantly, and even made motion pictures.

It was an ideal job for a young sideman. Today there are Glenn Miller Societies all over the world, and at this writing Miller albums record extremely high sales.[19]

It was only natural that new bands continually developed fronted by musicians who had been featured as solo artists in someone else's band. For example, from the Benny Goodman Band came Harry James, Gene Krupa, Lionel Hampton, Teddy Wilson, and others who became leaders in their own right.

Very often, the first recording of a new band would sound very similar to the band that the new leader had just left. This was because the new leader would hire friends from the band from which he had resigned to be on his first records. The musician's union had an established minimum salary that had to be paid to the musicians for recordings, so the new leader was wise to pay this to the experienced players rather than to those of lesser talents whom he was capable of hiring in his new band when first launching this new career.

A word should be mentioned at this time about pianist Stan Kenton's varied career. He organized and wrote arrangements in 1940 for a band to compete with the stylings of other swing bands. In his second stage, from 1945 to 1949, was a series of "Artistry" motifs. This was a large band that used harmonic and melodic advancements of the bop era, labeled "progressive." Pete Rugolo was the chief arranger. Next Kenton had a very large orchestra that included classical woodwinds, horns, and a full string section. Kenton called this phase "Innovations in Modern Music." His next band, in 1954, was a more normal-size swing jazz band, but he featured the very modern writing of Bill Holman, Shorty Rogers, Gerry Mulligan, and others. The 1960s saw Kenton in front of what he called his "Neophonic Orchestra," a most interesting experiment

14. Benny Goodman, *The Great Benny Goodman*, Columbia Records, CL820; *Carnegie Hall Jazz Concert*, Columbia Records, OSL–160; *The Great Band Era*, RCA Victor Records, RD4–25 (RRIS–5473).

15. Dave Dexter, *The Jazz Story: From the Nineties to the Sixties* © 1964. Reprinted by permission of Prentice-Hall, Inc., Englewood Cliffs, N.J., pp. 114–15.

16. Dorsey Brothers, *The Fabulous Dorseys Play Dixieland Jazz*, Decca Records, DL8631.

17. The Casa Loma Band, "Casa Loma Stomp," *Jazz Story*, vol. 4.

18. Woody Herman, *The Thundering Herds*, Columbia Records, C3L 25; "Misty Morning," *Jazz Story*, vol. 5.

19. *Glenn Miller—A Memorial*, RCA Victor Records, VPM 6019; *The Great Band Era*.

Glenn Miller and His Orchestra. Trombones (left to right): Paul Tanner, Jimmy Priddy, Frank D'Anolfo, Miller; trumpets: John Best, Steve Lipkin, Dale McMickle, Billy May; saxophones: Will Schwartz, Al Klink, Skip Martin, Ernie Caceres, Tex Beneke; drums: Moe Purtill; guitar: Bobby Hackett; bass: Doc Goldberg; piano: Chummy MacGregor; singers: Bill Conway, Hal Dickinson, Marion Hutton, Ray Eberle, Chuck Goldstein, Ralph Brewster.

involving many talented contemporary arranger-composers. For several more years Kenton remained one of the most energetic, exciting personalities in jazz with an exceptional band that toured the world. He died at the age of 67 on August 25, 1979.[20]

As the Swing Era emerged, the composer-arranger became important. Such excellent style-setting musicians as Fletcher and Horace Henderson, Don Redman, Duke Ellington, and too many others to list shifted the timbre of jazz from the early Paul Whiteman sounds to the sophisticated, swinging music of the large bands. Today fine textbooks by Bill Russo, Henry Mancini, George Russell, Van Alexander, and others deal with this art.

One of the oddities of big-band jazz was that soloists gained in importance also. Critic Joachim Berendt wrote of this situation:

Thus, the thirties also became the era of great soloists: the tenor saxists Coleman Hawkins and Chu Berry; the clarinetist Benny Goodman; the drummers Gene Krupa, Cozy Cole, and Sid Catlett; the pianists Fats Waller and Teddy Wilson; the alto saxists Benny Carter and Johnny Hodges; the trumpeters Roy Eldridge, Bunny Berigan, and Rex Stewart.

Often these two tendencies—the orchestral and the soloistic—merged. Benny Goodman's clarinet seemed all the more glamorous against the backdrop of his big band, Louis Armstrong's trumpet stood out in bold relief when accompanied by Louis Russell's

orchestra, and the voluminous tone of Coleman Hawkins' or Chu Berry's tenor seemed to gain from the contrast to the "hard" sound of Fletcher Henderson's band.[21]

The epitome of swing tenor saxophonists was Coleman Hawkins with his large full tone, flowing lines, and heavy vibrato.[22] A reassuring example of Hawkins's impeccable taste as an improviser is his recording of "Body and Soul."[23]

In comparing the early learning environment of two famous tenor saxophone players, Coleman Hawkins with Fletcher Henderson, and Lester Young with Count Basie,[24] Don Heckman has said:

Hawkins predated Young as an active participant in the jazz scene. As a member of the Fletcher Henderson Orchestra for ten years (1923–33), he was intimately

20. Stan Kenton, *The Kenton Era*, The Creative World of Stan Kenton, ST 1030.

21. From the *Jazz Book: From New Orleans to Rock and Free Jazz* by Joachim Berendt, translated by Dan Morgenstern, copyright 1975 Lawrence Hill & Co., Westport, Connecticut.

22. Coleman Hawkins, *The Hawk and the Hunter*, Mira Records, LPS–3003; *Coleman Hawkins*, Everest Records, FS–252.

23. Coleman Hawkins, "Body and Soul," *The Greatest Names in Jazz*, Verve Records, PR 2–3.

24. Coleman Hawkins (the Fletcher Henderson Orchestra), *A Study in Frustration*, Columbia Records, C4L–19; Lester Young (with the Count Basie Orchestra), *Lester Young Memorial Album*, Epic Records, SN 6031.

involved with what was probably the most famous jazz ensemble of the time. Henderson's orchestra typified the Eastern approach.

The Henderson, Duke Ellington, and Charles Johnson orchestras all played for a variety of musical events before audiences that frequently were all white. Although they were considered (with the exception of Ellington at the Cotton Club), to be primarily dance bands, the type of dance music they played was considerably more diverse than the bands further west. The Henderson group might be expected on any given night to play popular hits, tangos, Irish waltzes, and original jazz tunes. The music was usually written in complex arrangements, and the bands were carefully rehearsed. With some groups, in fact, well-drilled performances became more important than either improvisation or solos. Fortunately, this never happened with Henderson, who realized the importance of good soloists when Louis Armstrong joined the band in 1924. It was only logical that Hawkins' artistic growth would have been affected by such a musical environment.

. . . Young came into prominence in a completely different milieu. The Count Basie Band was the pinnacle of Kansas City and Southwestern jazz. Its music was blues-oriented, filled with riffing backgrounds, and frequently based on spontaneous head arrangements. The soloists had more opportunity to stretch out than the soloists in the more heavily orchestrated New York bands. Few of the Basie arrangements were very complicated; good intonation and well-drilled performances were not nearly as important as was the creation of a rolling, surging rhythmic swing. Kansas City jazz was dancing jazz, and the beat was the most important element. The revolutionary work of the Basie rhythm section made the Basie band something special. Their ability to generate a free-flowing, almost-alive pulse undoubtedly helped Young develop a rangy horizontal, i.e., melodic, playing style.[25]

Sometimes it is hard for young jazz enthusiasts to see how older players have influenced contemporary favorites, but the influences are there. Young's lines and Hawkins's tone can both be heard in Coltrane's recordings. Young's rhythmic and melodic outlooks can be heard on Ornette Coleman and Eric Dolphy records. In fact, it would not be an overstatement to say that every contemporary saxophonist is indebted to Young, Hawkins, and Parker.

The overall contributions of different swing bands to the development and future of jazz were varied. Benny Goodman's contribution was drive with an intense 4/4 rhythmic feeling. The Casa Loma Band featured ensemble arrangements specializing in the call-and-response pattern. Duke Ellington offered new sounds and colors built around the individual talents of his musicians and introduced larger forms into jazz. Glenn Miller proved that unerring precision was a possibility in jazz. Lionel Hampton played with chaotic swing. Bob Crosby preserved and expanded Chicago Style Dixieland music. Stan Kenton used more complex harmonies and brought recognition to such innovators as Shelly Manne, Shorty Rogers, Gerry Mulligan, and others too numerous to list. Count Basie contributed a type of relaxed ensemble setting with longer solo opportunities. Woody Herman aided the growth of jazz by continually adapting each new trend. His bands were always proving grounds for rising young instrumentalists.

There were good bands that pursued the showmanship aspect of the business with great energy; a typical example is Cab Calloway. This aspect of performance was at low ebb in jazz at one time, causing record executive Irving Townsend to proclaim, "For some reason, jazz thinks it doesn't need showmanship; it couldn't be more wrong."[26] In general, the many other swing bands of the period duplicated those already mentioned.

The small combo idea was never entirely discarded. Most large bands also had a small group made up of the better jazz players in the band. The smaller combo played during intermissions of the large band, and sometimes the small group built up its own personal following. In his band, Goodman had a trio, quartet, quintet, sextet, and even septet, depending upon the personnel in his band.[27] Artie Shaw's small "band within a band" was called The Gramercy Five and featured Johnny Guarnieri on harpsichord. Woody Herman had The Woodchoppers, Tommy Dorsey had The Clambake Seven, and so on. Throughout the swing years, Fifty-second Street in New York, with its numerous night clubs, was a real gathering place for small combos.

In July, 1944, Norman Granz organized a jazz concert at the Los Angeles Philharmonic Auditorium to aid in a fund for the defense of some Mexican-Americans who had been sent to San Quentin after a

25. Don Heckman, "Pres and Hawk, Saxophone Fountainheads," *Down Beat 30*, no. 1 (January 1963): 20.

26. Irving Townsend, "The Trouble with Jazz," *Down Beat 29*, no. 7 (March 1962): 14.

27. Benny Goodman, *The Great Benny Goodman; Carnegie Hall Jazz Concert.*

killing in Los Angeles. This concert was recorded and was the first commercial recording made in a public place instead of in a studio. It was a jam session recorded live, and it started a whole new phase in recording history. Jazz at the Philharmonic, as Granz's recording and touring package became known, was an extremely successful venture.

Because of the draft for military service and problems of transportation, the Swing Era came to an abrupt end at the beginning of World War II. Swing bands could not function unless they could play one-night stands. Though the bands took a financial loss on location jobs, they were necessary for radio time, a chance to record, and a chance to rest from the rigors of traveling. Then the bands went on the road again to recoup their losses. But World War II meant no gasoline and no automobile tires for civilians, and therefore all unessential travel came to a halt in this country. One other event contributed to the shutdown of employment for musicians. The federal government levied a 30 percent cabaret tax, and most cabarets simply closed their doors.

Swing is still with us, however, and most of the jazz we hear today stems directly from the developments of this eight- or ten-year period. The Swing Era must also be credited with many beneficial side effects: it absolutely rescued the record industry, and it allowed the musical instrument industry to grow to its present strength.

To reiterate: no style ever really dies out. For years Eddie Condon has run a nightclub that features nothing but Chicago Style Dixieland.[28] The Early New Orleans Dixieland revival of the late 1930s was mentioned previously in chapter 5.[29] Swing is still played all over the world. Not only is nostalgia of swing a salable product, but swing itself is a most communicative style of jazz.[30] There are books on the market today about the Swing Era alone.[31] It is indeed hard to be completely objective about this literature when one finds he is a part of that being discussed. The books are generally both interesting and informative. There are even books on the activities of just the Glenn Miller Band during the Swing Era,[32] and other books about this band are being written at this time.

Too many critics claim that organized, written arrangements cause jazz to lose some of its vitality, some of its "swing." These critics have not listened to Basie, Ellington, Herman, and others.

Additional Reading Resources

Allen, Walter C. *Hendersonia: The Music of Fletcher Henderson and His Musicians.*

Charters, Samuel B., and Kunstadt, Leonard. *Jazz: A History of the New York Scene.*

Dance, Stanley. *The World of Swing.*

Dexter, Dave. *The Jazz Story*, pp. 56–87, 105–20.

Feather, Leonard. *The Book of Jazz*, pp. 174–91.

Harris, Rex. *Jazz*, pp. 168–74.

McCarthy, Albert. *Big Band Jazz.*

Russell, Ross. *Jazz Styles in Kansas City and the Southwest.*

Schuller, Gunther. *Early Jazz: Its Roots and Musical Development*, pp. 242–317.

Shapiro, Nat, and Hentoff, Nat, eds. *The Jazz Makers*, pp. 175–86, 218–26.

Simon, George. *Glenn Miller.*

———. *Simon Says.*

———. *The Big Bands.*

Stearns, Marshall. *The Story of Jazz*, pp. 120–54.

Ulanov, Barry. *Handbook of Jazz*, pp. 15–26.

Walker, Leo. *The Wonderful Era of the Great Dance Bands.*

Note: Complete information including name of publisher and date of publication is provided in the Bibliography.

28. *History of Classic Jazz*, vol. 9.

29. *History of Classic Jazz*, vol. 10.

30. Live Concert, *Music Made Famous by Glenn Miller,* Warner Brothers Records, W 1428; *Those Swingin' Days of the Big Bands,* Pickwick Records, TMW–002; *The Great Band Era; The Big Bands Are Back Swinging Today's Hits,* RCA Victor Records, RD4–112 (XRIS–9501).

31. George Simon, *The Big Bands* (New York: Macmillan Co., 1967); George Simon, *Simon Says* (New Rochelle, N.Y.: Arlington House, 1971).

32. John Flower, *Moonlight Serenade* (New Rochelle, N.Y.: Arlington House, 1972).

Suggested Classroom Activities

1. In what ways did Fletcher Henderson influence the development of jazz in the Swing Era?

2. Describe the role of the music arranger in this era.

3. Explain why swing bands produced a fuller sound.

4. What jazz trombonist is considered the outstanding trombone virtuoso of the era?

5. Certain limitations were placed on the recordings of swing bands by the record industry. What were these?

6. Identify the band that was the most popular as well as the most successful.

7. What were some factors that resulted in the end of the Swing Era?

8. Was swing music primarily for listening or for dancing?

9. In order to enhance your aural perception of the big-band sound, listen to several recordings of thirty-seven top bands playing ten years of top tunes from the album *The Great Band Era* manufactured especially for *Readers Digest* by RCA.

10. Now listen to the swing band recordings in the album *Jazz* (Folkways Records FJ2808, vol. 8, Big Bands) and compare the arrangements of these earlier bands with the band sounds in the *Readers Digest* album.

Example 27

(Side 2, Band 2)

For complete arrangement see Appendix A.

Bop jazz was sometimes called *bebop* or *rebop*, but common usage shortened it to bop. In spite of some of the explanations of the origin of these words, the answer probably is that players sang the words *bebop* and *rebop* to an early bop phrase, as shown in example 28.

10
Bop
(1940–50)

Example 28

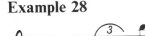

    Bop was a revolt against the confines of the larger bands. The short, stylized solos typical of the large bands of the Swing Era minimized the opportunity for exploratory expression. Soloists not only desired more freedom for experimentation, but also searched for a fresh and different approach to jazz. The young players were tired of reading written arrangements, tired of the clichés of swing, tired of the limitations of opportunity for improvisation, and so on. They also felt that many musicians with little creativeness were earning more than their share of fame and wealth and that the time had come for many changes. As an introduction to bop, listen to Side 2, Band 2 of the recorded examples (see example 31, p. 101 and Appendix A).

    Most bop players turned naturally to small combos. A quintet seemed to be the size Charlie Parker found most comfortable. It is interesting that the combos resembled, in appearance at least, the earlier dixieland bands—that is, a rhythm section with a sparse (by comparison to swing) front line. Without a doubt, the bop combo reflected Kansas City jam sessions. Regardless of claims, bop or any other style of music surely does not "begin" at any one place and at one time. It could not, for example, have been decided in October, 1940, at Minton's Playhouse in New York's Harlem, that bop was to be the next jazz style. Many unrelated events brought it about quite naturally. Just as Early New Orleans Dixieland jazz solidified in New Orleans years before, bop solidified in New York in the early 1940s. Charlie Parker said that an alto saxophone player from Dallas named Buster Smith was playing the beginnings of this free style. In the Southwest, Charlie Christian surely played saxophone-type lines on the guitar. In the St. Louis area, Jimmy Blanton was innovating on the bass. All this activity meant that the bop style developed not only in New York, but also in such places as Kansas City, St. Louis, Oklahoma City, and other cities.

Example 29

The shift to bop embraced the most radical changes in the development of jazz to this point. The draft and transportation difficulties during World War II favored the smaller band necessary for these new experimentations. In contrast to the musical arrangements of the Swing Era, notations for the bop bands were usually confined to unison lines for the melodic instruments. A standard format for performing tunes in the bop manner was to play the first chorus in unison (trumpet and saxophone usually), then the improvised choruses, followed by the unison chorus again. Therefore, if the tune had a chorus of thirty-two bars and a form of AABA, the first eight bars (A) would be composed, the second eight would be a repetition of the first eight (A), the third group of eight bars would be improvised (B), and the last eight bars would again be a repetition of the first eight bars (A). All of it added up to thirty-two bars and constituted the first chorus and last chorus. Therefore, all that had to be planned ahead was one eight-bar strain, the A part.[1]

For greater freedom of expression, these players used extended harmonies in their improvised choruses. The development of new harmonic resources for the jazz musician followed closely upon the heels of experimentations by classical composers. At the turn of the century, harmonies were enriched through the successive inclusion of higher members of the overtone series (see example 29). This resulted in an extensive use of ninth, eleventh, and thirteenth chords and beyond. Use of the flatted fifth became so ordinary that from this point on it was considered to be another "blue note" just as the third and seventh tones of the scale had been.

It was not until the Bop Era that the use of higher harmonics and their resultant complex harmonies became prevalent. Harmonic sonorities that were complex enough to be designated as polychords were used extensively. This harmonic construction can be best understood as a combination of two conventional chords. As long as these chords have a close relationship, such as common tones, they are perceived as one chord in the same key instead of in two separate keys.

In example 30, an A-major chord is placed directly over a G seventh chord.

Example 30

This type of sound was common to bop, and since the tones of the A-major chord are all contained in the higher harmonics of the G seventh chord, the players considered these extended harmonies and did not think of the sound as being in two different keys.

Substitute chords became important during the Bop Era. For example, C to C₇ to F could just as well be played C to G♭₇ to F, and it sounded more interesting at the time. The players were greatly stimulated by fresh chords inside of old progressions. An example is shown at the bottom of the page.

Bop playing in general employed faster tempos.[2] To create excitement by merely increasing the tempo would have been impractical with the large, unwieldy bands of the Swing Era. Bop was the first style of jazz that was not specifically for dancing. While the early jazz players used primarily quarter notes with four-toned chords or chords of the seventh, the bop players

1. Charlie Parker, "Yardbird Suite," *Bird Symbols*, Charlie Parker Records, PLP-407.

2. "Wee," *Jazz at Massey Hall*, Fantasy Records, 6003.

	B♭	Gm7	Cm7	F7	Gm7	E dim.	Cm7	F7	B♭
	↓	↓	↓	↓	↓	↓	↓	↓	↓
or	B♭9M7	D♭7	Cm7	B9	B♭9M7	Gm9	Cm7	F13	B♭9M7
	B♭9M7	E9	E♭M7	A♭13	B♭9M7	etc.			

often played sixteenth note rhythms with harmonies of greater complexity. One of the unusual phrasing idioms in bop occurred when there was a series of eighth notes:

The bop players accented the note in between the beats:

Compare the swing style:

Therefore, if the phrase were counted "one and, two and, three and, four and," the players would accent the "ands." Also at first, bop phrasing was heavily influenced by Kansas City-type short riffs; but soon the statements, both planned and improvised, became longer and less repetitive.

There was more tension in the music of this era than in the music of the Swing Era. Jazz, as well as the other arts, has always been influenced by the mood of the times, and this country was entering a war. The musical tension, then, was created by tonal clashes, unusual harmonies, and fast tempos with complex rhythms. To play bop well, the musicians had to have a good knowledge of harmony plus great technical facility. Even with these attributes, the hectic tempos and rapidly moving chords of many of the works caused some experienced players to merely run the chords (arpeggios) instead of creating interesting lines.

One of the major changes that occurred during the Bop Era was repertoire. The building of repertoire in bop was accomplished mainly by using the chords of a standard tune as the framework on which to compose a new melody. An example of this kind of borrowing is found in the selection "Ornithology," which is a melody improvised from the harmonies in the composition "How High the Moon."[3] Miles Davis and Thelonious Monk both recorded tunes based on "All God's Children Got Rhythm." Davis called his "Little Willie Leaps," and Monk's is titled "Suburban Eyes." Chords from "What Is This Thing Called Love" became "Hot House," "Indiana" became "Donna Lee," "Whispering" became "Groovin' High," "I Got Rhythm" became "Anthropology," "Koko" is from the chords

to "Cherokee," "S'Wonderful" became "Stupendous," and so on. Twelve-bar blues had such titles as "Relaxin' at Camarillo," "Parker's Mood," "Now's the Time," "Congo Blues," and others. In previous eras, the melody was usually stated in the first chorus, and improvisation began after that. The bop innovators, however, often disregarded the initial statement of the melody and began their improvisation at the beginning of the selection. Besides changing the harmonies, melodies, and rhythms, the bop players changed the approach to phrasing from neat symmetrical phrases to phrases that seemed uneven and unnatural compared to earlier jazz.

The assigned parts played by individual members of the rhythm section also underwent radical changes. Instead of the regular 4/4 steady rhythm heard in swing music, the drummer now used the bass and snare drums mainly for accents and punctuations. He usually maintained an overall sound by playing eighth-note rhythms on the top cymbal. If the accents were not spontaneous, then they were played on either the fourth beat of the bar or the fourth beat of every other bar. The more spontaneous punctuations were called *bombs* and had to be done with great discernment in order to aid the impetus instead of being a distraction. The piano player changed from playing 4/4 steady rhythm to chordal punctuations. Count Basie had played in this style for some time. These punctuations were played at specific moments to designate the chord changes and thus added to the overall musical excitement. With the advent of the amplifier, the guitar became a melody instrument and took its place with the trumpet, saxophone, and others. This left the sole responsibility for the steady pulse of the beat to the string bass. Although the string bass part now had a more interesting line, the line was secondary to the job of maintaining a rhythmic pulse.

The beauty of the bop rhythm section was that the individual members were freed from duplicating each other's role. In the swing style, all four players were forced mainly to keep the pulse because the bands were quite large and because the public wanted to feel the pure, unornamented, uncomplicated beat in order to dance. These bop approaches were, in general, not really new, as shown by Basie's piano work, Jimmy Blanton's bass playing with Ellington, and Charlie Christian's guitar work with Benny Goodman's orchestra. The bop players also added rhythm players from Cuba who not only aided the pulse assigned to the bass

3. Al Casey, "How High the Moon," *The History of Jazz*, vol. 4, Capitol Records, T796; Charlie Parker, "Ornithology," *Bird Symbols*, Charlie Parker Records, PLP–407.

player, but also brought new rhythmic excitement into jazz through improvised cross-rhythms. This addition pointed out the fact that the more intricate aspects of the West African musical tradition had been kept alive much more in Cuba than in the United States. Of course, Latin rhythms, as they were considered, were not new to jazz. For instance, there is a tango section in Handy's "St. Louis Blues," written about thirty years earlier.

Much of the leadership of this era must be attributed to Charlie Parker's fluid alto sax, Dizzy Gillespie's virtuosic trumpet playing, Thelonious Monk's melodies, and the brilliantly accented drumming of Kenny Clarke and Max Roach. The early bop sessions at Minton's Playhouse emerged from a band led by drummer Kenny Clarke. Charlie Parker was not there at first, but came later. Ex-bandleader Teddy Hill applied the Kansas City formula to Minton's style. He was the manager and hired a good contemporary nucleus of players with whom the performers of this advanced jazz enjoyed jamming. The musicians who played regularly at Minton's devised ways to discourage the unwanted from sitting in on the jam sessions. They would play tunes at such fast tempos, and play what at the time were such strange chords, that those musicians not really in the clique simply could not compete.

As Armstrong influenced many jazz musicians by 1930, Charlie Parker influenced almost all jazz musicians by 1950. Whereas Armstrong generally took the original melody and changed it subtly, Parker often merely implied the melody. Charlie Parker died in 1955, when he was less than thirty-five years old; yet he is considered to be one of the most significant of all jazz figures. The most notable followers of Parker are Sonny Stitt, Phil Woods, Jackie McLean, and Cannonball Adderley. (Parker is discussed also in chapter 18.)

Dizzy Gillespie, as talented a trumpet player as he is a showman, has combined great technique with fresh thoughts and extensive harmonic knowledge. Along with Parker, he was a leader in the style of jazz that he and his contemporaries labeled *bop*. Gillespie's trumpet playing stems from Louis Armstrong by way of Roy Eldridge. In passing we must note that not nearly enough is ever said about the versatile playing of Eldridge. He had played in a very fiery style for many years before bop came along.[4] Dizzy Gillespie's playing was so modeled on the talents of Eldridge that when Eldridge left the Teddy Hill band Gillespie was very naturally hired to replace him. Gillespie's first recorded solos were with this band in 1937. "King Porter Stomp" and "Blue Rhythm Fantasy" reflect the Eldridge influence most directly, and "Things to Come" was probably his most important record. There is no doubt that Gillespie was the most talked about bop musician at that time. Gillespie's playing seemed clear and well-defined while at the same time chaotic.

Gillespie's playing had been severely criticized earlier. The reactions to his style of playing ranged all the way from unqualified enthusiasm to pure indignation. Today he is highly regarded all over the world, and his contributions to modern jazz trends cannot possibly be disputed.[5] It seems obvious, however, that Gillespie has never taken himself as seriously as do his fans and followers. (Gillespie also plays the piano and feels that this helps greatly in his understanding of harmonic possibilities.)

The period from 1944 to 1947 was noted for the great jazz groups that worked in the clubs on Fifty-second Street in New York City. The first actual bop band on Fifty-second Street was formed by Dizzy Gillespie and bassist Oscar Pettiford in January of 1944. The Earl ("Fatha") Hines band had experimented in 1942 and 1943, but until the Gillespie-Pettiford band in 1944, bop had been confined mainly to Harlem's after-hours clubs such as Monroe's and Minton's, and to occasional improvised solos in big bands by such performers as Howard McGee, Charlie Parker, or Dizzy Gillespie. These choruses seemed out of context in the big swing bands—Cab Calloway's, Andy Kirk's, and so forth.

In 1945, Dizzy Gillespie organized his first big band. He preferred the larger band at a time when all other bop advocates were performing in combos. His first big band, called Hep-Sations of 1945, was short-lived. Gillespie became interested in Afro-Cuban rhythms after having performed with Cuban orchestras around New York City. In 1947 he added Chano Pozo to his band to bring Latin American and West African rhythms to jazz. With the addition of Chano Pozo the gap between bop and the 4/4 meter of swing became more apparent. The followers of Gillespie's trumpet excursions included Fats Navarro, Kenny Dorham, Miles Davis early in his career, Clifford Brown, Thad Jones, Donald Byrd, and Pete and Conte Condoli.

4. Roy Eldridge, *Dale's Wail*, Verve Records, MGV–8089.

5. Dizzy Gillespie and All Stars, "Leap Here," *Jazz Story*, vol. 5; "Groovin' High," *Folkways Jazz*, vol. 11; *Dizzy Gillespie*, RCA Victor Records, LPV–530; *Essential*, Verve Records, 68566; *The Greatest Names in Jazz*, Verve Records; "Carombola," *History of Jazz*, vol. 4.

Dizzy Gillespie. Courtesy of Ray Avery.

It should also be noted that Gillespie was the first to take a jazz band on tour for the United States State Department. His band, composed of both black and white musicians, helped relieve diplomatic tension in some parts of the world.

Both Charlie Christian and Jimmy Blanton became national figures on the jazz scene late in 1939. In the short span of time between 1939 and 1942 (both died of tuberculosis in 1942), Christian and Blanton changed entirely the concept of playing their respective instruments—Christian, the guitar, and Blanton, the bass.

Charlie Christian played mostly around Oklahoma City, Kansas City, and St. Louis before joining Benny Goodman when he was only nineteen years old. As influential as he was, speculation remains as to what he would have contributed had he not died so prematurely. Charlie Christian's guitar playing influenced all future jazz, and he must be placed in the same category as Gillespie, Parker, Lester Young, and Jimmy Blanton. He elevated the guitar from a strictly rhythm instrument to a solo melody instrument equal to other instruments. This is not to say that other guitarists did

not play extremely capable solos, but Christian, who came along about the same time as the introduction of the amplifier, was by far the strongest influence. Though he was involved in a new extension of chords, Christian's main innovation was that he played solos with long lines like those for a saxophone.

It is possible that most guitarists felt that the big moving chords of Eddie Lang, George Van Epps and other earlier players were beyond them. Also, the most perfect listening conditions were necessary for hearing guitar solos. Christian's single-note lines and the advent of the amplifier opened the door for many talented players such as Wes Montgomery, Barney Kessel, George Benson, Pat Metheny, and many more. It should be understood, however, that Christian's approach to solos—single-note lines instead of great moving chords—had been played earlier by the talented Belgium player Django Reinhardt. But there were few Reinhardt recordings at that time to document his technique.

Even in Charlie Christian's original and modern guitar playing, the blues influence was the most predominant feature. But unlike other blues guitarists,

Christian pioneered the use of the amplifier as early as 1937 in Oklahoma City. He joined the Benny Goodman band in 1939 in New York City. It was at this time that, after his performances every evening with Goodman, he became a regular performer at Minton's. The fact that he died in 1942 meant that he had very little time to develop his impressive legacy. The most mentioned of his recordings today are "Solo Flight" with the Benny Goodman orchestra, "Gone with What Wind" with the Benny Goodman sextet, and "Profoundly Blue" with the Edmond Hall quartet.[6]

Until Jimmy Blanton joined Duke Ellington in 1939, the bass player played either two or four notes to a bar and played very simple lines at that, mainly the roots and fifths of the chords. There was hardly ever a bass solo; solos demanded more technique from players as well as some entirely new techniques from recording engineers. In the Ellington band Blanton excited the jazz world with his solo "Jack the Bear" and his duets with Ellington—"Mr. J. B. Blues" and "Pitter Panther Patter." Blanton satisfied his listeners with the bass parts that he played, but while accomplishing this, he also played tasteful and interesting lines. He used eighth notes and sixteenth notes without ever sounding clumsy on the instrument, and he also proved that he could bow well. Though he died early, Blanton laid the foundations for all bass players who followed. Because of the path opened by Blanton, bass players were able to assume responsibility for keeping the pulse for the whole combo while weaving their way among the new, advanced chords. Blanton's solo on Duke Ellington's "Jack the Bear" was considered for a long time to be the greatest bass solo on record.[7]

One of the fine bass players to follow Blanton was Oscar Pettiford, who, with Dizzy Gillespie, formed the first bop band to appear on Fifty-second Street in 1944. There are many great bass players to be sure, but two must be singled out: Ray Brown and Charlie Mingus. Brown progressed so quickly that he had been out of high school only two years when he joined the famous Dizzy Gillespie sextet in 1946. Brown's style seems modern today, and even though he sounds relaxed, he displays great technical ability and fine musicianly taste. The musicianship of Mingus is ever present as he includes *ostinato* figures, pedal points, and double stops even during accompaniment. When Mingus solos, you are aware that he is also a good contemporary composer.

Ever since jazz musicians began hearing Thelonious Monk, they realized that he was an important pianist and jazz composer. Works written by Monk have to be considered "compositions" as opposed to the "lines" written by Charlie Parker, for example. Under some lines, the harmony can be changed, and over some chord progressions new lines can be invented. But with Monk's works, it seems necessary to use both his lines and his harmony. When Monk improvises, he does not simply play variations; he fragments lines sometimes and at other times he elaborates on them. He often starts with a basic phrase and, like Sonny Rollins on the tenor sax, plays the phrase in almost every conceivable manner. However, he received recognition for his composing before he was accepted as an innovating pianist. An example of Monk's strong influence is the effect he had on John Coltrane. When Coltrane joined Monk's combo he had to struggle with the repertoire. But after his experience in the group, he had the opportunity to become a really great musician and a most important influence himself. It was as if Monk were able to open Coltrane's ears and to point out possible directions as yet unconceived of by the saxophonist.[8]

Bud Powell, a seemingly logical piano heir to Art Tatum's reign, was one of the key figures in the development of bop. He was a regular on Fifty-second Street in the 1940s, playing with groups like John Kirby's and Dizzy Gillespie's. Unfortunately, Powell was constantly plagued by mental illnesses, beginning when he was only twenty-one years of age. In spite of this, repressings by both Verve and Blue Note Record companies, as well as recordings with Parker and Gillespie, attest to his contributions.[9]

Trombone playing did not contribute to the beginning of the bop style. Trombone players who had the virtuosity to play this style were not sufficiently interested at first. It required a highly developed technique plus understanding. J. J. Johnson proved to trombonists that the style was possible on the instrument. Kai Winding, Frank Rosolino, and many others quickly followed his lead.

6. *Charlie Christian*, Columbia Records, CL 652, G–30779; Charlie Christian (Edmond Hall's Quartet), "Profoundly Blue," *Three Decades of Jazz (1939–1949)*.

7. Jimmy Blanton (Duke Ellington's Orchestra), "Jack the Bear," *Historically Speaking—The Duke*, Bethlehem Records, BCP60.

8. *Thelonious Monk*, Prestige Records, 24006; *Brilliant Corners*, Riverside Records, RLP 12–226; *Monk's Dream*, Columbia Records, CL 1965; *The Thelonious Monk Orchestra at Town Hall*, Riverside Records, 1138; Miles Davis' Album, "Bags' Groove, Take 1," *Bags' Groove*, Prestige Records, 7109.

9. Bud Powell, *The Amazing Bud Powell*, vols. 1 and 2, Blue Note Records, 81503–4.

Thelonious Monk. Courtesy of Ray Avery.

When large bands utilized these bop harmonic and melodic developments, this jazz was labeled "progressive" jazz. At first, the only contributions in this direction were solos in big bands by such musicians as Gillespie and Parker, but soon entire bands were dedicated to these new directions. The progressive band leaders included Stan Kenton (who even adopted the label "progressive"),[10] Woody Herman, Earl Hines, Billy Eckstine, Boyd Raeburn, and bands led by Dizzy Gillespie himself. The Boyd Raeburn band played music as far removed from the earlier swing bands as could be envisioned.

Billy Eckstine, having built a following as a ballad singer with Earl ("Fatha") Hines, formed a band which had almost every leading bop player at one time. Between 1944 and 1946 his female singer was Sarah Vaughan. The Earl Hines and Billy Eckstine bands of this type reached their peak during a record ban, and hence there is not much recorded documentation of them. Record bans occur when the musicians' union strikes against the record companies. Eckstine's band

dates from June, 1944, to February, 1947. There were surely many frustrations, including limited audience appeal for the new music, bans on recording by the musicians' union, and lack of sympathy, cooperation, and encouragement from record companies when there was no ban. At times Eckstine's band was a financial success, but when the orchestra disbanded, Eckstine was left somewhat in debt. Gillespie was the musical director of Eckstine's band. Their first records sold mainly because of Eckstine's fine vocals. In fact, Eckstine's vocals, along with those of Sarah Vaughan, were the band's best means of communication with both the public and the recording executives. In 1944 when Gillespie left the Billy Eckstine band, he was first replaced by Fats Navarro and then by Miles Davis, who remained until the orchestra disbanded in 1947. Miles

10. Stan Kenton, *Kenton in Stereo*, The Creative World of Stan Kenton, ST 1004.

Stan Kenton. Courtesy of Ray Avery.

The band eventually recorded a variety of jazz for National Records including up-tempo works, ballads, and blues. Eckstine can even be heard on valve trombone solos. The trend was for vocalists to be more successful attractions than bands, and Eckstine surely must be considered one of the finest singers to come out of jazz or any other background.

Stan Kenton, who was continually an influential pioneer in jazz, had been working as a pianist in Los Angeles before organizing his first band in Balboa, California, in 1941. Kenton stated that he soon became aware of the adventurous excitement of jazz players and began to base his repertoire on the talents of the excellent musicians who passed through his band. Great credit should be accorded Kenton for having never compromised what to him was art for the comfort and safety of more commercial aspects of big bands. Kenton added Jack Costanzo to play Latin rhythms in 1948, furthering this direction in contemporary jazz.[12]

By 1944, Woody Herman had lost his dixieland trend and some of his Ellington influence as additions in his band began showing a heavy bop emphasis. For example, for a while his trumpet section was composed of Sonny Berman, Neal Hefti, Pete Condoli, and Conrad Gozzo.[13]

There were vocals, but the bop players primarily thought instrumentally. Earlier players played as they would have sung, seeming to work over a melody. Bop players were much more involved with working over the chord progressions.

By 1946, bop was being heard even in some commercial dance bands. Today, most good amateur or semi-amateur players improvise in the bop style. Even most name jazz players perform in a manner directly related to the bop school. Some more than others show the effects of having worked through the cool and funky styles since bop, but the phrases, harmonies, and the approach still seem to be quite clearly bop derived.

Bop did not have a chance to emerge gradually for public listening as had other styles previously. By the time the differences between the union and the record industry were resolved, bop was well advanced. One reason for its slow acceptance by listeners was that the public was saturated with bad publicity about bop that made the music appear more like a passing fad than an advancement in the development of jazz. An

Davis first joined this band for a short stay in 1944. George Hoefer of *Down Beat* has described what happened:

Trumpeter Anderson was taken seriously ill shortly after the band's arrival in St. Louis and was hospitalized. On the night the band opened at the Riviera, the first customer was a high school student with a trumpet under his arm. Gillespie asked him if he had a union card, and Miles Davis, 16, of East St. Louis, said that he did. The music director told him to go up on the stand and see what he could do.

"Miles," Eckstine later said, "he sounded terrible." Davis recalled, "I couldn't read the book, I was so busy listening to Bird and Dizzy." He played a few nights with the band and then headed for Juilliard in New York.[11]

11. George Hoefer, "The First Big Bop Band," *Down Beat* 32, no. 16 (July 1965): 21.

12. Stan Kenton, *Cuban Fire*, The Creative World of Stan Kenton, ST 1008.

13. Woody Herman, *The Thundering Herds*, vol. 1, Columbia Records, C3L–25.

Woody Herman. Courtesy of Ray Avery.

example is the way in which the followers of Gillespie imitated his dark glasses, goatee, and beret. Fan magazines even began advertising "bebop ties." After World War II, when bop started to be heard by more of the public, the radical changes from swing caused great consternation. Some of the older jazz players accepted the advancements, but most rejected bop, feeling that it lacked the more desirable jazz characteristics—emphasis on pulse, theme and variations approach, and so on. However, the real opposition appeared to stem from jazz critics, which seems to be the case as each new innovation arrives on the jazz scene. The adverse reaction to bop resulted in the revival of simpler forms of jazz like Early New Orleans Dixieland. Oddly enough, Parker and Gillespie were not terribly far from the early roots of jazz. Parker's earliest recordings were blues numbers; Gillespie's earliest recording was "King Porter Stomp," written by Jelly Roll Morton.

These changes in jazz, like the changes in classical music, were revolts against the preceding jazz styles. Musicians were constantly searching for new means of expression. As a consequence, they intentionally played melodic lines with unusual intervals. The absence of an easily recognizable melody has been one of the main obstacles to the acceptance of bop by the general public. The complexities of this style of jazz demand deeper concentration and more attentive listening. Rex Harris suggests that bop should not be dismissed at first hearing: "No worthwhile form of music will yield its secret so readily as that."[14]

Additional Reading Resources

Berendt, Joachim. *The New Jazz Book*, pp. 17–19, 61–70.

Dankworth, Avril. *Jazz: An Introduction to Its Musical Basis*, pp. 68–75.

Dexter, Dave. *The Jazz Story*, pp. 121–31.

Feather, Leonard. *The Book of Jazz.*

———. *Inside Jazz.*

Francis, André. *Jazz*, pp. 107–15, 124–30.

Hodeir, André. *Jazz: Its Evolution and Essence*, pp. 99–115.

Shapiro, Nat, and Hentoff, Nat, eds. *The Jazz Makers*, pp. 332–48.

Stearns, Marshall. *The Story of Jazz*, pp. 155–72.

Williams, Martin T. *The Jazz Tradition*, pp. 187–213.

Note: Complete information including name of publisher and date of publication is provided in the Bibliography.

Additional Record Resources

Be-Bop Era. RCA Victor Records, LVP–519.

Giants of Jazz. Atlantic Records, 2–905.

Gillespie, Dizzy. *Big 4.* Pablo Records, 23107.

———. *The Great Dizzy Gillespie.* Counterpoint Records, 554.

———. *In the Beginning.* Prestige Records, 24030.

Greatest Jazz Concert Ever. Prestige Records, 24024.

Jazz at Massey Hall. Fantasy Records, 86003.

Kenton, Stan. *The Kenton Era.* Creative World of Stan Kenton, 1030.

Smithsonian Collection of Classical Jazz. Columbia Special Products, P6 11891.

Suggested Classroom Activities

1. Explain the term *bop.*
2. In what ways was this direction in the development of jazz a change from the Swing Era?
3. Compare the arrangements of bop music with those of the Swing Era.
4. What is meant by "extended harmonies"?
5. Why were bop ensembles able to employ a faster tempo than swing bands?
6. Why is the word *tension* most appropriate in describing the feeling of bop music?
7. In what manner did the percussionist obtain the effect of accent and punctuation?
8. Listen to Dizzy Gillespie's rendition of "Things to Come" (*Dizzy Gillespie*, Galaxy Series, Longplay 4811), and in your own words describe your reactions to the music.
9. An excellent example of the true bop sound is found on the album *Jazz at Massey Hall* (Fantasy 6003), in the selection "Wee" as played by Charlie Chan, Dizzy Gillespie, Bud Powell, Max Roach, and Charles Mingus. Name the instrument featured in the solo spot that follows the short introduction. Do you hear the ascending and descending melodic playing of the string bass? Is the instrument bowed or plucked? Which instrument improvises next? What would you say about the range of tones this instrument realizes? What instrument is third? Finally, what instrument takes over in the wild, exciting climax?

14. Rex Harris, *Jazz* (Baltimore, Md.: Penguin Books, 1952), p. 188.

Example 31
(Side 2, Band 3)

For complete arrangement see Appendix A.

11
Cool
(1949–55)

The bop style was a revolt against swing, and the cool style of playing was a revolt against the complexities of bop. "Conservatism and understatement were the keys to this era. Jazz assumed . . . the form of a restrained chamber music."[1] The shock treatment of ten brass and five saxes would have been entirely out of place. What was needed was truly a chamber orchestra. Chico Hamilton, a drummer, was surprisingly a leader in the new direction.[2] Of course, Hamilton was no ordinary drummer, as indicated by his subtle rhythmic control and use of different drum pitches and timbres. One of his surprises was that he featured Fred Katz on cello.[3] As an introduction to cool jazz, listen to Side 2, Band 4 of the recorded examples (see example 33, p. 111 and Appendix A).

It is often thought that the violin and other stringed instruments do not make satisfying jazz sounds because these instruments, except for the plucked (pizzicato) bass, cannot be played percussively because they are usually bowed. This attitude reveals an oversight of some good jazz talent such as Jean Luc Ponty, Noel Pointer, Joe Venuti,[4] Stuff Smith, Eddie South, Ray Nance, and Stephane Grappelly.[5] Edgar Redmond, a woodwind player, has put forth a great effort to enlighten music educators along this line and has produced a very good album to prove his point.[6]

The tonal sonorities of these conservative players could be compared to pastel colors, while the solos of Gillespie and his followers could be compared to fiery red colors. Cool was a new ". . . kind of jazz which could be quite easily arranged . . . by conservatory trained musicians with a real feeling for contrapuntal jazz in an extended form."[7] By the extended form, Stearns refers to the fact that this new style was not restricted to twelve-, sixteen-, or thirty-two-measure choruses. Cool players devised a way to go even further

1. Barry Ulanov, *Handbook of Jazz* (New York: Viking Press, 1959), p. 158.

2. Chico Hamilton, *The Best of Chico Hamilton,* Impulse Records, A–9174; *Easy Livin',* Sunset Records, SUS–5215.

3. *Chico Hamilton Quintet,* Pacific Jazz Records, PJ–1209.

4. Eddie Lang and Joe Venuti, "Farewell Blues," *Encyclopedia of Jazz on Records,* Decca Records, DXSF–7140; Joe Venuti, *The Daddy of the Violin,* BASF Records, BASF–MPS 2120885–0.

5. Stephane Grappelly, *Django,* Barclay Records, 820105; Django Reinhardt Record, *Djangology,* RCA Victor Records, LPM–2319; *Violin Summit: 1966,* BASF Records, 20 626.

6. *Edgar Redmond and The Modern String Ensemble,* Disque Phenomenon Records, DP 2696.

7. Marshall Stearns, *The Story of Jazz* (London: Oxford University Press, 1958), p. 170.

Example 32

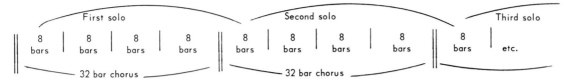

than bop players in the direction of freedom from the square-cut divisions of jazz music. For example, in playing a thirty-two-bar chorus, the soloist would play a little into the next player's chorus, causing the second soloist to play into the third soloist's chorus in order to play thirty-two bars, and so on (see example 32).

This helped the flow of the music as a continuous entity and erased the conception of a block type of form. By 1950, the acceptance of the long-playing record made possible the recording of longer works and longer improvisations.

This music sacrificed excitement for subtlety, and the players underplayed their variations. André Hodeir analyzed cool music according to three principal characteristics: "First, a sonority very different from the one adopted by earlier schools; second, a special type of phrase; and finally, an orchestral conception that . . . is not its least interesting element."[8] These three characteristics deserve examination. The most pronounced difference from the preceding eras was the more delicate attack used by the cool players. Little or no vibrato was used, and the wind players had a tendency to use the middle registers rather than the extremes. The delicate attacks used in the Cool Era and the lack of vibrato caused the playing to resemble that of classical playing, although relaxation was more salient to this style of jazz than to the classical performances.[9] It should also be noted that more and more schooled players were entering the jazz field.

In general, cool phrasing did not permit the player to deviate far from the original line. Some critics consider this backtracking rather than an advancement. Even with their melodic charm these lines often lacked the richness and boldness of music of the Bop Era. The cool players conceived their harmonic parts polyphonically. This approach gave the instrumentalist an independence of line not found in the Swing Era.

The chamber-type orchestral groups or combos were usually composed of from three to eight players. The introduction of instruments not previously associated with jazz changed the overall sound. The flute became important as a jazz instrument, as did the French horn, oboe, and cello. Important flute players include Paul Horn,[10] Buddy Collette, Herbie Mann,[11] Bud Shank, Frank Wess, and others. The soft sounds of the French horn fit beautifully with the general feeling of cool jazz. Nevertheless, there has been a scarcity of jazz French horn players. However, Willie Ruff, Johnny Graas,[12] Junior Collins, and Julius Watkins can be mentioned.

Playing jazz on a double-reed instrument is still not common. Bob Cooper began playing jazz on the oboe while he was with Stan Kenton. Today, good fresh blues and other jazz formats can be heard on the oboe on records by Yusef Lateef and Rahsaan Roland Kirk.[13] The oboe and other double-reed instruments, new to jazz, fit in very well with the more standard instruments (trumpet, trombone, saxophone) when the standard instruments are played in a cool manner as individual instruments instead of as parts of a section. The tuba was brought into jazz for the first time since the very early dixieland period, and was given slow-moving melodic lines instead of the familiar bass parts of marches.

The flügelhorn worked its way into the jazz scene mainly through the efforts of Miles Davis, Clark Terry, and Art Farmer.[14] The flügel, as it is often called, is in the same key and pitch as the B flat trumpet and cornet. It has a larger bore and as a consequence has a darker, more mellow sound; it is also easier to play at a low

8. André Hodeir, *Jazz: Its Evolution and Essence* (New York: Grove Press, 1956), p. 118.

9. Woody Herman, "Summer Sequence," *The Thundering Herds*, Columbia Records, C3L–25; "Early Autumn," *The History of Jazz*, vol. 4.

10. Paul Horn, *Profile of a Jazz Musician*, Columbia Records, CL 1922.

11. Herbie Mann, *Latin Mann*, Columbia Records. CL 2388; *Today*, Atlantic Records, SD 1454; *Stone Flute*, Embryo Records, SD 18035.

12. Johnny Graas, "Mulliganesque," *Encyclopedia of Jazz*, vol. 4.

13. Yusef Lateef, *Eastern Sounds*, Prestige Records, PR 7319.

14. Art Farmer, *Art*, Argo Records, 678.

Modern Jazz Quartet: John Lewis, piano and director;
Connie Kay, drums; Percy Heath, bass; Milt Jackson,
vibraphone. Courtesy of Ray Avery.

pitch and harder to play at a high pitch than the trumpet. The most enjoyable examples are the Clark Terry-Bob Brookmeyer recordings that team flügelist Terry with the very talented and tasteful valve trombonist Brookmeyer.[15]

The cool players established that jazz need not be confined to 4/4 and 2/4 meters and that choruses need not always be divided symmetrically. Many new meter signatures came into use in jazz, including 3/4, 5/4, 9/4, and others. Successful jazz compositions often utilized an interchange of signatures within a selection. Dave Brubeck stimulated interest by laying one rhythm, or more, over another, creating both polyrhythms and polymeters.[16] Don Ellis has, of course, carried the use of meters new in jazz much further (discussed further in chapter 13).

This school of jazz moved closer to classical music, even to the point of adopting such forms as rondos and fugues.[17] Sometimes the use of classical forms in jazz has been categorized as *third-stream music.* Sometimes, however, the Modern Jazz Quartet (and other groups) used the fugue and similar forms just to play good, swinging, subtle jazz and gave no

thought to third-stream music. It should be noted that the Quartet played classical forms quite precisely. For example, the fugues they played were truly baroque in form except that the exposition parts were improvised.

Critics who feel that the Cool Era lacked excitement should note that these players were seeking a more subtle means of jazz expression. The Modern Jazz Quartet, while being subtle, had the strength and vitality necessary for longevity; it lasted from 1951 to 1974.

The public seemed quite divided in its attitude toward cool players. Some people felt that the musicians were bored and arrogant, that they were disdainful and cold. Others considered the cool players to be

15. Clary Terry, *Bobby Brookmeyer Quintet,* Mainstream Records, 320.

16. Dave Brubeck, *Time Out,* Columbia Records, CL 1397.

17. Modern Jazz Quartet, "A Fugue for Music Inn," *The Modern Jazz Quartet at Music Inn,* Atlantic Records, 1247.

creative, hard-working, serious musicians, not clowns trying to be impressive. They understood that the players were in fact saying, "like my music for itself."

Cool developed gradually, as did previous styles. Saxophonist Benny Carter underplayed his attacks, Teddy Wilson played the piano with a delicate touch, Benny Goodman stopped using the thick vibrato of Jimmy Noone and other clarinetists. Miles Davis's solo on Charlie Parker's "Chasin' the Bird" in 1947 and John Lewis's piano solo on Dizzy Gillespie's record of "Round Midnight" in 1948 anticipated the Cool Era. However, it took Lester Young to prove that great swing could be generated without using any of the more violent aspects of jazz.

Near the end of the 1940s there were two large bands that seemed to have entirely different feelings and directions, yet both were quite influential in the beginnings of cool—Claude Thornhill's band from about 1946 to 1949 and the Woody Herman band of 1947 to 1949. Both were instrumental in directing the trend away from the hot feel toward the cool feel.

Woody Herman is the type of bandleader who always seems to make changes in his personnel that are responsible for keeping the band up to date. He formed a band in Los Angeles in 1947 after he had disbanded for three months. This band had a saxophone section that changed the concept of sax sections that followed. He hired Sam Marowitz on alto, Stan Getz, Zoot Sims, and Herbie Stewart on tenors, and Serge Chaloff on baritone. From this group (not using alto sax) came the famous "Four Brothers" sound. This was a tightly knit, beautifully blended section of four excellent jazz players who again disproved the theory that good improvisors are too individualistic to coordinate well. The tune "Four Brothers," incidentally, was written by another talented reed player, Jimmy Giuffre. Another boost for the cool advocate was the recording by the Herman band of Ralph Burns's "Early Autumn." This record alone was enough to launch the career of Stan Getz.[18]

The Claude Thornhill band, in addition to a tuba and a French horn player, had such talented musicians as Lee Konitz on alto sax, Gerry Mulligan on baritone sax and as arranger, and Gil Evans also as arranger.[19] The nucleus of this band made the first Miles Davis-Gil Evans records. One of the several recording bans was lifted in December of 1948, and the way was open for the three recording sessions in 1949 and 1950 for an album that was eventually called *The Birth of the Cool*.[20] An excerpt of a question-and-answer session with Gerry Mulligan throws a little light on these events:

Question: *Was the fact that so many men on the Miles Davis dates came from the Thornhill band coincidental?*

Mulligan: *No, the Thornhill orchestra was a tremendous influence on that small band. Because the instrumentation, when you get down to it, was a reduced version of what Claude was using at the time.*

Question: *Was this an attempt to get away from the conventional bop format?*

Mulligan: *No, the idea was just to try to get a good little rehearsal band together. Something to write for.*

Question: *Then it was more or less regarded as a workshop experiment?*

Mulligan: *Yes. As far as the "Cool Jazz" part of it, all of that comes after the fact of what it was designed to be.*[21]

As for his part in these recordings, Miles Davis believes that at the time he was interested in nothing more original than playing with a lighter sound; it was more expressive as far as he was concerned. At any rate, the recordings of this nine-man orchestra did set the tone for the Cool Era. Mulligan wrote "Jeru," "Venus de Milo," "Rocker," and "Godchild"; Gil Evans contributed "Boplicity" and "Moon Dreams"; John Lewis wrote "Move," "Budo," and "Rouge"; and John Carisi wrote "Israel."

The George Shearing Quintet also influenced the beginning of cool. Shearing, a classically trained blind pianist originally from England, can play in any style of jazz or classical music that he cares to. One of his favorite approaches is to play bop-type thoughts in a very subtle manner, thus making a good transition from one era to the next.[22]

The leading exponents of cool jazz were Lester Young, Miles Davis from about 1949 on, and Stan Getz, one of the few tenor saxophone players who compares well with Young in this style.

18. Woody Herman, *The Thundering Herds*.

19. Claude Thornhill, "Snowfall," *The Great Band Era*, RCA Victor Records, RD4–25 (RRIS–5473).

20. Miles Davis, *The Birth of the Cool*, Capitol Records, DT 1974.

21. Leonard Feather, "Cool," in *Jazz* (Los Angeles: Pacific Press, 1959), p. 26.

22. George Shearing, *Best of George Shearing*, Capitol Records, ST-2104; *Touch of Genius*, MGM Records, E 90.

Gerry Mulligan. Courtesy of Ray Avery.

Lester Young not only started a new style of playing tenor sax, but was also the epitome of an entirely new concept of jazz—hence his nickname Prez, president of the Cool Era of jazz.[23] Lester Young was born in Mississippi and matured during the 1930s in Kansas City where the jam sessions prepared him for all competition. Young first attracted attention when he was with the Count Basie band,[24] but there was much opposition to his playing at first. The big bands were very much oriented to the full-bodied Coleman Hawkins approach to tenor sax. Young seemed light and airy, even out of place, in the big Basie band. However, the younger players were more than impressed. Lester Young, the model for cool tenor saxophonists, played softer than Coleman Hawkins and was more abstract and subtle. Young himself was influenced the most by Rudy Wiedoeft (a nonjazz concert artist), Frankie Trumbauer, and Jimmy Dorsey.

Oddly enough, all were white alto saxophone or C melody saxophone players instead of black tenor saxophone players.

Young joined the Basie band for the second time in 1936 and stayed with him through 1940. During this time, he recorded 105 sides with Basie, plus many others with outside small groups. His first job as a leader was in 1941 on Fifty-second Street in New York City. However, he did return to the Basie band for a few months in 1943 and 1944 and, in 1944, was drafted into the army. Young was associated with Norman Granz's *Jazz at the Philharmonic* from 1946 until his death on March 15, 1959. Young had a beautiful, light, pure sound, but his biggest asset was his phrasing. He would carry melodic thoughts to their conclusion regardless of the bar lines. He recorded many solos with the Count Basie band that are available in repressings. But those that are most cherished by his army of admirers are the small combo records, including those backing Billie Holiday vocals.[25]

Miles Davis first came into New York in 1945 to study at Juilliard. He has said that when he started he played like anyone he could imitate, but states that Clark Terry was his main influence. It seems that no matter what Davis plays on his horn, it has a rather sad feeling to it. There is no doubt that he plays with the sound that he desires and that he simply would not trust his personal thoughts to any other type of sound. He seems to have a highly developed sense of communicative simplicity. At first, Davis could neither play high, loud, nor very fast. When he first arrived on the New York scene, he was young enough to be still in the process of developing strength in his lip muscles. But he felt that he could think better anyway if he were playing with a light sound; he was more relaxed with that approach. The critics of his bop efforts with Parker in 1945 should remember that eighteen-year-old Davis was only in his formative years.

Today, many fans are annoyed that Davis continually changes. These fans claim that just when they have become oriented to one style of his, the next time they hear him he seems to have changed to a different style. Davis, though, is a contemporary musician who is always searching for a new, fresh, exciting way to play his music. He does not feel obligated to older fans; after all, they can buy his previous albums and thereby

23. Lester Young, *Prez*, Mainstream Records, 56012.

24. *Lester Young Memorial*, Epic Records, SN 6031.

25. *The Essential Lester Young*, Verve Records, V–8398; *Giant of Jazz*, Sunset Records, SUM–1181.

Lester Young. Courtesy of Dave Dexter, Jr.

preserve the style that they prefer. Incidentally, these fans usually feel that the collaboration of the talents of Davis and Gil Evans is one of the highlights of music history. For interesting contrasts, listeners should compare the feelings on such Davis albums as *Sketches of Spain*, done with Gil Evans, and *Bitches Brew*, done with an electrified rhythm section as well as with an amplification of Davis's trumpet.[26]

Davis helped to make jazz more of a world music by incorporating flamenco-type works, African thoughts, rock feelings, and everything else that helped his self-expression. By the 1955 Newport Festival, Davis was not only the best paid and most successful musician in the world, but he had also paved the way for many of his illustrious sidemen, among whom are John Coltrane, Cannonball Adderley, Herbie Hancock, Bill Evans, Wayne Shorter, Chick Corea, Ron Carter,

Billy Cobham, John McLaughlin, Keith Jarrett, Tony Williams, and many others. Davis and Coltrane began to improvise from scales rather than from chord progressions, opening the door to more and more freedom in playing. Today, Davis is involved in electronic playing and still maintains his position as a leader and model for a great percentage of the jazz community.

Cool is a style of jazz that even the general public can agree is beautiful music. Very few players have contributed more to this beauty than tenor saxophonist Stan Getz. Getz was very heavily influenced by Lester Young, but, as time went on, he was able to establish an identity of his own that is quite distinctive. His

26. Miles Davis, *Sketches of Spain*, Columbia Records, CL1480; Miles Davis, *Bitches Brew*, Columbia Records, GP 26.

Miles Davis. Courtesy of Les McCann.

bossa nova excursions brought together a very moving Brazilian rhythm with pure tone and melodic charm, a combination that was readily accepted throughout the world.[27]

As cool jazz drifted farther and farther from bop and all other preceding styles, it reached the apex of subtlety when Jimmy Giuffre, playing low-register clarinet instead of tenor sax, decided to do away entirely with the steady pulse of jazz. Giuffre claimed that the beat of the music could be implicit instead of explicit. But when the listener experiences Giuffre's trio (clarinet, bass, and guitar) playing "Happy Man," the pulse can be felt quite readily—even though no instrument is relegated to the pulse alone.[28]

A word should be said here about west coast jazz. This term usually refers to Gerry Mulligan's pianoless band and his associates in California. The term itself has been generally dropped with the realization that this was merely a part of the cool movement. Miles Davis, Lester Young, and Claude Thornhill were located on the east coast, and it is quite easy to list players on the west coast who were much more involved in a hotter approach to jazz. Communication being what it is, it is hardly likely that any style of jazz was fostered exclusively in one area.

In considering cool jazz in retrospect, one realizes that the major problem of performing in this style is that no matter how cool the jazz becomes it must always have warmth—a problem the best musicians solved beautifully.

Additional Reading Resources

Berendt, Joachim. *The New Jazz Book*, pp. 19–24.

Cole, Bill. *Miles Davis*.

Francis, André. *Jazz*, pp. 130–49.

Hodeir, André. *Jazz: Its Evolution and Essence*, pp. 116–38.

Shapiro, Nat, and Hentoff, Nat, eds. *The Jazz Makers*, pp. 243–75.

Stearns, Marshall. *The Story of Jazz*, pp. 167–72.

Williams, Martin T. *The Jazz Tradition*, pp. 219, 233.

Note: Complete information including name of publisher and date of publication is provided in the Bibliography.

Additional Record Resources

Baker, Chet. *Cool Burnin'*. Prestige Records, PR 7496.

Davis, Miles. *Basic Miles*. Columbia Records, C 32025.

————. *Greatest Hits*. Columbia Records, CS–9809.

————. *Greatest Hits*. Prestige Records, S–7457.

————. *Miles Ahead*. Columbia Records, CL 1041.

————. *Miles Davis at Filmore*. Columbia Records, G 30038.

————. *Miles Davis*. Prestige Records, 24001.

Desmond, Paul, and Mulligan, Gerry. *Two of a Mind*. RCA Victor Records, LSP–2624.

Evans, Gil. *Out of the Cool*. Impulse Records, A–4.

Getz, Stan. *Best of Stan Getz*. Verve Records, V6–8719.

————. *Stan Getz Years*. Roost Records, RK–103.

Greatest Names in Jazz. Verve Records, Pr 2–3.

Modern Jazz Quartet. *European Concert*. Atlantic Records, 2–603.

————. *European Tour*. Atlantic Records, SD 20603.

————. *The Last Concert*. Atlantic Records, 909.

————. *Modern Jazz Quartet*. Prestige Records, 24005.

Mulligan, Gerry. *What Is There to Say*. Columbia Records, 32 16 0258.

Mulligan, Gerry, and Baker, Chet. *Timeless*. Pacific Jazz Records, PJ–75.

Smithsonian Collection of Classic Jazz. Columbia Special Products, P6 11891.

Young, Lester. *Young Lester Young*. Columbia Records, J 24.

27. Stan Getz, *Jazz Samba*, Verve Records, V–8432; *Jazz Samba Encore*, Verve Records, 68523.

28. Jimmy Giuffre, "Happy Man," *Seven Pieces*, Verve Records, MG V–8307.

Suggested Classroom Activities

1. What are some words that might be used to describe the feeling and tone of the Cool Era?

2. How does the cool type of tonal attack and vibrato influence the descriptive terms of activity 1?

3. What instruments became important in this era that were not prominent previously?

4. What instrument used in early dixieland music became more prominent and was used melodically in this era?

5. What new meters were used in place of 2/4 and 4/4?

6. Define the terms *polyrhythm* and *polymeter.*

7. Who were the leading exponents of cool jazz?

8. Two selections that are good examples of this jazz era are "Jeru" and "Moon Dreams" from the album *Miles Davis—Birth of the Cool* (Capitol Records, T1974). Compare and contrast these selections by answering the following:

   a. Are the instruments played mostly in the middle range or do you hear extremely high and low pitches?

   b. Do the instrumentalists use vibrato in solo spots?

   c. Compare the percussion rhythm with that of the Bop Era. How do you react to the rhythmic pulse of "Moon Dreams?"

9. An example of the use of alternating meters is "Three to Get Ready" in the album *Time Out—The Dave Brubeck Quartet* (Columbia, CL 1397). After the short waltzlike melody, the meter alternates between 3/4 and 4/4. Listen carefully and clap lightly two measures of three (heavy-light-light, heavy-light-light) followed by two measures of four (heavy-light-light-light, heavy-light-light-light) and continue to alternate.

10. Listen to "The Morning After" and "I Want to be Happy" from the album *Chico Hamilton Quintet* (Pacific Jazz Enterprises, PJ–1209), and identify by sound two instruments used in jazz for the first time.

Example 33
(Side 2, Band 4)

For complete arrangement see Appendix A.

12
Funky
(circa 1954–63)

At first, this style was called Funky Hard Bop Regression, but the style changed considerably and the title was shortened to funky. The word *funky* refers to the rollicking, rhythmic feeling of the style. The term *hard* means a performance that is more driving and less relaxed than cool jazz. The phrase *bop regression* implies a return to the elements of the bop style. "The funky idiom represented an attempt by the jazzman to rediscover his emotional roots. . . ."[1]

It may well be true that musical styles swing back and forth like a pendulum. But it must be kept in mind that the swinging of the music pendulum is not smooth. The swing toward complexity is fairly gradual. The players of the Swing Era added more musicians; the bop players played with extended harmonies and complicated melodies; the cool players brought in new instruments, time signatures, extended forms; and so forth. But the funky style that followed seemed to revert quite suddenly to the most basic of music elements, for example, the "amen chords" from religious services. As an introduction to the funky style, listen to Side 2, Band 5 of the recorded examples (see example 36, p. 116 and Appendix A).

Funky was a rawboned type of playing, with a highly rhythmical melody and a less complex harmony than that of the preceding era. This music had a happy sound and lacked tension and frustration. These performers utilized bop elements that were generally simplified because of having passed through the Cool Era. Today, the simplification has gone even further. Most of the bop sounds have been dropped in favor of elements that tend toward gospel jazz.

When funky was played in 2/4 meter, an important aspect was the accented second and fourth beats. In contrast to Chicago Style Dixieland, these accented offbeats had a lagging feeling, never as pushing as the Chicago style.[2] However, many successful funky works were written in 3/4 meter because the jazz player realized the possibilities of this meter during the Cool Era.[3]

The funky idiom embraces homophonic harmonic construction. Although the lines appear to be invented independently, as can be seen in example 34, they are actually planned homophonically. The lower note is played because of the sound of the specific

1. Martin T. Williams, "Bebop and After: A Report," in *Jazz*, eds. Nat Hentoff and Albert McCarthy (Holt, Rinehart & Winston, 1959), p. 297.

2. Richard "Groove" Holmes, "Living Soul," *The Best of Richard "Groove" Holmes*, Prestige Records, PR 7700.

3. Gerry Mulligan, "I'm Gonna Go Fishin'," Verve Records, V–1021X45.

Example 34

Example 35A

Example 35B

interval produced when it is played against the melodic note above it. Example 34 also points up the excessive use of the fourth and fifth intervals. Another identifying feature is the use of many blue notes, the E-flats and B-flats in example 34.

The homophonic construction of the Swing Era and that of the Funky Era are compared in examples 35A and 35B. Swing music was harmonized in a closed manner, as shown in example 35A by the blocks of chords. The funky players, while planning their music homophonically, developed a more open, loose setting, as demonstrated in example 35B.

This style was introduced by pianists but was quickly adopted by all instrumentalists. The funky style was brought to public notice by pianist Horace Silver and a group led by drummer Art Blakey called the Jazz Messengers.[4] Horace Silver made many records with his own combo.[5] Most pianists who play funky style music admit that Silver was the progenitor.

Berendt mentions Silver as the beginning:

The pianist-composer Horace Silver—and along with him a few others—has broken through with a manner of playing known as "funky": slow or medium blues, played hard on the beat, with all of the heavy feeling and expression characteristic of the old blues. Jazz musicians of all persuasions and on both coasts have thrown themselves into funk with notable enthusiasm.[6]

A good example of a big band playing in a funky manner is "Hey, Pete" on Dizzy Gillespie's album entitled *Dizzy in Greece.*[7] This album contains part of the music that Gillespie performed on the first State Department sponsored tour in jazz history. It is also excellent proof that the talented Quincy Jones could write good funky blues works for big bands. In addition, the album demonstrates the fact that the funky melodies were more rifflike and rhythmically and melodically more simple than in bop.

4.   Horace Silver (Art Blakey), *A Night at Bird Land*, Blue Note Records, 1521, vol. 1; *Horace Silver and the Jazz Messengers*, Blue Note Records, 1518.

5.   Horace Silver, *Blowing the Blues Away*, Blue Note Records, 4017; *Song for My Father*, Blue Note Records, 4185.

6.   From the *Jazz Book: From New Orleans to Rock and Free Jazz*, translated by Dan Morgenstern, copyright 1975 Lawrence Hill & Co., Westport, Connecticut.

7.   Dizzy Gillespie, "Hey Pete," *Dizzy in Greece*, Verve Records, MEV–8017.

Horace Silver. Courtesy of Ray Avery.

Critic Don Heckman has some different insights into these changes as he writes about the jazz of the 1960s:

Perhaps the most significant was the music that was called, variously, funk, soul, etc. Its roots in modern jazz could be traced to Horace Silver's efforts to translate the Blues-based forms, riffs, and rhythms of the Midwestern and Southwestern bands of the late '20s and early '30s into the idiom of the contemporary small group. Its roots in Negro society were less well defined but also important.

    Silver's work, however, was soon modified, simplified, and repeated—over and over. And few of the imitators understood the delicate balance of elements that was crucial to the music's artistic success. As often happens, the values Silver was seeking to express were discarded by most of his imitators in favor of the superficialities—the simple rhythms, the reduction of blues changes to their most simple form, and the distortion of Gospel-derived techniques.

The relationship between this music, which was considered by many to be a genuine expression of the Negro past, and the growing civil-rights movement was very close.[8]

The fact that funky music was a culmination of all previous styles leads one to conclude that this jazz must have been extremely complex music strictly for musicians. On the contrary, the return to jazz roots indicated by the less complex harmonies, excessive use of blue notes, and simpler rhythmic feeling enhanced communication between players and listeners. It is interesting that on early Horace Silver recordings the bop concept is prominent and the afterbeat accent hardly discernible. In the funky style the bop elements faded gradually as the accented afterbeat developed.

    The Hammond organ had been only rarely used before 1951 (Fats Waller and Count Basie) when Wild Bill Davis surprised everyone by performing real blues-oriented works on it. Jimmy Smith proved the real

8. Don Heckman, "Ornette and the Sixties," *Down Beat* 31, no. 20 (July 1964): 59.

potential of the instrument. For one thing, he used a larger variety of organ stops (effects) than any other player in the jazz field—and with incredible technique. The instrument was accepted wholeheartedly in the Funky Era.

Certainly one of the best funky piano players was Carl Perkins, who died much too soon to leave a legacy.[9] Les McCann paid tribute to Perkins by naming a tune after him.[10] Another notable funky artist is Ramsey Lewis.

André Previn adopted the funky style when he came on the jazz scene. There was considerable controversy concerning the worth or at least the sincerity of Previn's interpretation when he first entered the jazz field. Previn, however, continued to listen to good players and to associate himself with an excellent rhythm section (Shelly Manne, Red Mitchell, and others), and his playing improved rapidly to the point where it was no longer controversial. Today, Previn is capable of leading an entire tour as a jazz pianist, a classical pianist, or a classical conductor. He is, at this writing, the conductor of a symphony orchestra.

Just about the time that jazz musicians were deciding that they wanted to get back to communicating with the public (about 1953), a reputable critic of symphonic music, opera, and so on, Henry Pleasants, wrote a scathing book emphasizing that present-day composers of so-called serious music had lost touch entirely with their dwindling audience. "He [the contemporary 'serious' composer] finds it difficult to admit that he is simply not producing music that provokes a sympathetic response in his listeners. He forgets that it is the purpose of music to provoke such a response, and that all superior music in the past has provoked it."[11] The funky players agreed with Pleasants. Communication at the immediate level was truly important.

Additional Reading Resources

Williams, Martin T., ed. *The Art of Jazz*, pp. 233–38.
Note: Complete information including name of publisher and date of publication is provided in the Bibliography.

Additional Record Resources

Adderley, Cannonball. *Mercy, Mercy, Mercy*. Capitol Records, T 2663.
———. *The Best of Cannonball Adderley*. Capitol Records, SKAO 2939.

———. *The Cannonball Adderley Quintet Plus*. Riverside Records, 9388.
Holmes, Richard "Groove." *The Best of Richard "Groove" Holmes*. Prestige Records, 7700.
Lewis, Ramsey. *The In Crowd*. Cadet Records, S–757.
———. *The Best of Ramsey Lewis*. Cadet Records, S–839.
Morgan, Lee. "Sidewinder." *Three Decades of Jazz (1959–1969)*. Blue Note Records, LA 158–60.
Silver, Horace. *Best of Horace Silver*. Blue Note Records, 84325.
Smith, Jimmy. *Jimmy Smith's Greatest Hits*. Blue Note Records, BST 89901.
———. "Back at the Chicken Shack." *Three Decades of Jazz (1959–1969)*. Blue Note Records, LA 158–60.

Suggested Classroom Activities

1. In terms of rhythmic feeling, what does the word *funky* mean?
2. How would one describe the emotion or feeling of the music of the Funky Era?
3. What electronic instrument became popular in this era?
4. Listen to the excellent example of the funky style, "The Preacher," on *Horace Silver and the Jazz Messengers* (Blue Note Records, BLP1518). Give your reactions to the total sound. Is the melody recognizable? Do you hear the amenchord progression? Which of the two solo instruments, trumpet or saxophone, plays blue notes? Do you hear the musical conversation between the piano and ensemble near the end of the music?

9. Carl Perkins, "Too Close for Comfort," *Jazz Pianists Galore*, World Pacific Records, JWC–506.

10. Les McCann, "For Carl Perkins," *Les McCann Plays the Truth*, Pacific Jazz Records, 3075.

11. Henry Pleasants, *Serious Music and All That Jazz*, p. 26. Copyright © 1969 by Henry Pleasants. Reprinted by permission of Simon & Schuster, a Division of Gulf & Western Corporation.

Example 36
(Side 2, Band 5)

Complete arrangement in Appendix A.

13
The Eclectic Era

The jazz of today is a potpourri of some eighty years of continuous development. Each era through which the art has progressed had a definite impact upon all eras that succeeded it. Jazz musicians have borrowed from any source that they considered worthy. Contemporary experimentation is so widespread that present-day jazz must be considered to be going through an Eclectic Era. There are harmonic, melodic, and rhythmic advancements in improvisation; there are borrowings from classical music, rock 'n' roll music, and the church; there are important contributions from electronic devices; there are many free improvisation situations; and even the big bands seem to go on. Eventually another name may be given to the present era of jazz, but at present the authors feel that the most feasible is the Eclectic Era.

Gospel Jazz

Gospel jazz is an extension of the funky style. As the name implies, gospel jazz uses elements from, and has a definite feeling of, early gospel music.[1] A primary example of these elements is the constant use of the amen-chord progression (I, IV, I) (the plagal cadence). To hear extensive use of the amen chords listen to Les McCann's "Fish This Week."[2] In spite of the fact that this style is a return to prejazz music, gospel jazz has also been influenced by all preceding jazz styles including their harmonies, forms, and advanced musical techniques.[3] Rhythm, as well as emotional intensity, is highlighted in gospel jazz.

Many selections of this form of jazz can just as easily be performed in a church as in a nightclub. One is Les McCann's "A Little 3/4 for God and Company."[4] Big gospel bands sometimes perform in a hand-clapping, "shouting Baptist" manner as they enact a scene of baptism in a work such as "Wade in the Water."[5]

The first edition of this textbook spoke of this type of jazz as "soul jazz"; since then, the term has been used *ad infinitum*. If *soul* means *sincerity*, then certainly Armstrong's first recordings, or those of Jack Teagarden, must be included in this category. And no

1. Les McCann, *The Truth*, Pacific Jazz Records, 2.

2. McCann, *The Truth*.

3. The Jazz Brothers, "Something Different," *The Soul of Jazz*, Riverside Records, S–5.

4. McCann, *The Truth*.

5. Johnny Griffin, "Wade in the Water," *The Soul of Jazz*, Riverside Records, S–5.

Les McCann. Courtesy of Ray Avery.

performer was more sincere than Mahalia Jackson. But the term began to have some racial and revolutionary connotations. Therefore, as the music reverted more and more to church roots, the authors have seen the label for this kind of jazz gradually change to "gospel jazz."

Third-Stream Music

Third-stream music is a style of music that lies between the streams of jazz and classical music and embodies musical elements of both. An example of third-stream music is Robert Freedman's "An Interlude," a composition that uses polytonal and polymodal techniques.[6]

Leon Dallin defines a polytonal composition as one that emphasizes clearly two or more tonal centers at the same time.[7] Polymodal music uses two modes (i.e., major and minor) with the same tonic or two forms of the same chord simultaneously. Dallin calls it dual modality.

The phrase *third-stream music* is usually attributed to Gunther Schuller, but writer John S. Wilson is also credited with inventing the term. Schuller was

6. Robert Freedman, "An Interlude," *Jazz in the Classroom*, Berklee Records, BLPIA.

7. Leon Dallin, *Techniques of Twentieth Century Composition* (Dubuque, Iowa: Wm. C. Brown Company Publishers, 1974), p. 132.

CHART SHOWING SOURCES OF THE ECLECTIC ERA

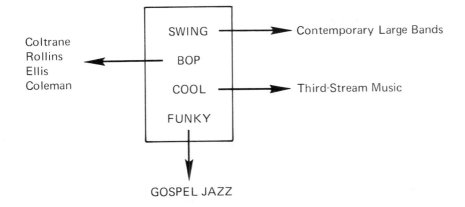

a French horn player with the Metropolitan Opera in New York City. His first involvement with jazz was with Miles Davis, Gerry Mulligan, and others for the album *Birth of the Cool*. Schuller is an excellent composer, both classical and third stream, and, at this writing, is director of the New England Conservatory of Music in Boston.

Third-stream music seems to have been influenced mostly by the techniques of the Cool Era. The jazz musicians play their instruments in a manner closely resembling the technique used by symphonic players, a technique that employs a precise tonal attack and a minimum of vibrato. Third-stream music also employs instrumentation new to jazz, except in the Cool Era. These instruments include the French horn, oboe, bassoon, and cello.

The harmonies used in third-stream music are similar to those associated with contemporary jazz. Musical forms such as the fugue, canon, theme and variations, and other extended types were borrowed from classical music.[8] The use of these forms by third-stream composers resulted in a return to a more polyphonic type of composition.

A controversy has developed over the fact that much third-stream music lacks a strong rhythmic pulse. Because of the absence of this element, many do not consider this music to be jazz.[9] We contend, however, that if enough of the other jazz elements are present in the music it must be considered jazz.

The acceptance of jazz as a musical art form has been broadened through the commissioning of jazz works for performance by various symphony orchestras. Examples are Brubeck's Dialogues for Jazz Combo and Symphony Orchestra,[10] Rolph Lieberman's Concerto for Jazz Band and Symphony Orchestra, and John Graas's Jazz Symphony No. 1. These new compositions fall into two distinct groups. First are compositions containing many jazz elements intended to be performed by a large symphonic orchestra using traditional instrumentation. Second are compositions following somewhat the form of the concerto grosso intended to be performed by a small group of seven or more players within a large symphonic orchestra. Too often, however, concerto grosso offers a little jazz and a little of the ensemble and no integrated effect. For an integrated third-stream feeling, listen to "Sketch" by John Lewis.[11] Neither the Modern Jazz Quartet nor the Beaux Arts String Quartet seem to lose their identity or basic characteristics when performing "Sketch." Listen to "All About Rosie" from the *Modern Jazz Concert* album to hear how George Russell has developed an extended jazz (or third-stream) work from a children's song-game.[12]

An early attempt at bridging the gap between jazz and classical music was made by the Sauter-Finegan Orchestra. Eddie Sauter was as well-known an arranger for the Benny Goodman Orchestra as Bill Finegan was for the Glenn Miller Orchestra. The semi-jazz of the Sauter-Finegan Orchestra, originally organized as strictly a recording orchestra, was strongly

8. Harold Shapero, "On Green Mountain," *Modern Jazz Concert*, Columbia Records, WL127.

9. Gunther Schuller, "Transformation," *Modern Jazz Concert*.

10. The New York Philharmonic Orchestra with the Dave Brubeck Quartet, conducted by Leonard Bernstein, *Bernstein Plays Brubeck Plays Bernstein*. Columbia Records, CL 1466.

11. The Modern Jazz Quartet, *Third Stream Music*, Atlantic Records, 1345.

12. George Russell, "All About Rosie," *Modern Jazz Concert*.

Gunther Schuller (standing) and Dizzy Gillespie.
Courtesy of Ray Avery.

influenced by Debussy and Ravel. Their most ambitious effort was the Lieberman work mentioned. It was extremely well received when performed by the Chicago Symphony Orchestra. Good early examples of third-stream music are Gunther Schuller's "Abstraction" and Larry Austin's Improvisation for Orchestra and Jazz Soloists.

In another approach to third-stream music a player draws directly from his classical background and inserts passages from Bach or Mozart into improvisations.[13] Sometimes complete works by classical composers are sung or played with jazz interpretation. Hubert Laws demonstrates his talents as a flute player on his recording of Stravinsky's *Rite of Spring;* other

contemporary composers are highlighted to great advantage on this same album. Chuck Mangione has merged his jazz quintet with a symphony orchestra and full choir on such albums as *Land of Make Believe.*[14]

13. Nina Simone, "Love Me or Leave Me," *Little Girl Blue*, Bethlehem Records, 6028.

14. Swingle Singers, *Bach's Greatest Hits*, Philips Records, 200–097; Metropolitan Pops Choir with Robert Mandel, *More of the Greatest Hits of Bach*, Laurie Records, LLP 2023; The Jacques Loussier Trio, *Play Bach Jazz*, London Records, 3289; Hubert Laws, *Rite of Spring*, CTI Records, 6012; Chuck Mangione, *Land of Make Believe*, Mercury Records, SRM 1–684.

While Gershwin, Gould, and others wrote a combination of jazz and classical music, Ellington's more pure jazz reflected a classical influence. Earlier, Stravinsky, Milhaud, Křenek, and many other classical composers had used jazz idioms very openly.

In the past, the typical jazz player did not have the educational background or advantages of today's performer. Now the jazz musician is usually well acquainted not only with Cage and Varèse, but also with Palestrina, Bach, and other fine classical composers. There is nothing wrong with the "jazz-is-happy-music" approach except that it contributes to the view that every new advancement is a step away from jazz. Third-stream music is still new, still relatively unexplored, when one considers its vast possibilities.

Advancements in Improvisation

At this point it is necessary to refer to specific musicians in order to examine additional contemporary trends. On the current scene, there are individual performers fostering advancements in improvisation.

Saxophonist John Coltrane's importance lies mainly in his use of expanded harmony. Coltrane utilized the higher harmonics of chords while usually playing on an instrument pitched in the register of the male voice (tenor saxophone). He often played long passages that used only one or two chords, which allowed the harmonic expansion to be more meaningful than if the chords changed rapidly. Sometimes Coltrane's experimentations concerned inventing melodic lines that used the twelve-tone scale to produce complex harmonic colors.[15] (Coltrane is discussed also in chapter 18.)

Tenor saxophonist Sonny Rollins's break with tradition is in the direction of melodic improvisation. He often improvises from a melodic line with apparent disregard for chord structure.[16] As was previously stated, an improvising player in the Swing Era usually had only a few measures in which to express his ideas. Rollins, on the other hand, often improvises for twenty or thirty minutes in order to develop his musical thoughts. He invents a short phrase and elaborates on it, expanding the idea in every conceivable direction as Mozart, Haydn, and Beethoven did. The concept is about five hundred years old.

Rollins's playing shows cool and bop influences repeatedly. For two choruses of "Limehouse Blues" he shows great economy of notes, playing only what he thinks the listener need hear. Then the bop influences become apparent, plus an occasional funky phrase.[17] On his recording of "St. Thomas," his solo flows extremely well as he establishes a short melodic thought and elaborates on it, changing it in every way that he can.[18] By little phrases he continually brings the listener back to thoughts that he has played earlier. Listen also to "Doxy" for this approach.[19]

An interesting aspect of Rollins's career was that after he had become a top nightclub attraction he became dissatisfied with his performance. He retired for two years, from the summer of 1959 to the fall of 1961 (and again in 1969), in order to practice. Such action takes great courage and dedication. Although the consensus seems to be that Rollins's absence did bring his coordination to real excellence, some writers still wonder whether his time away affected his playing. After his return, it seemed to take him a little while to adjust his directions into focus.

The key in Rollins's advancement is thematic improvisation rather than either improvisation on a chord progression or variations on an established melody. Rollins is more concerned with fragments of a piece than with the whole melody itself. He uses these fragments for his own personal expression. Many better-than-average musicians often use this approach, but Rollins seems to have brought it to a recognizable and usable level. The approach is described as thematic or motivic. Listen to the manner in which Rollins works the theme of "St. Thomas."[20] Rollins's recording of "Blue 7" is a clear example of how he (sometimes humorously) dissects a melodic line.[21] It is sometimes thought that this approach stems from the piano playing of Thelonious Monk—at least as far as Rollins is concerned. Therefore, another example of the thematic approach is Monk's development of a little three-note motif in "Bags' Groove."[22] Most musicians who had

15. John Coltrane, *Ascension*, Impulse Records, A–95.

16. Sonny Rollins, *Sonny Rollins at Music Inn*, Metro Jazz Records, E 1011.

17. Sonny Rollins, "Limehouse Blues," *Sonny Rollins at Music Inn*, Metro Jazz Records, E 1011.

18. Sonny Rollins, "St. Thomas," *Saxophone Colossus*, Prestige Records, LP 7079.

19. Sonny Rollins, "Doxy," *Sonny Rollins at Music Inn* and *Our Man in Jazz*, RCA Victor Records, LPM/LSP-2612.

20. Sonny Rollins, "St. Thomas," *Saxophone Colossus*.

21. Sonny Rollins, "Blue 7," *Saxophone Colossus*.

22. Thelonious Monk (Miles Davis record), "Bags' Groove (Take 1)," *Bags' Groove*, Prestige Records, 7109.

Sonny Rollins. Courtesy of Leonard Feather.

observed Monk's approach considered it valid but pianistic. After Rollins demonstrated that it was feasible and logical on a saxophone (which can be played only one note at a time), an entire school of wind players followed his lead.

Trumpeter Don Ellis was associated with talented Indian musicians during his study at the University of California at Los Angeles, among whom was Ravi Shankar, who taught at the university in 1965. Ellis and Harihar Rao (from India) formed what they called The Hindustani Jazz Sextet. It should be noted here that possibly the most intricate rhythmic system is that from India. The amalgam of jazz elements, the raga, and certain Eastern rhythms produced truly extraordinary jazz music. A raga is a melodic form, a succession of notes. There are thousands of ragas. Ellis was also intrigued by the Indian tala, a rhythmic series

that contains 3–108 beats. The particular tala to be played at a given moment is, of course, predetermined, but the rhythmic possibilities are almost endless. It should be kept in mind that these Indian musical fragments derive from speech patterns. This is also true in the African musical culture.

In Ellis's belief that young children in some countries sing and dance in meters unnatural to jazz is the implication that meter is a matter of conditioning, a difference between cultures.

Ellis directed a successful large band that featured many unusual meters such as 19/4, 11/8, and so on.[23] Ellis subdivided the measures; for example, the

23. Don Ellis, "332221222," *Don Ellis Orchestra Live at Monterey,* Pacific Jazz Records, P–J–10112; Don Ellis, "Upstart," *The Don Ellis Orchestra Live in 3⅔/4 Time,* Pacific Jazz Records, PJ–10123.

Don Ellis. Courtesy of Ray Avery.

very title of the selection in 19/4 meter is the subdivision "332221222." Ellis recorded a number called "New Nine," in which the subdivision (the manner in which the measures are counted and played) varies: 2223, 2232, 2322, 3222, and 333.[24] His "Blues in Elf" (in 11/4) is counted 3332.[25] Ellis's "Indian Lady" is in 5/4 and touches on gospel, rock, and free improvisation.[26]

Ellis was an excellent trumpet player, and also soloed well on drums. Not only did Ellis advance rhythmic techniques, become an educated and acknowledged performer of jazz/rock, and introduce interesting uses for electronic devices, but he also devised a trumpet with an extra valve that allowed him to play quarter tones. Such pitches may seem odd when compared to the well-tempered twelve-tone European scale, but in Eastern cultures they are quite suitable. Ellis died in 1978.

In England, saxophonist Joe Harriott and his jazz quintet collaborated with John Mayer and a quintet of Indian musicians to record an interesting album called

24. Don Ellis, "New Nine," *Monterey*, Pacific Jazz Records, P–J–10112.

25. Don Ellis, "Blues in Elf," *Tears of Joy*, Columbia Records, G 30927.

26. Don Ellis, "Indian Lady," *Electric Bath*, Columbia Records, CL 2785.

Indo-Jazz Suite.[27] On "Raga Megha," Harriott improvises over an authentic raga format. It is not hard to play a given raga, but mastery of improvisation is very difficult.

Elements other than rhythms have been borrowed from Indian music. Yusef Lateef makes both scales and ragas part of his personal expression, using them as points of departure for improvisation.

Free Form

While some directions in jazz are extensions and advancements of everything in jazz that has preceded, there were those musicians who felt that all assumed approaches should be closely reevaluated and replaced by newer thoughts that would further self-expression in the field of jazz.

Free form is often called *free improvisation* or even the *new thing*. Free form really means no form at all. This music is performed in its truest sense when one musician begins playing and the others react, with the original musician then reacting to the others. The greatest empathy possible is necessary for this means of performance to be successful. Also, the old axiom, the more freedom allowed, the more discipline necessary, is pertinent to this style. Without discipline, a performer might merely make unusual sounds unrelated to music instead of reacting in a musical sense to his fellow performers.

In an age when the finished product is the only criterion for judgment, it is refreshing to have a situation where it is the process, not the product, that is really important. This one fact makes free-form jazz difficult to accept. The listener must observe conscientiously and attempt to empathize with the players in order to appreciate the activity. This type of music can be more readily understood and appreciated at a live performance than by listening to a recording because it is easier to develop a feeling of being a part of the performance when the listener can also see the players. This type of music can be compared to action painting or nonrepresentational painting, such as a Jackson Pollock work. Listen to Red Mitchell (bass) and Shelly Manne (drums) as they attempt to communicate with Ornette Coleman (and vice versa) on "Lorraine."[28] Alto saxophonist Joe Harriott has been called an abstractionist. Harriott claims to have worked in this idiom before there could have been any Ornette Coleman influence. It would not be illogical to hold that free-form jazz started to develop during the very beginnings of jazz. The jazz pioneers seemed headed toward freedom by improvising.

One of the most controversial, present-day jazz players is Ornette Coleman. Critics who have examined his work fall into one of two distinct groups. One group is composed of staunch admirers, while the other group views his work as unworthy of any consideration. These adverse opinions are due to Coleman's complete disregard for all tradition.[29] It is said that he refuses to comply with restrictions normally imposed by rhythm and meter, chord progressions, or melodic continuity, and that he desires the freedom to play any thought that occurs to him at any time, regardless of context. There are many misunderstandings concerning Coleman's playing. One is that he turns to free form because he is incapable of anything else. To say that Coleman "doesn't sound good" is too loose a statement. Questions immediately arise: good compared to what? other saxophonists? European scales and harmony? Coleman shows on "Part I" that he can play both melodically and rhythmically.[30] In fact, in the authors' opinion, Coleman is very melody oriented. Coleman phrases freely. He feels no obligation to contain or extend his musical thoughts so that they fit neatly into a certain number of measures, which is logical since he does not use a chord progression. Also, he is not involved in keeping a certain pulse; after all, his music is not for dancing. Coleman's melodies have pitch relationships even for the uninitiated, but his metrically invented phrases are placed over a free rhythm with no identifiable chord progressions, and this approach tends to lose those who have not listened to free form to some extent. The shift from a steady pulse to a free-flowing rhythm can be traced first to Lester Young and then to Gerry Mulligan and others as they attempted to avoid constraint within the bar lines.

Because there is no chord progression, some players feel free enough to avoid a key center and play with an atonal feel. This sense of not being in a key is not quite the same as the twelve-tone system of Schoenberg, where each tone has equal importance and no key center is implied. Rather, these players seem to have no home base, which many listeners seem to need. However, there is no reason to argue about atonality

27. Joe Hariott and John Mayer, *Indo-Jazz Suite,* Atlantic Records, SD 1465.

28. Ornette Coleman, "Lorraine," *Tomorrow Is the Question,* Contemporary Records, M 3569.

29. Ornette Coleman, *Tomorrow Is the Question,* Contemporary Records, M 3569.

30. Ornette Coleman, "Part I," *Free Jazz,* Atlantic Records, 1364.

Ornette Coleman. Courtesy of Blue Note Records.

in jazz. It is to be remembered that many of the roots of jazz, such as the field holler, were in no specific key. Some authorities consider the lack of a steady pulse or beat to be a new rhythmic concept, while others consider it no concept at all. One of the more appreciated concepts of this new music is the way in which musical thoughts and attitudes from the entire world are incorporated. Obviously, these young musicians feel that older musical concepts are too rigid, too predictable, and certainly too cliché laden.

Because of the lack of adherence to established rules, the question is often asked if free form is jazz and, indeed, if it is music. Each listener must decide for himself. At a time when free form was still fairly new in jazz (in comparison to most styles), Dan Morgenstern took a perceptive look at the controversy:

But is it jazz? Some of the main elements are lacking. There is little of what we have come to know as "swing." There is often none of the formal organization found in most jazz—rhythm section and melody instruments, solo versus ensemble, strict time, etc. Yet, the sound and feeling is often of a kind peculiar to jazz as we have become accustomed to it, and it is certainly not "classical" music in any sense of that ill-defined word. Whatever it may be—and one often has the feeling that even the musicians don't quite know what they have hold of; it is a music in flux, if anything—it must not be burdened with comparisons that are unwarranted.[31]

To accuse a drummer of not swinging when he doesn't want to achieve swing in the sense that his critic has in mind is unfair and pointless. To demand adherence to formal patterns that the musicians are obviously rejecting is as foolish as taking a painter of geometric abstractions to task for being nonrepresentational.[31]

In spite of the debate as to whether the performance is jazz, the free-form manner of expression must be the ultimate in improvisation. Coleman was the leader in this direction, but now followers have extended this experimentation much further—notably Eric Dolphy and Ken McIntyre.[32]

Coleman was the first jazz player to go all the way into harmonic freedom. This idea had been examined earlier by classical composers, but in an entirely different way. Coleman's approach was through improvisation. To say that Coleman was the first is only partially true. Actually he was only the first to receive widespread recognition. At the time Coleman organized a quartet in 1957 in Los Angeles, Cecil Taylor was playing in a free manner at the Newport Jazz Festival. And Charlie Mingus had invented free sounds even earlier. The term *free form* first appeared on a Coleman album with Eric Dolphy entitled *Free Jazz.*

Faulty intonation has been one of the criticisms leveled at Coleman. It could be that the fault lies in the well-tempered scale of European classical music. Reference could be made to the blue areas or blue notes and questions could be raised about the cultures that do not subscribe to the European concept. Possibly in any emotional music in which notes are constantly pushed this way or that way, there is faulty intonation.

Some performers gain recognition today who make no pretense to any connection with past musical styles. They specify that they play "emotion," which is entirely different from playing lines, keys, modes, and rhythms.[33] Players of free form are considered the most radical musicians since the Bop Era. They feel that music in general and jazz in particular should show the emotion of the player, and that the older types of jazz do not adequately show today's deep emotion. Coleman and other free-form players think that jazz should also express feelings not previously reflected. After an interview with Archie Shepp, Leonard Feather wrote, "Shepp's music—empassioned, fierce, often atonal, almost totally free of rules of harmony, melody and tone that have governed most music of this century—reflects the turmoil and frustrations that

bedevil him."[34] Whether free form is "hate music," "love music," or whatever, it is still a means of expression.

We suspect that it is mainly the critics and musicians who simply cannot go along with these new expansions who call free-form jazz "hate music." Of course, it was mainly the jazz critics who chose to label it "hate music." Some of the music on Coltrane's recordings is in fact quite religious. There were many jazz critics who would neither support nor condemn free form for fear of eventually being proven wrong or at least foolish. No matter what it is called and even though many claim it to be chaotic, this music has found an audience.

The free-form players thrive on controversy. Those free-form advocates who acknowledge that this style has not developed a large following argue that a man should have the right to fail. But failure is not always the result for free-form players. There are even those who are financially successful—witness Ornette Coleman's Guggenheim Foundation Grant.

Some musicians believe that if a performer does not experiment constantly he cannot be considered creative. Once again, John Coltrane must be considered. At the time of his early death, Coltrane was experimenting with free form and free improvisation. Because of his complete mastery of the instrument as well as of other facets of music, most musicians considered him to be the leader of this contemporary aspect of jazz.[35]

Coltrane came to these attitudes slowly and did not rush straight into free playing, as have some players who followed. He began improvising from modes and scales instead of from chord progressions when he was with Miles Davis in the 1950s. He worked next with Thelonious Monk for four or five years, developing his ear training to a high degree, and then began to hear directions for his improvisations that had not occurred to him previously. Even with the new avenues that opened to him, Coltrane never seemed to lose his feeling for playing long, melodic thoughts.

31. Dan Morgenstern, "The October Revolution—Two Views of the Avant Garde in Action," *Down Beat 34*, no. 30 (November 1964): 33.

32. Eric Dolphy, "Out to Lunch," *Three Decades of Jazz (1959–1969)*; Ken McIntyre and Eric Dolphy, *Looking Ahead*, Prestige Records, 8247.

33. Albert Ayler, *Bells*, E.S.P. Disk, 1011.

34. Leonard Feather, "Archie Shepp Jazz: Portrait in Passion," *Los Angeles Times*, 10 April 1966, p. 23.

35. John Coltrane, *Ascension*, Impulse Records. A–95.

Coltrane was a tremendous help in furthering the careers of other contemporary free-jazz players like Archie Shepp and Pharaoh Sanders. Coltrane and Coleman were at the top of most musicians' poles in the middle of the sixties, especially in Europe.

McCoy Tyner played piano for Coltrane for almost six years (1960 to 1965), and it took him almost eight years after that to free himself to the point where he was an individual expressing his own thoughts. When he started his group, they played set forms. Later they became much more flexible and free.[36]

There are contemporary groups who deserve special mention because of their highly experimental nature: the Archie Shepp Quintet, the New York Art Quintet, the Albert Ayler Quintet, and the Jazz Composers Workshop (later Jazz Composers Orchestra) with Carla Bley and Mike Mantler. There is also a great deal of this type of activity in Europe.

Each musician's method of performance is individual and a compilation of his entire background plus his attitudes toward contemporary art forms. The most recent Miles Davis recordings point this out quite graphically. Davis rose to great popularity as a jazz musician typical of the cool style. But he is also an example of a contemporary man who seeks constantly to find new means of self-expression. His newest recordings to this date involve free improvisation, plus his cool background and what he personally hears and enjoys in other types of music, for example, the rock rhythmic feeling. Listen to Miles Davis's *Bitches Brew* to hear talented performers react to one another.[37]

There are many variations of free form. Sometimes one or two musical elements are predetermined—for example, the tempo and the key center. This is not entirely free. However, only two aspects are controlled, and these works still lack melody, chord progression, and form. Miles Davis's *Bitches Brew* is free except for the tempo and key feeling. Cecil Taylor's "Luyah" feels as though the rhythmic feeling is the only predetermined element.[38] Even without the other musical aspects being established, Taylor is able to generate great momentum.

It appears as though the freer aspects of jazz, at least, have somewhat reduced the freedom acquired in the sixties. Most successful recording artists today construct their works in this way: beginning with a strain with which listeners can relate, following with an entirely free portion, and then returning to the recognizable strain. The pattern may occur several times in a long selection, giving listeners pivotal points to cling to. At this time, listeners accept this—they can recognize the selection while also appreciating the freedom of the player in other portions. Players, meanwhile, are tending toward retaining a key center for the seemingly free parts. It is as if the musician has learned that entire freedom is not an answer to expression, that he needs boundaries, bases, from which to explore. Some of the better players with this attitude are Miles Davis, Cecil Taylor, Herbie Hancock, John Klemmer, Keith Jarrett, Chick Corea, Pharaoh Sanders, McCoy Tyner, Alice Coltrane, Gato Barbieri, Wayne Shorter, Anthony Braxton, Joe Zawinul, Don Cherry, and Sun Ra.

Arista Records, a new recording company, devotes most of its energies to this new type of free-form jazz. Company executives say this effort is for both prestige and integrity, implying their confidence in the honesty and validity of this means of expression in spite of opposition. The company has also released some avant-garde jazz recorded in Europe (Anthony Braxton, for example) so that Americans as well as Europeans can become aware of these artists. Strangely, Europeans have always appreciated this American art form more than have Americans. Perhaps efforts such as those of Arista will win the stamp of validity for free jazz.

American musicians should be aware of the work with the freer aspects of jazz being done at Woodstock, New York. Composer-percussionist Karl Berger is director of the Creative Music Foundation, a study center for contemporary music. Included on the faculty are such adventurous young musicians as bassist Dave Holland, multi-instrumentalist Jack De Johnette, and woodwind players Sam Rivers and Lee Konitz. The workshops are held in the spring and winter and are eight weeks long. Students meet in groups and also study individually. Briefly, their overall attitude is that improvisation has gone beyond the mere playing of choruses with rhythmic feeling. They are also deeply concerned with discipline, precision, and skilled listening, in spite of their commitment to free form. It is enlightening to know that Berger and the others are very concerned about audience appreciation. They think that the clinics and workshops they conduct in schools throughout the country will enhance audience appreciation and understanding. They feel that their endeavors entirely disprove the notion that their type of music is appreciated elsewhere more than in America.

36. McCoy Tyner, *Sama Layuca*, Milestone Records, M9056.

37. Miles Davis, *Bitches Brew*, Columbia Records, GP 26.

38. Cecil Taylor, "Luyah," *Looking Ahead*, Contemporary Records, S 7562.

The free-form player places the importance of individuality of self-expression considerably ahead of popularity or acceptance by general audiences. His claim to musical artistry is often through music unrelated to any previous approach to music.

Disco

The authors are questioned constantly about disco music. This music has become so popular that everyone has been touched by it to some degree. Record companies are spending millions of dollars on disco records, and at this date there are reported to be twenty thousand disco clubs.

There are two attitudes as far as the jazz aficionados are concerned. One attitude is quite negative and relates disco strictly to rock 'n' roll or rhythm and blues music. This group points out that disco music is usually played at only one volume, that there is most often an indistinguishable vocal, that there is a complete lack of subtlety, a lack of creativity, and surely no durability. They point to the fact that the ponderous rhythm track can be taped; then an endless amount of tapes can be made by dubbing over vocalists and instrumentalists using the same rhythm track. Truly, this approach does limit individuality.

On the other side of the argument, instrumentalists throughout the history of jazz music have always adopted any rhythmic feeling that encourages the listener to move. Disco music is primarily played for that one reason—to encourage the listener to move. The jazz player adopted the 2/4 feeling of ragtime and used it in Chicago Style Dixieland and funky. The driving 4/4 rhythm satisfied swing dancers and bop listeners. Jazz players are very comfortable playing eight beats to the bar in boogie-woogie. As described in chapter 14, the main ingredient to come to jazz/rock from rock 'n' roll was the effervescent pulse that gives that kind of music such great momentum.

Where then is the problem? Is disco music played so loudly that some jazz players have difficulty being inventive under such conditions? Is the heavy beat too confining? Does it restrict the directions open to the player? Disco is music to dance to, but all jazz up to bop has been music to dance to, and dance once again became important in jazz with funky and gospel jazz.

Some earlier aspects of music were considered at the time of their inceptions to be unworthy if they were even remotely associated with jazz. For example, ragtime was outlawed by the musicians' union at one time. Of course all this has passed, but at the same time

controversy has returned with the rise of disco. The authors maintain that just because some music has a disco beat, it is not necessarily bad, or good for that matter. An examination of many great jazz artists of the past proves that they created as they entertained, and that music that compels the listener to move is important.

Disco, as jazz, rock 'n' roll, and many other types of music have, is going through the trauma of acceptance. It has been said that all jazz sounds alike, all classical music sounds alike, all rock sounds alike, and so on. Many antirock people thought that music would just go away, especially when Elvis Presley went into the military service. Disco is here, and there is good and bad in it just as in any other music. Disco is extremely popular going into the 1980s, partly due to the success of the film *Saturday Night Fever*. The success of disco records depends on the sale of singles and audience response to them. Many disco hits are by black artists, but it may surprise many people to know that some of the biggest disco hits are by Henry Mancini, Barbra Streisand, and Boz Scaggs. Most disco records are produced exclusively for dancing. The records are often long and unsuitable for radio. However, almost one quarter of the records on the 1978 popular charts were disco records and eight Grammy Awards for 1979 went to disco records.

The disco rhythm is surely not good for all tunes, or all settings of any given tune; but used at the right time with sensitive choices concerning volume, interesting chords, creative orchestration, and so on, a fusion of jazz and disco rhythm should not be overlooked. The question at the moment is whether the jazz players will utilize disco's moving energetic rhythm just as they did rock's effervescent pulse, or whether they will stay away from disco's commerciality because their individuality may be lost in the many tracks of background instruments. There really is no answer; there is only the fact that, up to the end of the 1970s, it was difficult to find albums of many reputable jazz players involved with disco music. So far, it seems that only George Duke, Herbie Hancock, Herbie Mann, Lonnie Liston Smith, and a very few others have satisfied themselves and their listeners in this direction.[39]

39. George Duke, *Follow the Rainbow*, Epic Records, 35701; Herbie Hancock, *Feets Don't Fail Me Now*, Columbia Records, 35764; Herbie Mann, *Super Mann*, Atlantic Records, SD 19221; Lonnie Liston Smith, *Erotic Mysteries*, Columbia Records, 256541.

Contemporary Large Bands

Due to either nostalgia or a desire for large full sounds or both, a great percentage of the public still wants the sounds of the Swing Era. Consequently, large bands are extremely important on the current jazz scene. Some were organized during the swing days and have continued to progress, staying abreast of the changes in jazz. As a result, they have broadened their performance to include most new advancements in jazz, as well as the better musical features of the last forty years.

Among contemporary big bands are some that go back to the forties, thirties, and even twenties. Some of these bands play modern musical thoughts, while others are quite successful with a revival approach. There is no denying that nostalgia is a saleable product. Among the bands whose names have been prominent to the public for a number of years (not all sell nostalgia) are the bands of Duke Ellington (now directed by son Mercer), Count Basie, Woody Herman, Stan Kenton, Maynard Ferguson, Gil Evans, Ray Charles, Charlie Mingus, Dizzy Gillespie, Les Brown, Harry James, Tex Beneke, Louis Bellson, and others.

The contemporary big band list also includes some that started out as rehearsal bands, with no thought of public performances. A rehearsal band is usually made up of very good musicians who do not have an opportunity to play the music that they enjoy best while performing the music that they are paid to play. A rehearsal band becomes mainly an emotional release for its members. Among such groups is the band of Gerald Wilson and the fine Thad Jones-Mel Lewis orchestra.[40] The largest source of players for big bands today remains the schools, colleges, high schools, and junior high schools.

Sometimes a large band is considered old-fashioned or at best a nostalgia treat, surely not the case for most contemporary large bands. In these bands contemporary harmonies, contemporary tunes, and contemporary sounds predominate. Such bands as the following are proof that big bands do not die but, on the contrary, remain in full bloom: the Quincy Jones band playing *Walking in Space*; the Thad Jones-Mel Lewis band playing the popular, swinging *Potpourri*; and the Toshiko Akiyoshi-Lew Tabackin band playing the modern, culture-crossing sounds on *Kogun*.[41]

The Basie band has changed very little over the years. It has always had a style that swings and communicates. The only changes are those wrought by contemporary soloists. Even the arrangers stay within the traditional Basie approaches. Basie feels that performer innovation is not truly honest, that the way to play is to relax, be yourself, and let the writers worry about innovation.

Some bands start from present-day style and go forward using all previous jazz innovations: the bands of Don Ellis, Tommy Vig, Doc Severinsen, Quincy Jones, and the fine Toshiko Akiyoshi-Lew Tabackin bands are examples.

Ever since many new instruments entered the jazz scene during the Cool Era, jazz musicians (mainly woodwind players) have had the added responsibility of performing proficiently on more than one instrument, in some cases, several instruments. It should also be noted that harmony, melody, and rhythm have all progressed a great deal since the Swing Era.

Latin Jazz

One of the important areas of jazz at the present time is *salsa*, a term used to designate a new approach to a combination of jazz and Latin music. The usual meaning of *salsa* is "a hot, piquant sauce." The term "salsa" has become so accepted today that there are often sections in large record stores strictly for this music. A combination Latin jazz and "soul" music has appeared that is being labeled "soulsa."

Latin rhythms have been a part of the jazz scene almost from the beginning. In fact, this element can be traced back easily to prejazz (see chapter 3). Jelly Roll Morton often used the tango as a means of expression. There is a tango section in W. C. Handy's "St. Louis Blues." Dizzy Gillespie and Stan Kenton both featured Latin rhythms in the forties. And the bossa nova in the fifties and sixties brought Brazilian rhythms to public notice.

Kenton disbanded briefly in the 1950s, and many of his musicians were absorbed by Réné Touzet and his band. Touzet used what were primarily vocal musical patterns on which the rhythm section could build to ecstatic heights. The jazz-oriented, powerful brass section from Kenton's band soon made these patterns a driving force.

Reggae, a Jamaican brand of rhythm and blues, is another major influence. Artists as diverse as Paul Simon, Eric Clapton, Elton John, and Stevie Wonder

40. Thad Jones and Mel Lewis, *Central Park North*, Solid State Records, SS 18058.

41. Quincy Jones, *Walking in Space*, A & M Records, SP 3023; Thad Jones and Mel Lewis, *Potpourri*, Philadelphia International Records, KZ 33152; Toshiko Akiyoshi and Lew Tabackin, *Kogun*, RCA Victor Records, 6246.

utilize reggae's captivating beat. Audiences are now showing their willingness to accept the "real thing" in reggae. Jazz with rock, jazz with disco, and jazz with reggae are now finding public acceptance.

There are such technical interrelationships between what are called Latin rhythms, African rhythms, or Cuban rhythms, that it is impossible to distinguish these exciting pulsations.

In New York City especially, Latin bands mix Afro-Cuban rhythms, jazz improvisation, and other contemporary jazz thoughts with exciting results. Carlos Santana, Willie Bobo, Tito Puente, Johnny Pacheco, and Willie Colon are recognized leaders in the field, but Ray Barretto, an energetic percussionist, receives the most publicity. His audiences are mainly bilingual and are very much at home with jazz and such rhythms as the mambo. Carlos Santana is another dynamic leader whose playing of both Latin music and jazz is accepted by fans of both idioms. If it were possible to hear only two examples of this exciting music, we suggest that they be Santana's *Caravanserai* and Barretto's *Carnaval*.[42]

The School Scene

The rise of jazz/rock has whetted the enthusiasm of many young players who might otherwise not have taken quite so readily to jazz. One of the problems today is the lack of organizations to serve as proving grounds for young musicians. There is no better way for them to improve and refine their playing than to work with and learn from the more experienced musicians.

In 1976, there were reported to be at least twenty thousand jazz bands in the United States just in high schools and junior high schools, and this number is growing. The type of music that is in style with these bands is a swing band format with a rock rhythm section.

In 1965, only twenty-five colleges gave accredited courses in different phases of jazz. In 1971, the number of colleges offering jazz courses was approximately five hundred. By 1976, jazz researchers had simply stopped counting. From 1978 to 1979, the number of four-year colleges that were involved in what they called "commercial music" doubled their course offerings. There are schools giving degrees in the study of jazz: Berklee College of Music in Boston, North Texas State in Denton, University of Miami in Coral Gables, Florida, and the University of Utah in Salt Lake City. Many more schools are heading in this direction.

All movements are begun by individuals. In the school jazz band movement, great credit should be given to the following: Gene Hall for his work in Texas and other areas, Matt Betton for work in the Midwest, Bob MacDonald for efforts in Southern California, and Stan Kenton for his clinics. Music publishers and instrument manufacturers should be grateful to these musicians, as well as to the National Association of Jazz Educators, for their exciting, hard work. The National Association of Jazz Educators has organized the teaching of all facets of jazz at all levels of education. This group aids others in the school field who are trying to work with jazz. Although they have accomplished much, they realize that work in the field has barely started.

A big controversy has been brewing for quite some time within the National Association of Jazz Educators. One faction feels that the ideal performance vehicle for students is the big band. The attitude of this group is that there are not many mature, or even good, improvisers at the school level, and that with a large band (and there are excellent models to draw from) more students would be involved, or better yet, fewer students would be discouraged from having a jazz experience. This group points to the aesthetic musical values to be attained by playing fine musical arrangements with good balance, intonation, and so forth. The other faction believes in the development of the individual by participation in a small combo setting. They maintain that this situation is the only way to learn to improvise, hence, achieve self-expression through jazz. If it is possible, the authors recommend that students involve themselves with both large bands and combos; so much can be gained from participation in both settings. With a good arrangement, a large band generally sounds acceptable in competitive situations; whereas a small group taxes individual talents, which are very exposed. Instructors should realize that the most important jazz players throughout the history of this music have in general been the best improvisers; this art can best begin in the school situation today.

Two notable exceptions to schools offering jazz studies, and these are generalities, are music conservatories and black colleges. To qualify that, it must be mentioned that there is very extensive, excellent jazz work done at Eastman School of Music and some at the New England Conservatory. Some black colleges

---

42. Carlos Santana, *Caravanserai*, Columbia Records, KC 31610; Ray Barretto, *Carnaval*, Fantasy Records, 24713.

are overcoming the misguided notions they have about jazz being sinful and from more humble beginnings than European classical music. Black administrators have told us that their music departments must prove themselves by European standards and then can teach anything that they wish.

The performance of jazz is by far the most important aspect for most jazz educators; the history and theory of jazz take a backseat. Some schools, have more than one jazz ensemble. North Texas State has more than ten very fine bands. Although the authors realize the risk of singling out a few of the many fine college jazz bands, at least five more should be mentioned: the bands at the University of Miami, the University of Illinois, the University of Indiana, Berklee College, and the Eastman School of Music.

The National Association of Jazz Educators met with executives of the John F. Kennedy Center for Performing Arts in December 1971 in Washington, D.C. As a result of the meeting, the Association was given authority, responsibility, and funding for the American Jazz Festival first held in May, 1972. This is a nationwide event and all colleges having jazz activities are invited to participate. Festivals (by both school groups and strictly professional players) are now an established part of the jazz scene.

Stan Kenton believed that the future of almost all creative music in the United States lay in the hands of the universities.[43]

Jazz in Other Countries

Since its inception jazz has been considered an American phenomenon. While there can be no question that jazz originated in the United States, jazz and the American musician are no longer synonymous as they were once considered in other countries. The first thing to consider is that jazz has always been appreciated more in foreign countries than in the United States. More jazz records are sold in Japan than in any other country in the world. More jazz festivals are held each year in Europe than jazz publications can mention. In 1975, several jazz festivals were held, including the Fifteenth Annual Jazz Festival in Molde, Norway, the Ninth Annual Festival in Montreaux, Switzerland, the Seventh Festival in Bergamo, Italy, and the Tenth Festival in Helsinki, Finland. There were also jazz festivals in Antibes, Nice, Dijon, and Nancy in France and in Copenhagen, Denmark, not to mention the San Sabastion Festival in Spain, the Laren Festival in Holland, the New Castle Jazz Festival in England, the Berlin Jazz Days, and on and on. One is hard pressed to find a single country not supporting at least one major jazz festival. There was a jazz festival in Hawaii for the first time in 1975.

Prior to the 1970s, the jazz played by American musicians was superior to that played by musicians of other countries. Large foreign bands had the sound of the late thirties, and other styles were weak copies of the originals. There were exceptions, of course, such as Django Reinhardt and George Shearing. But generally speaking, American jazz musicians were ahead of the rest of the world.

All that has changed now. Jazz players in other parts of the world are equally creative. There are fine contemporary large bands all over the world: the Clarke-Boland Band in Europe and the Daly-Wilson Band in Australia, to name two.[44] The world is beginning to become aware of talents from Japan, such as Toshiko Akiyoshi, Sadao Watanabe, and others.[45] Exciting rhythms emanate from South America. At the Berlin Jazz Days only dixieland jazz was played, and the best players in that style in Europe and the United Kingdom were brought together. At one time, jazz was taboo in countries whose political ideology differed from that of the United States. Today, there is so much jazz talent in Poland that in 1975 the Ministry of Culture and Art in Prague presented eleven awards for Meritorious Cultural Activity to Polish jazz players.

Author and jazz musician Josef Skvorecky, in his book *The Bass Saxophone*, says that although the Nazis condemned jazz, no number of Nazi decrees outlawing jazz could stop its underground expression. So when the Russian Red Army marched into Czechoslovakia, no party politics could keep down the beat of the jazz players. He goes on to remark that in recent history, the Cambodians were allowed to sing only ideological phrases. Skvorecky feels very strongly that if a people's religion and music are taken away, they are left with only two choices: death or revolt.[46]

One of the interesting aspects of jazz in Europe is that free-form jazz has been accepted more readily there than in the United States. As a consequence, not

43. Stan Kenton, "Big Band Jazz: Look to the Colleges," *Down Beat* 29, no. 25 (September 1962): 19.

44. Clarke-Boland Band, *Big Band Sound*, BASF Records, MC-25102; Daly-Wilson Band, *The Exciting Daly-Wilson Big Band*, Elephant Records, ELA-7002.

45. Akiyoshi and Tabackin, *Kogun*.

46. Thomas Sanchez, "Eastern Europe, Where Music Is the Food of Freedom," *Los Angeles Times*, 1 April 1979.

only have good free-form players developed there, but players from this country have gone to Europe in order to find an audience for their kind of jazz. The efforts of Artista Records and other forward-looking companies have made it possible for some of those players (for example, Anthony Braxton) to return to the United States and be able to support themselves. There are many talented free-form players, but the preference among contemporary European musicians is to play large-band free form. It appears that Europeans tend toward collective free-form performance in contrast to American musicians who favor individual free-form style.

Rock and jazz are played together successfully everywhere, but there are territorial differences such as the Scandinavian taste for a cooler type of jazz.

Many musicians from other countries now have international reputations, whereas in the past only American musicians were well known. Among the most talented are the following: in Germany, Albert Mangelsdorff on trombone, Peter Brötzmann on tenor saxophone, and Gunter Hampel and Karl Berger on vibraphones; in France, Jean Luc Ponty on violin; in Denmark, Niels Pedersen on bass and John Tchicai on alto saxophone; in Holland, Willem Breuker on tenor saxophone and Chris Hinze on flute; in Norway, Jan Gabarek on tenor saxophone; in England, Evan Parker on tenor saxophone, Bob Downes on flute, and John McLaughlin on guitar; in Argentina, Gato Barbieri on tenor saxophone; in Bulgaria, Simeon Shterev on flute; in Haiti, Andrew Hill on piano; in Africa, Dollar Brand on piano; in Austria, Joe Zawinul on piano; in Czechoslovakia, Jan Hammer on piano; in Hungary, Gabor Szabo on guitar; and in Brazil, Laurindo Almeida on guitar. The point to be noted is that jazz has spread throughout the world, and there are now talented jazz musicians in all parts of the globe.

There are many organizations today made up of people who have a mutual interest in jazz. The organizations vary in the makeup, purpose, and interests of the membership. Some organizations are made up of fans, like the Society for the Preservation of Dixieland and the Glenn Miller Society of England with 125,000 members. Other organizations are composed of musicians, like Jazzmobile and Jazz Heritage in New York City. Other groups in New York and Chicago are interested primarily in the contemporary directions of jazz. Still other groups are business oriented and concerned with recording and broadcasting.

Other Considerations

There are musicians who play such a variety of styles that they cannot be categorized in any specific era. In the authors' opinion this attribute is a good one because it shows these musicians' versatility. Oscar Peterson is such a musician. If one wished to point to an artist who is a logical descendant of Art Tatum, one could easily pick Peterson. Some authorities feel that Peterson is the finest all-around pianist today. While he does accompany other players, his solo works and those with his trio show such drive, imagination, and technique that there is no question of the high position he has reached in the history of jazz.[47]

There are also players who play very well but not in a recognizable jazz style. Each player's style is completely individualistic. There is certainly nothing wrong with this individuality. Erroll Garner was one player who could not be classified. He played only like Erroll Garner. He can be heard on recordings made with some of the bop advocates during that era, but he did not attain fame until he began making records under his own name with his own group in a style that cannot be called bop or any other style of jazz.

Garner relied on two distinct styles. One is a very rhapsodic approach to performing ballads. This style seems to have very little to do with jazz in general or even with Garner's own other more rhythmic approach. The second style, a rhythmic approach, is so individualistic that aspects of it are readily copied by players who are less creative. With the left hand Garner played a strumming effect in which the chords were just slightly broken, while with the right hand he played charming melodic thoughts. The most unusual characteristic was that the two hands did not seem to keep time with each other. Listen to his theme on the album *Concert by the Sea*, which clearly shows that the right hand and the left hand play independently.[48] When two players neglect to keep time with each other, the music loses its momentum or swing. However, this was not the case with Garner. His two hands did not seem to be playing together, yet the music moved extremely well. Garner did not read or write music, but this did not restrict his composing. His most notable composition is the beautiful "Misty." Erroll Garner died in 1976.

One of the most refreshing aspects of jazz is the constant revolution against standard approaches to performance. This complicates life for jazz critics and

47.   Oscar Peterson, *The History of an Artist,* Pablo Records, 2625–702; *The Trio,* Pablo Records, 2310–701.

48.   Erroll Garner, *Concert by the Sea,* Columbia Records, CL 883.

Erroll Garner. Courtesy of Bob Asen, Metronome Magazine.

jazz historians because it changes their criteria. But it is surely a source of excitement for those interested in new avenues.

Today, jazz is moving in two general directions. One emphasizes communication with audiences, while the other is based on esoterica. In the former category are gospel jazz, jazz/rock, and many of the contemporary big bands. The latter includes most third-stream music and free form.

Through the years, jazz has made whole groups of avid fans very disgruntled when "their style" was replaced by a newer innovation. Many fans of the Early New Orleans Dixieland bands were disturbed by Louis Armstrong's solo style. Both Armstrong's followers and the earlier fans were shocked by the written arrangements of the Swing Era. The bop fans were disdained by and disdainful of all earlier groups. And so on to the present time. Fans are never unified, and therefore new styles develop and become the "in" way to perform jazz.

Also many jazz fans are bigoted; intolerance exhibited by those who disapprove of jazz altogether is outdistanced by cultish intolerance of jazz aficionados. Jazz traditionalists become nostalgic antiquarians and jazz modernists frequently resort to pharisaical haughtiness. Such clannish bickering serves to diminish the value of music which is meant to be heard, not claimed or possessed.[49]

Followers of more contemporary jazz and classical styles can be divided into four general groups: (1) those who like what they know and are suspect of the unfamiliar, (2) those who embrace new ideas and new personnel simply because they are new, (3) those who are staunch fans of particular performers, and (4) those who want to learn.

Acceptance of any change is not easy, a fact jazz has struggled against throughout its history. The acceptance of free form (the "new thing") is as hard won as the acceptance of bop was during World War II. Critic Stanley Dance offers this example:

. . . the oblique complexities of the avant-garde, such as are found in Cecil Taylor's Unit Structures *[Blue Note 4327], are consistently avoided.*

Taylor's music [performed by a septet] and his piano playing are as eccentric as his liner notes, which offer no real explanation of the abrasive noises the album contains. The new jazz revolutionaries prattle incessantly about freedom, but a better word for what they practice would be anarchy. The anger, bitterness and frustration, or whatever it is they are individually seeking to express, emerge too often as exhibitionist displays of musical gibberish. A sadistic pleasure in the making or discharge of it may be conceded, but its patent ugliness and explosive discontinuity are rewarding to this listener only in the new appreciation of silence that the end of each record brings. Similar arguments are undoubtedly advanced against early primitive jazz, but that at least had rhythmic value and a function as dance music—it made people want to dance. It is conceivable that devotees of the New Thing, who find it "stimulating," require it in the same way that manic-depressives require electrical shock treatment.[50]

When changes such as those made by Coltrane, Rollins, Ellis, and especially Coleman began to be at least recognized, it became obvious that some of the new directions would not be appreciated by occasional or casual listeners of jazz and by some critics. Don Ellis, while agreeing that experimentation is of great importance, felt that those musicians whose work

. . . could be classified as truly in the forefront of the art would be playing music characterized by the following:

Music based on solid audible structural premises (the opposite of the musical doodling now so prevalent).

Music that is well conceived and thought out (as opposed to the "don't bother me with technical details, man: I don't need to develop my ear, artistic sensitivity, musical knowledge, instrumental technique—I'm playing pure emotion" school).

Music with new rhythmic complexity, based on a swinging pulse with new meters and superimpositions.

Music with melodies based on principles of musical coherence, utilizing the new rhythms along with new intervals (pitches).

Music making use of new harmonic idioms based on principles of audible coherence (in contradistinction to the everybody-for-himself-with-12-tones-go! school).[51]

However, Ellis would agree that listening to all approaches to jazz with the same attitudes and set of standards would be comparable to viewing Pollock, Miro, and Picasso, and Rembrandt, Michelangelo, and da Vinci with the same attitudes and set of standards.

Thelonious Monk has often stated that his modern style is directly rooted in James P. Johnson and old blues—surprising, considering the angularity and dissonances of Monk's music. Contemporary jazz players seem to have a real attachment to the early roots—the blues has not faded at all.

The survival of dixieland seems assured. At this writing, at least eight organizations in southern California meet at least once a month to enjoy this kind of jazz.

So many directions are now open to jazz players. Diversity of age among both performers and listeners means that there must also be a diversity of jazz. No

49. Rudolph Landry, "Jazz 1984: Two Voices," *NAJE Educator* 4, no.2 (December-January 1971–1972): 6.

50. Stanley Dance, "Jazz," *Music Journal* (March 1967): 90.

51. Don Ellis, "The Avant-garde Is NOT Avant-garde," *Down Beat* 33, no. 13 (June 1966): 21.

one style could possibly satisfy everyone. Regardless of what style in the past was called *mainstream*, the bop style seems to be the most-used approach in improvisation today.

Kenton was adamant about the importance of jazz:

I think that jazz came along and all of music will never be the same again because of jazz music because it has given all of music a whole new dimension and I think that in order for music to come close to satisfying the aesthetic needs of modern man or of man in the future, no music is ever going to come close to that unless it has the ingredients of jazz. Jazz has completely changed the whole concept of playing music, of communication through music.[52]

Too often jazz is thought of as entertainment and classical music as something to be understood especially by an elite. In the first place, even if jazz is entertaining, this by no means detracts from its aesthetic values or its importance. In the second place, communication is very important in most jazz, which surely cannot be said for contemporary classical music.

John Tynan quotes William Grant Still expressing his thoughts about contemporary styles in music:

No composer should confine himself to one school of thought or to a single style or form of expression if he has the inclination to expand. There is some value in everything; it is mainly the exclusive use of dissonance, formlessness, and stunts that I deplore, in addition to the fact that proponents of this sort of expression apparently have closed their minds to any other sort of expression.

In summation, I would say these things: 1. Music's true function is greater than that of merely expressing harsh and uninteresting sounds. 2. The new is not necessarily better than the old. 3. Intellect isn't always more desirable than emotion, and unintelligibility can never supplant simplicity and understandability.[53]

The virtuosity of today's younger players as they mix jazz, rock, classics, and electronics seems to be the first proof of Ellington's prediction that someday there will be just "music," with no categories.

Only time will authenticate or invalidate the merits of the contributions made by the players discussed in this chapter. We contend that efforts such as these should not be quickly dismissed, because innovators protect the art from stagnation.

Additional Reading Resources

Budds, Michael J. *Jazz in the Sixties.*
Jost, Ekkehard. *Free Jazz.*
Note: Complete information including name of publisher and date of publication is provided in the Bibliography.

Additional Record Resources

Adderley, Cannonball. *Cannonball Adderley Quintet and Orchestra.* Capitol Records, ST-484.

Ayler, Albert. *Vibrations.* Arista Freedom Records, AL 1000.

Braxton, Anthony. *New York, Fall 1974.* Arista Records, AL 4032.

Coleman, Ornette. *At the "Golden Circle" Stockholm.* Blue Note Records, 4225.

————. *Science Fiction.* Columbia Records, KC 31061.

Dankworth, Johnny and the London Philharmonic Orchestra. *Collaboration.* Roulette Records, SR 52059.

Energy Essentials. Impulse Records (6 sides), ASD-9228.

Evans, Bill. *Bill Evans Trio with Symphony Orchestra.* Verve Records, V6-8640.

Hancock, Herbie. *Maiden Voyage.* Blue Note Records, 84195.

Handy, John III. *Quote, Unquote.* Roulette Records, R 52124.

Herman, Woody. *Giant Steps.* Fantasy Records, 9477.

————. *Thundering Herd.* Fantasy Records, 9452.

Jazz Composers Orchestra. JCOA Records, 1001/2.

Jones, Quincy. *Walking in Space.* A and M Records, SP 3023.

Kirk, Roland. *Rip, Rig, and Panic.* Limelight Records, LM 82027.

Lewis, John. *European Windows.* RCA Victor Records, LPM-1742.

Lewis, Ramsey. *The In Crowd.* Argo Records, LP-757.

McCann, Les. *Beaux J. PooBoo.* Limelight Records, LS-8625.

52. Landry. "Jazz 1984: Two Voices," p.23.

53. John Tynan, "Take 5," *Down Beat* 28, no. 24 (November 1961): 40.

Martin, Skip. *Scheherajazz*. Somerset Records, P-9700.

New Wave in Jazz. Impulse Records, A-90.

Outstanding Jazz Compositions of the Twentieth Century. Columbia Records, C 2S 831/C2L 31.

Rollins, Sonny. *Blue 7*. Prestige Records, LP 7079.

———. *Sonny Rollins* (two vols.). Blue Note Records, 1542/1558.

Sanders, Pharaoh. *Deaf Dumb Blind*. Impulse Records, AS 9199.

Schuller, Gunther. *Jazz Abstractions*. Atlantic Records, S-1365.

Severinsen, Doc. *Doc Severinsen's Closet*. Command Records, RSSD-950-S.

Shepp, Archie. *Four for Trane*. Impulse Records, A-71.

———. *On This Night*. Impulse Records, A-97.

Smithsonian Collection of Classic Jazz. Columbia Special Products, P6 11891.

Taylor, Cecil. *Silent Tongues*. Unit Core Records, 30551.

———. *Unit Structures*. Blue Note Records, 84237.

Vig, Tommy. *The Sound of the Seventies*. Milestone Records, 9007.

Suggested Classroom Activities

1. Present-day jazz is a potpourri of many years of continuous development. Name the sources and kinds of music jazz musicians adopt today.

2. Listen to Les McCann's rendition of "Fish This Week" in the album *Les McCann Plays the Truth* (Pacific Jazz Records, PJ2) to discover how he uses the plagal cadence harmonies in gospel jazz.

3. What are some characteristics of third-stream music? Name the jazz era it stemmed from.

4. Listen to the Modern Jazz Quartet playing with a string quartet to produce third-stream music in the selection "Sketch" from the album *Third Stream Music* (Atlantic 1345). How would you describe the total effect? What musical elements seem to be most prominent in the string quartet's part? What jazz elements are most prominent in The Modern Jazz Quartet's part?

5. Listen to "Blues for the Orient" on the album *Yusef Lateef Eastern Sounds* (Prestige Records, PR 7319). Identify the solo instrument that is used in this style for the first time. Is the percussionist playing a flat-four or a 2/4 rhythmic feeling? What musical element gives you the feeling of Oriental music?

6. Describe the improvisatory contributions of Coltrane, Rollins, and Ellis.

7. What relationship exists between the attitude one has toward free-form jazz and one's understanding of the way the musical elements are used by the performer in expressing his musical thoughts?

8. Explain two variations of free-form technique used by performers playing this type of jazz.

9. What do the terms "salsa," "soulsa," and "reggae" mean in relation to Latin jazz?

10. Should a school jazz combo listen to and play large band arrangements in addition to those it regularly performs? Why or why not?

11. In what ways do the contemporary large bands differ from the large swing bands?

14
Jazz/Rock

Although the amalgamation of jazz and rock is a prime example of eclectic jazz, we believe that the jazz/rock style is now important enough to warrant a separate chapter. In fact, terms have come into being to describe the activity, *crossover* and *fusion*, which refer to the interchange of elements between jazz and rock music. Their use by both the recording industry and music journals and related publications is widespread. Although *crossover* and *fusion* are usually used to mean the combination of jazz and rock, it should be noted that jazz is also being combined with all other kinds of music except country music, where crossing-over remains minimal. *Crossover* and *fusion* are also used to describe any style of music that appeals to more than one type of listener or record buyer. Jazz players increasingly attract followers of rock music, and performers of rock music have enlarged their audience by appealing to jazz lovers.

Some players use jazz/rock crossover merely to increase the number of their listeners and are more concerned with popularity than with good musicianship. However, musicians who play jazz/rock well can increase their chance for financial success considerably.

Jazz musicians have borrowed from anywhere and everywhere throughout the history of this music, and the same is true of rock 'n' roll musicians. Now there is a healthy interchange between these two musics. The most obvious borrowings by rock from jazz are instruments not previously associated with rock, along with jazz-type improvisations and improved and generally more sophisticated musicianship. Jazz, on the other hand, has not only borrowed repertoire from the rock field but, more important, has borrowed rock's exciting rhythmic feel and new rock sounds born mainly from electronic advances.

Irving L. Horowitz, a professor of sociology at Rutgers University, wrote the following about the merging of jazz and rock:

Many recent bands [Blood, Sweat and Tears, Chicago, and Cold Blood, for example] are highly reminiscent in their instrumentation of such earlier groups as Miles Davis' Tentet in the late '40s. And the loud, brassy arrangements are direct descendants of Count Basie. A promising new group, Ten Wheel Drive, provides a mixture of Big Mama Thornton blues and a tenor sax reminiscent of Coltrane, all set to tight arrangements that remind one of the Jazz Messengers with Art Blakey and Horace Silver.[1]

1. Irving L. Horowitz, "Rock on the Rocks—Bubblegum Anyone?" Reprinted from *Psychology Today,* January 1971. Copyright © 1971 by Ziff-Davis Publishing Company. All rights reserved.

Jazz players have never objected to new rhythmic directions as long as momentum was also added. Rock double-time feeling is as moving as any rhythmic feeling ever incorporated into jazz. It is contemporary and it communicates. The simple rhythms and meters of rock gave jazz the needed impetus to avoid public apathy at a time when a large portion of the public resented the lack of a definite pulse in some contemporary jazz.

At this point, to say that a specific group is a rock group with added jazz elements or a jazz group with a rock rhythmic feeling reflects the opinion of the speaker only.[2] Musicians are often involved in both types of music (if labeling of music can be considered valid). Happily, many young jazz musicians came immediately to grips with the merging: for example, Gary Burton, Larry Coryell, Tom Scott, Donald Byrd, Grover Washington, Herbie Hancock, Chuck Mangione, Freddie Hubbard, Don Sebesky, and even Miles Davis. At first, these players seemed to be oddities because they worked so well in both jazz and rock. There are many such musicians today.

One style deeply involved in crossover is free-form jazz. The steady pulse of rock rhythm is the one element that makes partial free form acceptable to the general public. Miles Davis undoubtedly led the way.[3]

At one time rock players felt that jazz—especially free form—was too esoteric, was hard to understand, and failed to communicate with listeners. On the other hand, jazz musicians avoided rock because they thought that it was too primitive and did not require good musicianship. Crossovers have proved both groups wrong. The primary reason why these opposing views have been resolved is that both musics have borrowed from the same sources—blues forms and sounds, spirituals, gospel songs, and so forth.

The changes in the rhythm section today are as definite as those in the Bop Era, when the means of displaying the pulse was revolutionized. Rock or jazz/rock bass players now usually play an electric bass or bass guitar instead of a traditional string bass. This allows them to play faster and to invent more complex lines. The rhythm guitar now plays the chordal punctuations that had been assigned to the piano. Don Ellis explained the manner in which the drummer plays in this idiom:

In the drums, whereas in bebop the sound went to the cymbals, in rock music (although the cymbals are still used) the opposite has happened, and the basic patterns have gone back to the drums. One of the reasons, I suspect, is that because of the high level of volume at which a great deal of rock is played the cymbals *give no definition to the time and merely add a blanket to the overall sound. So the burden of time-keeping has now come back to the snare and bass drums. This also gives it a more solid rhythmic feel. For anyone who likes to swing hard, I think this is a definite step in the right direction.*

The patterns the snare drum and the bass drum are playing, instead of being sporadic, are now more regular in the sense that they are played continually.[4]

Ed Shaughnessy, percussionist with a fine large band of his own, says that drummers today should have a good solid base in older techniques of playing rhythm but must also learn to play intricate rock patterns.

The rock drummers continued the trend of becoming more pitch conscious. This concern with pitch dates back to the cool drumming of Chico Hamilton, to the drumming of Kenny Clarke and Max Roach during the Bop Era, and, later, to the drumming of Elvin Jones, Tony Williams, and others.

The rhythm section is the main element in the crossover product as far as the jazz player is concerned—not only drum patterns, but also electronic advancements for keyboards, guitars, and basses. It should be remembered, however, that electric sounds have been used in jazz for quite some time. Charlie Christian played the electric guitar in 1939, and Ray Charles used the electric piano in 1954, whereas rock bands did not incorporate it into their battery of amplification until about 1968.

Two of the earliest rock 'n' roll groups that featured jazz solos were Chicago (Chicago Transit Authority) and Blood, Sweat and Tears. The public became aware of jazz/rock with the hit record "Spinning Wheel," which included a jazz trumpet solo.[5] The musicians in the group Chicago say that they were into the jazz aspect first but that the *Blood, Sweat & Tears* album was produced ahead of their album. There is a difference in their instrumentation. Chicago used a seven-man group, in which three members play instruments as in a jazz combo. The ratio for Blood, Sweat and Tears was nine to five.

Talented young saxophonist Tom Scott tends to borrow from any source that he considers musically valid. On the recording "The Gospel of No Name

2. *Blood, Sweat & Tears,* Columbia Records, CS 9720; *Don Sebesky and the Jazz-Rock Syndrome,* Verve Records, V6–8756.

3. Miles Davis, *Bitches Brew,* Columbia Records, GP 26.

4. Don Ellis, "Rock: The Rhythmic Revolution," *Down Beat* 36. no. 24 (1969): 32.

5. *Blood, Sweat & Tears,* Columbia Records, CS9720.

City," he borrows from rock and from rhythm and blues, playing a fairly light, cool type of jazz as well as a very heavy, driving style reminiscent of Coltrane.[6]

Don Sebesky has a large band with the standard trumpet, trombone, and saxophone sections, plus a rock-type rhythm section. This combination generates great excitement; listen to the tune "Big Mama Cass." Sebesky features guitarist Larry Coryell on "The Word." Coryell is a very fine rock guitarist, and the record shows that he is comfortable in a jazz/rock setting. Coryell played with Gary Burton, who also crosses all musical lines. The Sebesky album also displays the talented saxophonist Richard Spencer.[7]

Buddy Rich has been able to maintain a big jazz band with a rock rhythmic feeling. Of course, the fact that Rich is such an excellent, driving drummer gives him complete control of the rock aspect.[8]

Bill Chase's album *Chase* is a good example of jazz/rock.[9] Chase had been a featured jazz trumpet player in several name bands. His group consisted of four trumpets, a rock rhythm section, and an organ. To hear this group was a moving, exciting experience, and the group itself was a challenge to all groups with pretensions to jazz, rock, or jazz/rock.

One should not think that jazz/rock groups do not experiment in other directions. The advances in electronic sound are obvious. Chase and similar groups use new meters such as 7/4. These two new kinds of innovations merge excitingly on the Marvin Stamm album *Machinations*.[10]

The jazz/rock direction is surely not without criticism. "Most 'Jazz/Rock' bands fall into one of two categories. Either it's a jazz band trying to play rock without any real affinity for or identity with the idiom, or it's a group of rock musicians whose conception of jazz has not progressed far beyond Basie riffing and watered-down copies of the great creative jazz soloists."[11] If a player has not really assimilated the feel of both jazz and rock, his performance of jazz/rock will probably lack a great deal.

The word most bandied about in discussions like this is *communication*. While there is no magic formula for making a best-selling recording, chances are much better if the music has that elusive, ambiguous quality "communication." Crossover has increased the chance for universal appeal. Two of the first players to use crossover to improve communication with listeners were Herbie Hancock, a talented keyboard artist, and Donald Byrd, a seasoned, schooled trumpeter. Some musicians who have played well for years are finally achieving success by using a crossover approach. A case in point is Stanley Turrentine. His records are heard on jazz radio stations, rock radio stations, and soul music stations.

One indication of jazz/rock's growing audience appeal is that in New York City there are now almost one hundred clubs providing work for jazz players, whereas in the late 1960s there were only a few. Another indicator is the sellout crowds for jazz concerts at Carnegie Hall, Avery Fisher Hall, Philharmonic Hall, and so forth.

In June of 1979, jazz demonstrated the great impact and upswing in popularity it has experienced recently. In Los Angeles, during a two-day period, 30,200 fans crowded into the Hollywood Bowl to hear jazz artists perform. One evening the crowd numbered a capacity 17,200. Six years before, a jazz concert at this same Hollywood Bowl lost $50,000. There is no doubt about the popularity of this diverse musical art called jazz.

It is possible to cite specific records to show how deeply the recording industry is involved in crossover. *Billboard* magazine conducts a weekly survey of radio stations and record stores to determine which records are sold and which are played each week. Their survey uses the same categories used by record stores and radio stations. In August 1975, of the forty top jazz albums, five appeared in both the pop (rock) and soul categories: Grover Washington, *Mister Magic;* Freddie Hubbard, *Liquid Love;* Weather Report, *Tail Spinnin';* Esther Phillips, *Esther Phillips w/Beck;* and Nancy Wilson, *Come Get to This*.[12] Seven other jazz albums among the forty also appeared on the rock charts: recordings by Hubert Laws, the Brecker Brothers, Chuck Mangione, Phoebe Snow, Keith Jarrett, and the Eleventh Hour. And two other jazz albums appeared on the soul charts: albums by Cannonball Adderley and the Blackbyrds.

6. Tom Scott, *Paint Your Wagon*, Flying Dutchman Records, FDS–114.

7. Don Sebesky, *The Jazz Rock Syndrome*, Verve Records, V6–8756.

8. Buddy Rich, *Mercy, Mercy*, World Pacific Jazz Records, ST–20133; *Big Swing Face*, Pacific Jazz Records, PJ–10117.

9. Bill Chase, *Chase*, Epic Records, E 30472.

10. Marvin Stamm, *Machinations*, Verve Records, V6–8759.

11. Joe H. Klee, "Dreams Come Through," *Down Beat* 37, no. 22 (November 1970): 16.

12. Grover Washington, *Mister Magic*, Kudu Records, KU 2051; Freddie Hubbard, *Liquid Love*, Columbia Records, PC 33556; Weather Report, *Tale Spinnin'*, Columbia Records, PC 33417; Esther Phillips, *Esther Phillips w/Beck*, Kudu Records, KU 2351; Nancy Wilson, *Come Get to This*, Capitol Records, ST 11386.

Most of the jazz/rock groups feel that they offer a variety of music that needs a sincere listening audience as well as people who want to move. They consider their best audiences to be college audiences.

At this writing, 17 percent of the record industry sales are fusion, or crossover, recordings. The jazz/rock crossover is now considered an established, accepted phase in the history of American music. Blood, Sweat and Tears, Chicago, and other groups have had such success with mass audiences that jazz artists such as Grover Washington, George Benson, Chuck Mangione, Ramsey Lewis, Chick Corea, Herbie Mann, Billy Cobham, Freddie Hubbard, Bob James, George Duke, and Eddie Harris now use this broader approach. None seem to be sacrificing creativity or personal feel. Some players, like the eclectic Tom Scott, are not concerned with how their music is labeled but with putting their best efforts into each tune they play.

Several specific trends that affect crossovers should be noted. One is the current interest in jazz. Bop, cool, and avant-garde performers of the forties, fifties, and sixties often achieved popular success and still played for their own gratification, or at least this was the opinion of the recording industry. But during the late fifties and sixties jazz was overtaken in popularity and prominence by rock. Recently, however, jazz groups like Earth, Wind and Fire and the Blackbyrds have attracted attention with a mellow, tuneful, widely accepted style. George Benson, a jazz artist for years, is only now achieving widespread popularity in different record markets. In 1976, Benson's album *Breezin'* was number one in jazz according to the industry's charts, number two in soul, and number four in all albums. The jazz/rock fusion of Herbie Hancock and others also appeals widely to the young.

Jazz players have always searched for new sounds and new dimensions. This is probably just as true in other kinds of music.

Additional Reading Resources

Coryell, Julie, and Friedman, Laura. *Jazz-Rock Fusion.*
Note: Complete information including name of publisher and date of publication is provided in the Bibliography.

Additional Record Resources

Chicago Transit Authority. *Chicago.* Columbia Records, KGP24.
———. *Chicago Transit Authority.* Columbia Records, GP8.
Feldstein, Saul. *Jazz-Rock.* Alfred's Music Records.
Winter, Edgar. *Edgar Winter.* Epic Records, BN 26503.

Suggested Classroom Activities

1. Select two recordings in your school record library that you think would be good examples of jazz/rock. Give reasons for your selections.
2. What is meant by the terms "crossover" and "fusion" as they relate to jazz/rock? Be specific.
3. Who led the way for a fusion of rock rhythm and free-form jazz?
4. In a jazz/rock percussion section, what rhythmic role is assigned to the snare and bass drums in contrast to the electric bass or bass guitar? Why?
5. Identify two of the earliest rock 'n' roll groups that featured jazz solos.

15 Electronic Advancements

Jazz players have always experimented with any means to expand the possibilities for personal expression. Some electronic advancements can be and have been exploited as gimmicks. Fortunately, most jazz players have the good taste necessary to reject directions that do not actually enhance their performance. It should be noted at this point that it is neither within the intent of this text nor within the authors' abilities to give a highly technical explanation of these electronic devices.

A small microphone can be placed on or in any instrument, with the wire leading into an amplifier. From that point the possibilities are limitless. Of course, the sound of the instrument can be made much louder, but also the higher and lower overtones of each pitch can be made louder or softer. This makes the tone brighter or darker, whichever is desired. Instrumental and vocal sounds can be made, electronically, to sound larger, deeper, more penetrating, and so forth.

The pickup can be run through a divider, and any overtone or undertone can be amplified. The usual way involves setting the divider so that it plays along with the natural instrument, except that it is one octave lower. The volume of the divider can be adjusted so that only a hint of that lower octave is heard, or the divider can be turned up so loud that the original natural instrument can no longer be heard in its true sound.

The pickup can be run through a tape loop. The player plays a phrase and a short loop of tape repeats the phrase several times. Don Ellis experimented considerably with the tape loop, or delayed tape process. Listen to the trumpet cadenza that he plays on "Open Beauty."[1] Here he uses the divider and plays in octaves with himself, adding echo and reverberation with the loop in operation. With the loop, he was able to improvise two, three, four, or more parts at one time. Eddie Harris uses the divider on his tenor saxophone on Les McCann's "Compared to What." Buddy Terry demonstrates it on "Alfie," Sonny Stitt on "Laura," and so on.[2]

Electronic advancements allow "overdubbing" to a considerable extent. A player can play all four parts of a quartet, for example. One of the best examples of this technique is by the extremely talented trombonist Lloyd Ulyate, in which he plays ten trombone parts himself.[3] No wonder the blend is perfect.

1. Don Ellis, "Open Beauty," *Electric Bath*, Columbia Records, CL2785.

2. Les McCann, "Compared to What," *Swiss Movement*, Atlantic Records, SD 1537; Buddy Terry, "Alfie," *Electric Soul*, Prestige Records, PR 7525; Sonny Stitt, "Laura," *Parallel-A-Stitt*, Roulette Records, R 25354.

3. Lloyd Elliott (Ulyate), *Lloyd Elliott and His Trombone*, Ava Records, A-18.

As the jazz players became accustomed to these devices, they stopped thinking of them as novelties and began thinking of ways to put them to good creative use. Listen to the introduction of Bill Chase's "Open Up Wide" as he starts with one trumpet with an extreme amount of echo, then gradually dissolves into four trumpets in unison with no echo.[4] The effect is most interesting.

Electronic devices do not replace musicians, but they do produce new sounds and control and reshape old sounds. Machines have no emotion and therefore cannot replace human beings in an emotional idiom. However, the advancements certainly expand musical possibilities, not only in opening up new directions but also in offering to older concepts new, broader dimensions. An example of the expansion of an older sound is the electrified harpsichord.

Herbie Hancock demonstrates the advantages of a new instrument called a Vocoder. Hancock sings—in any pitch—into a microphone built into his glasses; but what the listener hears coming out of the amplifier are Hancock's syllables pronounced in the pitches chosen and elicited from a synthesizer. Hancock is not a great singer, but because he is so talented as a keyboard player, the result is infectious and musical.[5]

Musicians now seem to take sides in considering the attributes of the electric piano compared to those of the acoustic piano. The authors believe that the two instruments should not be compared at all. They really have only one aspect in common—both are keyboard instruments. Advocates of the electric piano point out that many electrical devices can be attached to it, thereby making possible a wider palette of sounds and colors. Among such players are Herbie Hancock, George Duke, Joe Zawinul, and Jan Hammer (from Czechoslovakia). Other people involved in jazz maintain that all musicians sound alike on the electric piano and consequently greatly prefer the acoustic piano, even when it is played by such diverse artists as McCoy Tyner and George Shearing. Sometimes, players like Bill Evans switch back and forth from one instrument to the other on the same tune.[6] By overdubbing, vibraphonist Gary Burton was able to accompany himself on both electric and acoustic piano on the album *Alone at Last*.[7]

Some performing groups are traveling electronic studios. Their equipment of amplifiers and speakers also includes "fuzz boxes," filters, echo chambers, and reverberators. Their electronic instruments include pianos and organs, along with the guitars and basses.

While strongly advocating the use of the Varitone, a divider, and other electronic devices, George Wiskirchen warns:

One thing that must be made clear about the Varitone or any electronic instrument is that it is dependent for its efficiency on the technique of the player and is not automatically going to improve the player or give him new techniques. What was bad tone, bad intonation, bad phrasing before is going to remain and be electronically exaggerated.[8]

Much heated discussion continues among musicians concerning the great volume of sound many contemporary bands use. Some feel that the original sounds of most instruments are no longer played and long to hear again the familiar sounds made by talented guitar players, bass players, saxophone players, trumpet players, and so forth. They want at least occasionally to hear pure sounds as a relief not only from the volume but the distortion of electronically amplified instruments.

On the other hand, defenders of the electronic age are very convincing when they state that volume is necessary for physical, visceral communication. They also argue that electronic amplification now makes it possible to hear the softer instruments, such as the guitar and flute, over the percussion (except when the percussion is also amplified!). The authors are performers and can vouch for the fact that the feel of performing music loudly is truly different from performing it softly. However, we think the aggressive feeling of loud playing is somewhat lost if the loudness comes from the turn of a dial instead of from the physical action of the performer.

The advocates of electronic devices have a point when they say that technology makes it possible to devise new instruments from old ones. For example, the amplified guitar is simply not the same instrument as the unamplified guitar, and players do not want to play the same sounds on both instruments. Thus, it is apparent that electronics ushered in an entirely new art, with many directions possible. What one person considers noise may be a pleasing increase in volume and different approach to another.

4. Bill Chase, "Open Up Wide," *Chase*, Epic Records, E 30472.

5. Herbie Hancock, *Feets Don't Fail Me Now*, Columbia Records, 35764.

6. Bill Evans, *Bill Evans Album*, Columbia Records, 30855.

7. Gary Burton, *Alone at Last*, Atlantic Records, 1598.

8. George Wiskirchen, "Electronics in the Big Band," *Down Beat* 35, no. 20 (October 1968): 36.

Some musicians who have been successful in one style of jazz have now gone deeply into electronics. A good example is Les McCann, a hard-swinging, effervescent acoustic piano player who was an early funky stylist. He went from funky straight into gospel jazz, making heavy use of the amen chords. McCann is at present an electric player in every sense of the word. He is associated with a manufacturer of electronic instruments and seems to use them all. He is extremely creative and finds ways to use each device, enjoying the new sounds of each. It is interesting to note that whether McCann plays a synthesizer or a clavinet, uses tapes, or whatever, he still manages to sound as funky as ever. It seems as if his personality demands the funky style of playing, and he cannot fight it even if he cared to.

To spend an evening with the talented Eddie Harris is to experience an unbelievable electronic display. Not only does he do everything possible electronically with the saxophone and keyboard, but his guitar player plays a "guitorgan," an instrument that looks like a guitar and requires guitar techniques, but sounds like an organ.

Among the many talented leaders in the field the following should be mentioned: Herbie Hancock, Chick Corea, John McLaughlin, George Duke, Klaus Doldinger, Larry Coryell, Umir Deodato, Monk Montgomery (the pioneer and a true artist on the electric bass), and Carole Kay.

At first, the synthesizer was called a Moog (rhymes with *vogue*) because the instrument built by scientist Dr. Robert Moog was the first of its kind of which the musicians and public became aware. A recording that is not really (in the authors' opinion) an aesthetic experience but one that demonstrates the synthesizer quite clearly is *Switched On Bach*.[9] A synthesizer is a nonacoustical instrument. That means that without electrical current it cannot be heard at all. With current, it generates, modifies, and controls sounds. It differs from the electric guitar, electric piano, electric bass, and so on, in that these instruments do create a very soft sound even when not plugged into an electrical outlet. They require current to amplify their sound, to make them louder; the synthesizer needs current to actually produce a sound. By controlling pitch, volume, attack, duration, and timbre, musical sounds are "synthesized." Some say that this control has made the synthesizer into the most expressive electronic instrument.

Synthesizers use what is known as an oscillator. This component oscillates electrical currents—in lieu of vibrating materials like strings, metal, or wood—to produce sounds. By increasing or decreasing frequencies, pitch is controlled. By amplifying frequencies, the volume can be raised. By initiating or terminating frequencies, the duration of the note is controlled. By filtering frequencies, timbre, or the quality of tone, is controlled. Synthesizers are capable of producing pitches that are higher or lower than the pitches any traditional instrument can produce, and they are capable of producing an endless variety of timbres. Through the use of what is called a "noise generator," synthesizers can invent or reproduce extramusical sounds such as the sound of thunder, the howling of a storm, the gentle rush of the surf on a beach, and hundreds of other effects ranging from eerie to exciting.

So far, the number of accomplished synthesizer performers is small. The instrument is so new that only a small percentage of those who own synthesizers have taken the time to learn how to play them proficiently. However, the synthesizer will need only a fraction of the time it took the piano, for example, to gain widespread acceptance. Up to this time, most musicians have performed on the synthesizer as if its capabilities were limited to a few electronic sounds. They usually preset the controls to obtain a specific sound, then play the synthesizer keyboard as they would play an electric piano or organ. In order to do justice to the instrument, the performer must play the keyboard while simultaneously moving the various sliders, switches, and dials.

The synthesizer's potential has not even been approached in live performance. It can sound like another instrument, like a chorus of instruments, or like no instrument ever heard before. One of the first priorities, however, is that the manufacturers do a better job in helping the musician to "see" how he is creating certain sounds—the controls must be made easier to read and to manipulate.

Improvisational synthesizer work makes up the bulk of recorded synthesizer music at the present time. People like Stevie Wonder, George Duke, Joe Zawinul, and others record but do not write music specifically for other synthesizer players. Considering the dozen or so synthesizer models available in this country, any sort of standard notation seems to be years away.

The art of live synthesizer performance, as stated before, is still in its infancy. With a few exceptions, most performers are not yet able to realize more than a fraction of the potential inherent in this instrument. However, through the talents of Herbie Hancock, Jan Hammer, Les McCann, Joe Zawinul, and others, the synthesizer will become a well-established jazz instrument. There is even talk today of a guitar synthesizer, which would surely revolutionize approaches to the guitar.

9. *Switched On Bach*, Columbia Records, MS 7194.

Some musicians use synthesizers to reproduce, more or less, the sounds of instruments already in existence. This kind of use seems to show a lack of creativity and imagination. The synthesizer holds endless possibilities for going far beyond what are considered conventional musical sounds. And the opportunities for organizing these new sounds and colors are limitless.

There are now synthesizer kits. The electronically inclined musician can now organize his own instrument so that it includes the components most adaptable to the musical directions of his interest. Those who write or speak about the different parts (modules) of this equipment usually have very little feeling for the lack of understanding that most music, or nonmusic, people have for the technicalities of the modules. There are currently periodicals that are essential to anyone undertaking the kit approach: *Synapse, the Electronic Music Magazine,* published in Los Angeles, and *Polyphony,* published in Oklahoma City.

Since about 1950, when records began being recorded directly on tape, splicing of the tape has been very important. A final record can consist of a number of short segments spliced together. Imagine the advantage in using the best part of performance number one, the best part of number two, and so on. Even bad notes can be removed.

Even with the advantages of recording on tape, there is a trend of returning to what is called "direct to disc" recording. This is precisely the manner in which recordings were made before the advent of tape. However, if a listener has very fine equipment on which to play his records, he will be ecstatic at the beautiful fidelity of these records—so much has recording equipment improved since 1950. If the reader has good phonographic equipment, a suggested album would be Buddy Rich's *Class of '78.*[10] If the listener does not have excellent playback equipment, the extra cost of the "direct to disc" recordings would be money foolishly spent.

At the end of the 1970s, spokespersons for the recording industry were making recurrent predictions that records with grooves would become obsolete and possibly even collector's items. One new system that is generating a lot of enthusiasm is digital recording—a computer-augmented means of recording sound. This new system promises to change the size and shape of albums, as well as the equipment upon which they are played. Audio signals are picked up by a computer and converted into numerical symbols. In other words, numbers are used to represent sounds. The computer then recalls the numbers, reassembles them precisely as recorded, and converts the sound into a master tape, free from distortion. The "albums" are small pieces of plastic the size of a postcard. The card is covered with numbers that are scanned by an optical (or laser) scanning system. The biggest problems with conventional recording have been distortion, tape noise, surface noise, print through, and limited dynamic range. There is a loss of quality through editing and copying. At present in digital recording, over 50,000 computer-fed numbers per second can be generated, corresponding to minute variations in pitch and tonal quality. The sounds of a live concert performance embrace approximately 640,000 variations per second. Some record stores are already beginning to stock conventional albums (not the plastic cards) made by the digital process, and the fidelity is outstanding. There are digital processors that allow home video cassette machines to play digital recordings. The three-by-five-inch plastic cards will be easier to store than the conventional albums or tapes, permitting the public to enjoy more albums of their favorite jazz and other music performers. The recording industry spokespersons suggest that this new system will be accepted by the public by about 1985.

Although there is no doubt about the importance of technological advancements, there is a considerable difference of opinion as to whether this progress frees the artist to pursue new creative directions or whether he is so involved in the technology that creativity becomes secondary.

One situation that has arisen because of more advanced techniques is that there are now fans of the electronic recording and playback advancements who will listen to anything that is recorded well, regardless of the talent or lack of talent displayed. The more musically discerning listeners will listen to the *music,* regardless of the recording deficiencies. The avid collector of older records often desires the surface noise produced by the older phonographs. Obviously, the ideal situation would have excellent music being recorded under optimum conditions (this refers mainly to the equipment used) and played back on the best possible audio system. A glance at the new recording techniques seems to reveal a definite trend toward less interference between what is performed and what is actually heard on records. This by no means implies fewer electronic musical instruments.

Electronics has introduced a new concept to music. Now, there is music played in which the significant element is the invention of a specific sound. In other words, there has been a change from using a

---

10. Buddy Rich, *Class of '78,* The Great American Gramophone Co., GADD 1030.

certain sound primarily as a vehicle to showcase thematic material to an emphasis on the individual sound and color being produced. In a way, this new concept can be related all the way back to when musicians first became aware of jazz interpretation or even to the prejazz field hollers—remembering the overworked expression: "It's not about notes, it's about feelings."

Even though there is so much more involved, to many musicians and the public electronics equals amplification which equals louder volume. The music in general surely has become much louder—even instrumental backgrounds for featured vocalists are often so loud that the often-touted vocal "message" can never actually be imparted. In defense of the higher decibels, the performance setting has generally altered to the point that, in this type of music, intimacy is simply not as important as it was previously.

Players deeply involved in amplification and all its implications (certainly more than volume) say that they plan to move into further creative arenas, that they want to invent colors never before heard, and that such broadening will attract a wider audience. Most mature contemporary musicians agree that a good balance between acoustic and electronic music is healthy.

Electronic music is surely here to stay. We must therefore maintain a reasonable attitude toward this endeavor at expanding the perimeters of music. (Listen to Frank Comstock's *Music from Outer Space* for interesting electronic experiments.)[11]

Additional Reading Resources

Baird, David. *From Score to Tape.*

Friend, David; Perlman, Alan R.; Piggott, Thomas G. *Learning Music with Synthesizers.*

Drake, Russell; Herder, Ronald; Modugno, Anne D. *How to Make Electronic Music.*

Muro, Don. *An Introduction to Electronic Music Synthesizers.*

Note: Complete information including name of publisher and date of publication is provided in the Bibliography.

Additional Record Resources

Synthesizer Recordings

Hammer, Jan. *Melodies.* Nemperor Records, 35003.

Hancock, Herbie. *Sunlight.* Columbia Records, 34907.

Mahavishnu Orchestra. *Birds of Fire.* Columbia Records, KC 31996.

———. *Inner Worlds.* Columbia Records, PC 33908.

Weather Report. *Heavy Weather.* Columbia Records, PC 34418.

Wonder, Stevie. *Songs in the Key of Life.* Tamla Records, T 13–34062.

Direct to Disc Recordings

Herman, Woody. *Road Father.* Century Records, CRDD-1080.

Herman, Woody, and Phillips, Flip. *Together/Flip and Woody.* Century Records, CRDD-1090.

Miles, Barry. *Fusion Is.* Century Records, CRDD-1020.

Torme, Mel, and Rich, Buddy. *Together Again—For the First Time.* Century Records, CRDD-1100.

Woods, Phil. *Song for Sisyphus.* Century Records, CRDD-1030.

Suggested Classroom Activities

1. In producing a tone, how does the synthesizer function in contrast to an electric piano? In contrast to an acoustic piano?

2. Give the title of a recording that uses the synthesizer.

3. What is a guitorgan?

4. For an exciting new sound, listen to "Open Beauty" as played by the Don Ellis Orchestra on the album *Electric Bath, The Don Ellis Orchestra* (Columbia, Stereo CS 9585). In this composition Ellis weaves a psychedelic effect by using an electric piano with reeds and brasses. What electronic effect was used to create the sound of many parts occurring at one time?

5. Who was noted for his mix of electronics and the singing voice?

6. Name the musician who was highly successful while identified with a particular style of jazz and now is associated with electronics. Has his entrance into electronics changed his earlier style of jazz playing? If so, how?

7. What is digital recording?

11. Frank Comstock, *Music from Outer Space,* Warner Brothers Records, 1463.

16
Jazz in Television and Motion Pictures

Since the beginning of sound movies, composers have been attempting to compose, and critics have been attempting to write about, a combination of jazz and classical music for this medium. Some European composers like Ravel were constantly amazed that American composers had not drawn more from jazz sources. Gershwin was headed in this direction; in fact, movie composers borrowed heavily from Gershwin in order to set urban scenes. However, too many American composers have been reluctant to borrow from the obvious folk source, jazz, knowing full well that European composers whom Americans respect and often emulate have borrowed from folk sources for centuries. Early European composers even utilized the soloists' ability to improvise; not so in America. The result of this apparent inhibition has been that when American classical musicians attempt this mixture of jazz and classical music, the results have been fairly awkward; the styles seem to have been juxtaposed but not integrated well.

As has been pointed out earlier in the text, Gunther Schuller coined the label "third-stream music." This music, however, has not remained in serious favor with the public except as it appears as background music on television and in motion pictures. For about the first thirty-five years of the movie industry, jazz was not considered right for movie music; music that was closer to classical meant a loftier, more ideal image for that industry. For example, when Benny Carter broke into film scoring, he was used mainly to write backup arrangements for black singers. Any hint of jazz was used to indicate something on the order of a sexy woman. The artists who perform today on the sitar have an "image" problem because television and movie composers overused the instrument for setting scenes that involved drug users.

Jazz began to break through its image dilemma toward the end of the 1950s. The conjecture is that a newer generation of executives who had grown up during the Swing Era came into power in the television and movie industry. They did not make the error of associating jazz with the seamier aspects of life, because they remembered their own good times with big band music and saw no reason to keep out this enjoyable means of expression.

Jazz performers have been a part of the movies for years. Bessie Smith made the film *St. Louis Blues* in 1929. In 1934, Duke Ellington and his orchestra were in Earl Carroll's *Murder at the Vanities*. Louis Armstrong appeared in movies in the late 1930s and early 1940s. In fact, many movies have been made that center on a jazz player or an entire jazz band. There have been movies based on the lives of Bix Beiderbecke,

148

Scott Joplin, Red Nichols, Billie Holiday, Louis Armstrong, and others. During the Swing Era, Glenn Miller made two films featuring his band: *Sun Valley Serenade* with Sonja Henie, and *Orchestra Wives*. Jimmy Stewart played the title role in *The Glenn Miller Story* a dozen years after Miller's disappearance during World War II. Movies were made featuring Paul Whiteman, Benny Goodman, Tommy Dorsey, Artie Shaw, Gene Krupa, and many others.

In the early 1960s, the public began hearing jazz used in films as background music to establish scenes and moods. Elmer Bernstein used Shorty Rogers's "Giants" in *The Man with the Golden Arm,* and Johnny Mandel used Gerry Mulligan's "Quartet" in *I Want to Live.* Both films, however, did deal with unpleasant aspects of life: the first was about a drug addict and the second about a girl accused of murder. Nevertheless, these creative composers used jazz throughout the entire pictures for dramatic purposes—certainly a step forward.

Henry Mancini's movie score for a romantic comedy, *Breakfast at Tiffany's,* proved the feasibility of jazz as background music for movies. This film was followed quickly by Mancini's scoring of the Pink Panther films, *Two for the Road,* and even the African adventure *Hatari.* Duke Ellington scored *Anatomy of a Murder* in 1959, *Paris Blues* in 1961, and *Assault on a Queen* in 1966.

Mancini truly opened the door for television scoring with his jazz-oriented music for the "Peter Gunn" and "Mr. Lucky" series. In addition to his wonderful scorings using jazz, the talented, eclectic Mancini uses classical music, rock, electronics, and anything else that his good taste allows. His up-tempo sequences sound similar to contemporary large bands, while his more romantic underscoring is quite reminiscent of the Cool Era of jazz.

It is possible to mention only a few of the outstanding artists who have contributed to the field of television and motion picture scoring. Quincy Jones wrote the television scores for "Ironside," "Sanford and Son," "The Bill Cosby Show," and too many well-known films to mention. Patrick Williams scored the music for "The Mary Tyler Moore Show," "The Bob Newhart Show," and "The Streets of San Francisco." One of the latest film scores by Williams was for a picture called *Cuba,* whose score is replete with Afro-Cuban rhythmic sounds. Lalo Schifrin wrote the score for "Mission Impossible," "Mannix," and such movies as *Bullitt* and *Dirty Harry.* Oliver Nelson scored for the television shows "Matt Lincoln," "Longstreet," "The Six Million Dollar Man," "It Takes a Thief,"

"The Name of the Game," and many films. Benny Carter scored television specials such as "Bob Hope Presents" and "The Sarah Vaughan Special," and his film credits include *A Man Called Adam, Buck and the Preacher,* and *Louis Armstrong: Chicago Style.* Among Pete Rugolo's credits are "Thriller," "The Fugitive," and "Run for Your Life." Billy May's work was heard on "Naked City," Earle Hagen's on "The Mod Squad." Resourceful arranger/composers like the highly respected Dave Grusin and Billy May have done much "ghostwriting." Composers whose time pressures have placed them in an impossible position will call in ghost-writers to do the assignment for them. Billy May wrote a great amount of music for producer Jack Webb, often receiving no screen credit. John Barry combined the Mancini style of jazz with the English approach to rock for the James Bond films. It has become quite natural to hear the infectious creations of jazz trumpeter Harry "Sweets" Edison on Nelson Riddle's scores. For the film *The World of Insects,* Lalo Schifrin wrote no score; instead, he let the players improvise from sequences, clusters, twelve-tone rows, and motifs. Marvin Hamlisch won an Oscar for the music for *The Sting,* although the score consisted mostly of Scott Joplin ragtime tunes. André Previn furnished the music for *The Subterraneans* by calling a group of his friends to the studio to improvise behind the scenes of this low-budget movie. His friends included Gerry Mulligan, Art Farmer, Art Pepper, Shelly Manne, and Red Mitchell.

Sometimes the composer must write in such a way as to make the producer feel secure about his product, and film producers seem to want their offerings to the public to have the most contemporary sounds available. This situation, along with the mood of the specific scenes to be underscored, will on occasion cause a talented composer to write certain music that he might not otherwise invent. In the opinion of the authors, the score for *Star Wars,* written by the talented John Williams, is an example of this situation.

One of the authors was in an orchestra that recorded weekly for "The D.A.'s Man," one of the early dramatic shows that used jazz-oriented background music. The show was produced by Jack Webb, and the fine scoring was done by Frank Comstock, formerly with Les Brown's band.

Jazz players have found quite remunerative employment on staff bands for talk shows and variety shows. For example, the personnel of Doc Severinsen's band on the "Tonight Show" includes some of the best jazz players in the world. Fine jazz could be heard on Dean Martin's variety show—Bob Hardaway improvised on the tenor saxophone over the credits in such an exciting way that musicians would listen to the show specifically to hear Hardaway's creativity. One of the authors was on the staff of the American Broadcasting Company for sixteen years and played for many series of variety shows with good jazz players.

One of the great advantages of scoring a film with jazz, as far as the producers were concerned, was that a smaller musical group could be used—representing quite a financial savings. Also, repairs in the studio (new cuts or additions to the film) could be accommodated much more easily, sometimes involving merely the improvising skills of the players. Consequently, a new breed of musicians evolved out of this situation, musicians who can play any type of music at any time under the pressure of recording.

Today, there is an organization named "The Orchestra," comprised of about one hundred of the best and most well rounded musicians in the world. The organization was established by two men, Jack Elliott and Dr. Allyn Ferguson, who are intelligent, contemporary, musical, and imaginative. These two men collaborated in writing music for television shows such as "Charlie's Angles" and "Barney Miller." They also use jazz constantly in their film scoring. For example, Benny Goodman's "Sing, Sing, Sing" plays a very important part in the movie *Birds of Prey*. In George Burns's movie *Just You and Me, Kid*, earlier jazz styles set mood and plot. Elliott and Ferguson have gathered together musicians from the movie and television studios, augmented their own compositions with those of David Grusin, Billy May, Robert Farnon, Lyn Murray, Hugo Friedhofer, Roger Kellaway, Patrick Williams, Sam Nestico, Greg McRitchie, Michel Legrand, and others, and performed concerts with overwhelming success. Offerings of bookings are coming much faster than they can be accommodated. The Orchestra's debut performance was at the 1979 Academy Awards. The reason for this success is simple: the most versatile musicians ever assembled are playing music written by the very best of contemporary American composers. There is no thought of whether the results are jazz or third stream or something else; but it is not difficult to imagine the thrill of a moving Bud Shank improvisation in the middle of a symphonic setting. Ferguson has assured the authors that recordings will soon be available.

These television and movie composers are not attempting to write concert music. They are writing music to establish moods, set scenes, cause reactions, whether the music is intended to convey sadness or joy, light or darkness, fear or courage. That is their goal, that is what they have trained themselves for. Fortunately for those involved in jazz, these talented artists realize that this kind of music can express any emotion and is readily accessible to the listening audience. In fact, it is rare today to watch any movie or television show that is not backed by jazz-oriented music.

17
Future
Directions

Because of the ease of present-day communication, changes in the styles of playing jazz occur more frequently now than in the past. As long as people want to dance there will be a demand for dance music, and providing music for dancing has been the most important function of jazz since its inception. Ballrooms have been a chief source of employment and financial gain for the jazz musician. However, not as many people dance today as did prior to World War II. As a consequence, there are fewer ballrooms in operation and this decline has gradually diminished the dance band field.

Nightclubs offer steady employment for smaller groups of musicians, while the large bands travel the ballroom circuit. Two major disadvantages of the nightclub atmosphere are bad acoustics and long working hours. The advantages, however, appear to outweigh the disadvantages. The intimate surroundings together with the *esprit de corps* developed through long hours of playing together foster experimentation and the development of jazz.

With the advent of the Swing Era, jazz became an important theater attraction. In 1938 it moved into the concert halls. But television took business away from the theaters, thus diminishing a major outlet for jazz performance. At first the concert hall was considered an ideal showplace for the art, but it soon became evident that the attendance was erratic. Concert hall promoters paid high salaries, but were interested only in name attractions. One other problem with the larger concert halls was communication. The difficulty was due to the distance between the players and the listeners as well as to the fact that footlights screened the reactions of the audiences from the performers, thus lessening the rapport so necessary to the performing musicians.

In the authors' opinion, the most logical place for the presentation of jazz today is in a small concert hall or theater-in-the-round. In such settings, there are few communication problems, and intimacy and attention are guaranteed. The only disadvantage in this setting is the lack of accommodation for dancing.

The large jazz music festival is one of the best means of furthering interest in jazz. Two successful festivals are the Newport Jazz Festival, which is held in New York, and the Monterey Jazz Festival (California). Other jazz festivals, such as the one held in New Orleans, are also very successful. Because the festivals are a summer activity they cannot be a source of year-round employment for jazz musicians. One great advantage of the festival is that it can present jazz to multitudes. Unfortunately, promoters of the festivals often substitute commercialism for creativity.

The festival movement continues to grow and to be accepted all over the world. More countries held jazz festivals in 1979 than ever before.

Jazz authorities differ as to the direction that the music itself will follow. One possibility is that jazz will merge completely with classical music. Gunther Schuller states that "the deeper blending of jazz and classical music is only a matter of time."[1] John Lewis feels that jazz and classical music will never merge. Berendt thinks that jazz is approaching atonality.[2] The jazz player, following Ornette Coleman's lead, wants at least to break with harmonic predictability. Obviously, the jazz/rock crossover is one of the important continuing directions. Duke Ellington believed that all categories would be abolished and that there would eventually be just one music. The answer can be substantiated only when the matter is viewed in retrospect.

The ease of world travel will definitely affect the future of jazz. In addition to the exchange of ideas among the various countries, there will be new markets for jazz. Through State Department tours American jazz musicians have been enthusiastically received in all parts of the world, including those that have had practically no exposure to jazz. These touring musicians, in turn, have been impressed and influenced by the native music of foreign countries. Dizzy Gillespie claims that jazz has progressed as far with European influences as is possible and rightly states that influences will come from such sources as Indian scales. One of the authors heard jazz performed on authentic Eastern instruments in Bangkok in 1971.

Jazz does seem to be attempting to escape from the transitional 1960s and 1970s in order to develop new structures. However, the more traditional approaches appear to be the most durable and flexible. The new approaches add greatly to the possibilities of jazz and do attract attention, but they seem to get absorbed into the mainstream of jazz stylings. There are many jazz groups that defy categorization. The authors applaud those players who refrain from either following in someone else's footsteps or remaining in a small niche. It is refreshing to hear jazz artists who can perform contemporary music but are also looking ahead and behind themselves, who continue to experiment while retaining an understanding of and devotion to the past. The key word in jazz today, as always, is "creativity."

We have attempted to show innovations, mergings, borrowings, and other influences on jazz from its primitive beginnings to the present. No jazz style has ever completely disappeared. In most contemporary jazz performances definite fragments of several eras can be found. Even the most avant-garde of the innovations stems from some eighty years of development.

Additional Reading Resources

Feather, Leonard. *The Book of Jazz*, pp. 245–62.

Hentoff, Nat, and McCarthy, Albert. *Jazz*, pp. 327–42.

Stearns, Marshall. *The Story of Jazz*, pp. 227–30.

Note: Complete information including name of publisher and date of publication is provided in the Bibliography.

1. Marshall Stearns, *The Story of Jazz* (London: Oxford University Press, 1958), p. 227.

2. Joachim Berendt, *The New Jazz Book* (New York: Hill & Wang, 1962), p. 25.

Louis Armstrong (1900–1971)

If we make a list of truly great jazz men, it should begin Louis Armstrong and Duke Ellington. Armstrong—the intuitive improviser—and Ellington—the creator who held improvisation and written part, soloist and orchestra, in delicate balance in his work, a balance in which each contributed to a total development, a whole greater than the sum of its parts.[1]

18
Five Out of Many

If the one most influential musician in the entire span of jazz had to be chosen, the choice would be Louis Armstrong. The other four artists discussed in this chapter made permanent contributions for sure, but if jazz is considered from the very beginnings, the selection would be Armstrong.

Daniel Louis Armstrong was born on July 4, 1900, as close as any researcher has been able to discover. He was born in a poor neighborhood in New Orleans. Armstrong's parents were separated when he was very young. His father worked in a factory and his mother was a cleaning woman. Armstrong was placed in the Colored Waifs Home for boys at the age of thirteen years because he playfully fired a revolver in the air while celebrating New Year's Eve, and he remained there for 1 ½ years. At the Waifs Home, Peter Davis taught him to play the bugle and then the cornet. He joined the band and the chorus and played for social affairs outside the home.

After leaving the home he first played with an orchestra of youngsters under Joe Lindsay. The king of New Orleans trumpet players around 1917 was Joe Oliver. Oliver took an interest in Armstrong and made him his protégé. When Oliver left for Chicago in 1918, he placed Armstrong in his chair with a band directed by trombonist Kid Ory. Armstrong stayed with Ory for eighteen months and then joined Fate Marable's orchestra on a Mississippi steamboat in 1920. He was briefly married when he was eighteen years old. In 1922, Oliver sent for Armstrong to join him in Chicago at the Lincoln Gardens. Armstrong married Lil' Hardin (the second of four wives) in 1924. She was the pianist with Oliver, but she encouraged Armstrong to organize his own band. However, Armstrong always remained grateful to Oliver and considered him his idol.

Another of Armstrong's early idols was B. A. Rolfe, a white virtuoso trumpeter who later on conducted a Paul Whiteman-type radio orchestra, and who was never associated with the mainstream of jazz.

---

1. Martin T. Williams, *Jazz Masters in Transition* (London: Macmillan & Co., 1970), p. 39. Copyright © by Martin Williams.

153

Louis Armstrong. Courtesy of Ray Avery.

Armstrong heard in Rolfe a good tone and sensible control of melodic thoughts. In Armstrong's opinion, both of these elements are missing in the performance of most contemporary jazz players.

One of Armstrong's greatest thrills was at his first recording session when the engineer placed him twenty feet behind the other musicians (including King Oliver) because Armstrong's tone was so powerful. Armstrong left the Oliver band in 1924, and the band declined. (Oliver did make some good recordings in 1926 and 1927.)

Armstrong joined Fletcher Henderson at the Roseland Ballroom in New York City in 1924. At this time he recorded frequently with Clarence Williams's Blue Five accompanying singers. With Henderson, he accompanied Bessie Smith and Ma Rainey. He was a remarkable influence in the Fletcher Henderson band. Because of his spirit and inspiration, he was a true catalyst.

In 1925 he returned to Chicago and was billed as the World's Greatest Trumpet Player. Also in 1925, he started to record under his own name. The next four years are notable for the Hot Five and Hot Seven records. With these records (classics in this music), jazz was turning from ensemble-oriented music to solo-oriented music.

By 1926, Armstrong was considered the greatest trumpet player that had ever lived. His tone, stamina, range, creativeness, and technique were envied by all jazz performers. At that early age, he became the ideal, the model of how to play jazz improvisation.

In 1929 he headed for New York City again—this time with his own band. Here he continued to record and play nightly on radio as well, which helped to spread his fame. In 1930 he was in Hollywood, and in 1931 he returned to Chicago. Then he went to England and Europe, where he was, of course, a tremendous success. Armstrong was the first jazz player to achieve international fame.

Armstrong's career remained very solid throughout the Swing Era and even included several motion pictures. He had a large swing band that was usually led by someone else—Louie Russell, for example. The band was usually only a showcase for the talents of Armstrong himself. His big band phase was not as productive nor nearly as creative as the earlier and later small band phases. He seemed to be most comfortable with the small band format.

His career hit a new high in 1947. He returned to using a combo, which included at one time or another Jack Teagarden, Earl Hines, Cozy Cole, Barney Bigard, Sid Catlett, Arvell Shaw, Dick Cary, Billy Kyle, Joe Darrensbourg, Tyree Glenn, and Trummie Young. With his All Stars, Armstrong toured the world in the 1950s and 1960s and became known as the Ambassador of Good Will. As late as 1964, he had his biggest record success, "Hello Dolly." Fortunately he lived to be both wealthy and famous. He died July 6, 1971.

Armstrong was the first great jazz soloist. Here is Martin Williams's assessment (with which most other writers agree) of Armstrong:

Armstrong's music has affected all our music, top to bottom, concert hall to barroom. No concert composers here or abroad write for brass instruments the way they used to, simply because Armstrong has shown that brass instruments, and the trumpet in particular, are capable of things that no one thought them capable of before he came along. Our symphonists play trumpet with a slight, usually unconscious vibrato that is inappropriate to Beethoven or Schubert because Armstrong has had one.

"Louis changed our whole idea of the band," said Henderson's chief arranger at the time, Don Redman. So did he change everyone's idea of every band, and every soloist's idea of himself. From that, the era and the style took its name: swing. From the Henderson band itself came the Benny Goodman style, and, directly or indirectly, most of the popular big bands of the swing era. American music was not the same after it became swing, and what made it different was the influence of Armstrong.[2]

In the 1920s, playing high C on the trumpet was extraordinary. Armstrong, however, often amazed his audiences by playing 100 high Cs (with the band shouting out the count on each one). Then Armstrong would soar upward to a high F. In the twenties and thirties that alone was an incredible feat, but Armstrong would follow this display with an outstanding version of a blues or some tune of the day. The moment was one to be remembered.

Armstrong was also considered one of the best jazz singers. He was very concerned with pleasing his audiences, and he became a great showman and even a comedian. Too often, praise for Armstrong is divided between Armstrong the artist and Armstrong the entertainer, as if artists do not entertain. It is almost inconceivable that the man who was probably America's greatest natural musician, the man who was so personally responsible for a way of playing and listening to music, should be remembered as an affable clown. Is it possible that without Armstrong there would have been no jazz? There may have been jazz, but it truly would have developed in an entirely different way than it did. Armstrong always felt that even if music was one's whole life, it was meaningless if it could not be presented to and appreciated by the public.

It must be gratifying to their fans to know that during their lifetime both Armstrong and Ellington received the public acclaim they deserved. Armstrong was undoubtedly one of the best-known and most highly respected personalities in the world. He was probably the first to be recognized as an artist—about 1925—in a music that was at that time considered merely entertainment.

Today's researchers benefit greatly from the fact that Armstrong's recordings are a real documentation of his career and his permanent worth. The most mentioned solos are "West End Blues," "Savoy Blues," "Potato Head Blues," "Hotter Than That," "Weather Bird," "Muggles," "Beau Koo Jack," "I'm Not Rough," "Cornet Chop Suey," "Struttin' with Some Barbeque," "Heebie Jeebies," and "Mahogany Hall Stomp."

In Armstrong were combined well-developed technique, rhythmic feel, intuition, good tone, and high register, as well as personal warmth and an ability to communicate. Each solo, no matter how deep into improvisation, sounds cohesive and well-planned but

2. Martin T. Williams, "For Louis Armstrong at 70," *Down Beat* 37, no. 13 (July 1970): 22.

still spontaneous. In spite of being a great improviser, Armstrong's chief talent was his ability to inject rhythmic feeling into a melodic line, whether that melodic line was an improvised line or a written line. The tunes that he recorded were often quite banal until he transformed them into a worthwhile listening experience.

He was a genius at improvisation, and his improvisations showed more than anything else that simplicity leads directly to communication. As great as his trumpet playing was, Armstrong's chief asset was his ability to communicate.

Although he often seemed gregarious and extroverted, Armstrong could play a blues that was lovely and sad at the same time. Almost every player who improvises plays phrases that can be traced back to Armstrong and his influence. Somehow, he almost single-handedly set the stage for the jazz soloist, maybe the stage for jazz. In fact, most musicians agree that Armstrong was the leader that all other jazz players followed. ". . . Daniel Louis Armstrong, the man from whom has flowed so much good music and so much good will that the world will never fully realize just how deeply it is in his debt."[3] Armtrong's approach to jazz or to life has never been out of style. Somehow Armstrong made everybody happy!

Duke Ellington (1899–1974)

Just as Armstrong crystalized and popularized the solo aspect of jazz, Duke Ellington, more than any other single musician, proved that orchestrating jazz was an art of the highest level. However, it should be pointed out that Ellington's music was always a combination of solo and ensemble playing. He, like Basie, drew the thoughts of his soloists together into the orchestral whole, accomplishing the feat from the piano. On the other hand, the musicians playing for Ellington did not lose their identity. The Ellington orchestra was always made up of the *individual* talents of his players. It cannot be emphasized enough that listeners are always aware of the personalities of the players (Johnny Hodges, Lawrence Brown, Rex Stewart, Harry Carney, and so on). Yet the band always sounded like Ellington regardless of changes in personnel over the years. This is one of the most important aspects of the band: allowing individuals to retain their own identity and to expand and explore their own directions. Ellington's band always sounded like a well-knit unit expressing the feelings and personality of Ellington. Whenever one heard his band, it always sounded like Ellington.

Edward Kennedy ("Duke") Ellington was born in Washington D.C., on April 29, 1899. He did not come from a poor family, as did Armstrong, and he had educational advantages that many musicians his age lacked. He received his nickname from a high school friend. He was a better than average young painter and won a scholarship to study at the Pratt Institute in Brooklyn, New York. His art career was superseded, of course, by music.

Ellington listened to and was influenced by ragtime piano players in the Washington area. It is possible to hear ragtime and stride in Ellington's extended piano solos, especially at the faster tempos. The influence of Fats Waller, Willie ("The Lion") Smith, and James P. Johnson is evident. Ellington played piano, but most jazz writers agree that the orchestra was his real instrument. By the age of seventeen years he had a five-piece combo called The Washingtonians.

In 1919, Duke Ellington's son Mercer was born. He became a trumpet player, composer, and arranger—a talented musician in his own right. Mercer now leads the Ellington band.

Ellington, with his drummer Sonny Greer and saxophonist Toby Hardwicke, made an abortive attempt to move to New York City in 1922 to join the orchestra of Wilbur Sweatman. Financial problems caused Ellington to return to Washington until Fats Waller encouraged him to try to move again in 1923. This time Ellington and his friends went to work in New York's Harlem where Ellington began his career as a leader of exceptional talent, pianist, and composer-arranger.

Around 1926, the Ellington personnel began to solidify, and, as a consequence, his style, his sound, was established. Personnel changes were rare from then on. Complete sections of the orchestra remained constant for an entire decade. It is no wonder that they worked so very well together. Baritone saxophone player Harry Carney joined the band in 1926 when he was seventeen years old and remained in the orchestra until he died in 1974. Johnny Hodges joined the band in 1928, and, except for a period from 1951 to 1955, stayed with the band until his death in 1971.

A move that really established the orchestra was the booking at the Cotton Club in Harlem from 1927 to 1932. Ellington's influence from that point on has always been quite definite. His musical pictures were considerably ahead of their time, and the band could swing. Ellington's band at this time featured what were called "Jungle Sounds," with much "growling" on the

3. Leonard Feather, "The Real Louis Armstrong," *Down Beat* 29, no. 5 (March 1962): 23.

Duke Ellington. Courtesy of Ray Avery.

instruments. As a consequence, the very elaborate floor shows of the Cotton Club were designed around the music that the band played. Once again, the sounds of the individuals were woven into the tonal colors of the entire group, an attribute that was evident throughout Ellington's career.

Ellington actually had four rather different styles that pervaded his repertoire. One was the previously mentioned "jungle style" built around the raucous playing of Bubber Miley, and then of Cootie Williams on trumpet and Tricky Sam Nanton on trombone. Ellington also had a "mood style" that is identified with the beautiful ballads played by saxophonist Johnny Hodges. Some of the selections like "Solitude" are very well known to the public, but other works like "Prelude to a Kiss" and "Lotus Blossom" are known

and loved only by musicians. Another Ellington style could be called his "concerto style," in which he featured Cootie Williams on trumpet or Jimmy Hamilton or Barney Bigard on clarinet. The other style was a rather "standard style" in which he approached his arrangements in much the same manner as other large bands. However, he always sounded exactly like Ellington, something no one else could accomplish.

In 1933 the American depression prompted Ellington to make a most successful trip to Europe. He returned home a recognized international attraction. When Ellington first went to England, he was surprised to find out how well known he and other American jazz players were. He realized the importance of jazz as an

American export, but also was aware that popularity at home somewhat determined his effectiveness abroad. There is no need to expound on his success during the Swing Era. His band was by far the most colorful of the large bands during a time when large jazz bands were attracting a multitude of followers. Ellington may not have been quite as popular with the public as he could have been because he did not receive the radio coverage that some bands enjoyed and did not concern himself as much with the popular tunes of the day as other bands did.

In 1943, Ellington gave the first of a series of annual concerts in Carnegie Hall in New York City, introducing the longer forms into jazz that became a recognized part of his repertoire (an example is "Black, Brown and Beige," fifty minutes in length). He seemed to expand his thinking without altering his music. Ellington's recording of "Reminiscing in Tempo" in 1935 foreshadowed later directions. He used the concerto form in jazz to write "Barney's Concerto" (for clarinetist Barney Bigard) and "Cootie's Concerto" (for trumpeter Cootie Williams).

Ellington toured constantly, which kept his image alive in the entire world. He continually recorded historically important works written by him and Billy Strayhorn. The collaboration of Ellington and Strayhorn led to some of the most charming music possible in any category of the art. Sometimes while composing a piece of music, it would occur to either of these musicians that a specific member of the orchestra was in need of a work on which he would be featured, and this fact would influence the composition. Sometimes it worked just the opposite: the work being composed would need a specific player in order to be interpreted to the greatest advantage.

Ellington's innovations include the following: the wonderful ensemble sound (developed using individuals in the band), the larger forms in jazz (which often ignored the three-minute limit on recordings that dictated the repertoire of most bands), his more than skillful orchestration, the use of voices as instruments (as far back as 1927 with singer Adelaide Hall on "Creole Love Song"), and many, many innovative jazz tunes starting with "Mood Indigo" (first recorded as "Dreamy Blues" in 1930), "Sophisticated Lady" (1933), and "Solitude" (1934). Ellington often changed the titles of his tunes: for example, "Rumpus in Richmond" was changed to "Harlem Air Shaft." This puts the liner notes on some albums in a very suspicious light since some record company employee tried to explain the final title as if it were Ellington's idea of daily life in New York's Harlem.

Those listeners who challenge all changes disturbed Ellington to a point. His later music was sometimes compared unfavorably with that which he had played in the past. Ellington's answer to the "time test" (comparing jazz to other music) was that he was not interested in writing or playing music for posterity; he wanted his music to sound good at the very moment that it was performed.

The earliest Ellington recording available is an album called *The Birth of Big Band Jazz*. These sides were recorded in 1923 (some writers place the date at 1925). The album called *Early Ellington* comprises recordings made between 1927 and 1931. Most writers feel that Ellington's greatest recordings were made between 1940 and 1942: such records as "Jack the Bear," "Warm Valley," "Cotton Tail," "Chelsea Bridge," "Take the A Train," "C Jam Blues," and so on.

True, Ellington did perform his "standards"—he was almost required to. But it cannot be said that his repertoire did not have good variety. He performed in so many different situations (dance halls, large clubs, theaters, festivals, concert halls) that he had to be diversified.

It is worth noting that Ellington, while feeling that his music was always primarily black music, never felt ethnic ties to the point of using only black musicians in his band—as witnessed by the white drummer Louie Bellson.

Ellington's band, his music, and his recordings are proof of his belief that though jazz borrowed from any and every source available, it still remained personal. His ensemble was an integrated whole; yet, no one's orchestra has ever been based so much on the talents of its individuals. Some jazz writers actually credit Ellington's success to his brilliant sidemen. The sidemen themselves, however, always point to Ellington's composing, arranging, piano playing, and leadership in general. In 1962, Leonard Feather wrote of Ellington: "We see him today as the most challenging, most provocative, most brilliant, and most irreplaceable paragon in the sixty-year history of jazz."[4] That statement is still true.

Benny Goodman (1909–   )

Rave reviews for an artist who was probably the universal symbol of jazz thirty-five years earlier dominated the media in 1975. It is true that when Benny Goodman plays a concert today many of his listeners

4.   Leonard Feather, "The Duke's Progress," *Down Beat* 29, no. 12 (June 1962): 19.

Benny Goodman. Courtesy of Popsie and Phoebe Jacobs.

experience great feelings of nostalgia, but, on the other hand, some who thoroughly enjoy his mastery of the clarinet, his vibrant rhythmic feel, and his effervescent improvisations are too young to feel any nostalgia for his music. He is truly a master of his art.

Benny Goodman was born May 30, 1909, in Chicago, the eighth of eleven children of an immigrant tailor. Just as jazz is a product of America, Benny Goodman's rise from poverty to global fame is a typical American story.

His early musical training was in a synagogue orchestra and at Hull House in Chicago. He next studied privately with Franz Schoepp of the Chicago Symphony Orchestra. By the time Goodman was sixteen years old, word of his excellent musicianship had spread even to California, and Ben Pollack asked him to join his band. He had built a considerable reputation by the time he left the Pollack band in 1929 at the age of twenty. For the next five years he played on radio and for recording companies in New York City.

In 1934 Goodman organized his first band for a theater restaurant, the Music Hall, owned by Billy Rose. At the same time, Goodman played on a series of Saturday night, three-hour radio shows. It should be noted that the two jobs coincided with his association with Fletcher Henderson who created most of the musical arrangements that were such an integral part of Goodman's success.

In the winter of 1934–35 Goodman began a tour across the United States that seemed to consist of one failure after another. No one appeared to know or care about his band. The farther the band traveled from New York City, the more worried became Goodman, the band, his bookers, and the manager of the Palomar Ballroom in Los Angeles—their destination. In fact, it has often been rumored that had the manager been able to locate Goodman during that tour he would have canceled the booking. Fortunately, the booking was not canceled. Goodman opened at the Palomar Ballroom in May of 1935 and was an immediate success. Whether the swing type of jazz started earlier than this is beside the point. Goodman's engagement at the Palomar is designated by most jazz writers as the beginning of the Swing Era.

Goodman's band played a hard-driving type of swing in comparison to other bands at that time. He often rehearsed the band without the rhythm section—reasoning that if an arrangement could swing well and have momentum without the rhythm section, the music would offer much more when the rhythm section was added. The band also played a soft, more subtle jazz—a chamber music sort of jazz—by using trios, quartets, quintets, and so forth.

The Goodman trio consisted of Teddy Wilson on piano, Gene Krupa on drums, and Goodman himself on clarinet. The group was enlarged to a quartet in 1936 with the addition of the exuberant Lionel Hampton on vibraphones, and in 1939 it became a sextet when Charlie Christian on guitar and a bass player were added. These smaller groups also included at various times Red Norvo, Cootie Williams, Roy Eldridge, and George Auld. The small units played during the intermissions of performances by the large band and also recorded separately. Some fans consider these recordings to be as important as those of the large band.

In 1938, the Benny Goodman band became the first swing band to play a concert in Carnegie Hall. Record sales of his Carnegie Hall concerts alone grossed more than a million dollars and continue to sell today.

Mention should be made of Goodman's classical solo work. He commissioned and recorded a solo clarinet composition by Béla Bartók, commissioned clarinet concertos by Aaron Copland and Paul Hindemith, and performed works by Mozart, Debussy, Brahms, and other composers with such distinguished orchestras as the Boston Symphony, the Rochester Symphony, the NBC Symphony, the Cleveland Symphony, the Budapest String Quartet, and the American Art Quartet. Goodman is one of few musicians who moves easily between classical music and jazz—with distinction in each field.

In 1955 Universal-International Studios made a motion picture based on his life, and Goodman himself recorded the music and acted as musical director.

Goodman has toured in many parts of the world on behalf of the State Department. In 1956 he played to sellout audiences in Hong Kong, Singapore, Tokyo, and Bangkok. In 1958 and 1959 his overseas tours took him to Belgium, Germany, Sweden, Denmark, France, Switzerland, Austria, England, Australia, Central America, South America, and Alaska, and his reception was as great as ever each time. The Goodman band was chosen to be the first band to make a State Department tour of Russia. His triumph there was proof of his artistry, the durability of the swing style, and the worldwide popularity of this American music.

Today, Benny Goodman enjoys a truly international popularity. The mere announcement that he will perform in a country causes great excitement among the jazz enthusiasts there, a fact probably more true about Goodman than about any other living musician.

Since the middle 1960s Goodman has appeared regularly at jazz festivals and even at some of the more plush night spots. At the end of the 1960s he toured the United States with both jazz and classical groups and recorded in both the United States and England.

Through the 1970s Goodman continued to tour in Europe, the United States, and Canada. Sometimes he appeared with a full band, sometimes with a sextet, and sometimes with members of his original quartet. The reception is the same: he is the King of Swing, a jazz immortal, the clarinet image for the world, and an international celebrity to jazz fans of all ages.

Goodman was the first band leader to force the issue of integration. Black musicians and white musicians jammed together in after-hours clubs and recorded together, but neither the white public nor the black public would go to see a "mixed" band. In 1936 when Goodman hired Teddy Wilson and Lionel Hampton, he had to pretend that they were not regular members of his band but only an act. Finally, he simply acknowledged that these musicians were part of his band and gave notice that the public would have to see and hear his music on his terms. He stated very simply in a nonpolitical way that he was not selling prejudice or integration but music.

Goodman continues to play jazz in a most exemplary manner and still leads the world on clarinet. He performed a concert at Carnegie Hall in 1974, thirty-six years and eight months after his first concert there. The authors saw and heard Goodman at a jazz festival in 1975 where he received a standing ovation as he walked on stage. As he played he proved conclusively that he truly deserved the applause.

Besides being King of Swing, and besides almost single-handedly cutting through racial barriers in music, Goodman was instrumental in making it possible for jazz musicians to earn a decent wage. He brought jazz out of back rooms into the best night spots, into the greatest theaters where young people screamed and danced in the aisles. Still, for a man whose name is synonymous with the Big Band Era, Goodman is extremely low-key, never flamboyant. His playing is a combination of great wit, precise musicianship, beautiful subtleties, and never-ending swing.

Down Beat magazine nominated Benny Goodman to its All Time Jazz Hall of Fame, and the National Academy of Recording Arts and Sciences

Charlie Parker. Courtesy of Orrin Keepnews.

placed his recording of "Sing Sing Sing" in its Hall of Fame. He has also collaborated on four books: *The Kingdom of Swing, BG—Off the Record, BG—On the Record,* and *Benny: King of Swing.*[5]

Goodman inspired musicians when he was only sixteen years of age and in 1980 he still inspires them. He is as unique in his field as any great actor, writer, or other type of artist is in his field. It is important to remember that Goodman did not follow the changing fads in jazz. He attributes his continued overwhelming success to the fact that he simply plays "good" music.

Charlie Parker (1921–1955)

Charlie Parker, called "Yardbird"—or more often simply "Bird"—was born August 29, 1921, in Kansas City, Kansas. He moved to Kansas City, Missouri, at the age of seven. As a youngster, he listened a great

5. Benny Goodman and Irving Kolodin, *The Kingdom of Swing* (New York: Frederick Ungar Publishing Co., 1939); Benny Goodman and D. R. Connor, *BG—Off the Record* (Fairless Hills, Pa.: Gaildonna Publishers, 1969); Benny Goodman, D. R. Connor, and W. W. Hicks, *BG—On the Record* (New Rochelle, N.Y.: Arlington House, 1969); Stanley Baron, *Benny: King of Swing* (New York: William Morrow & Co., Inc., 1979).

deal to saxophonists Lester Young and Buster Smith. An important predecessor of Parker, Smith was from the Kansas City School. After Benny Moten's death, Smith was at first coleader with Basie of Moten's group. As far back as 1932, Buster Smith recordings foreshadow Charlie Parker. There is no doubt about the strong influence that altoist Smith and tenor saxophonist Young had on young Charlie Parker. But what is surprising is that Parker himself credited five white saxophonists with having the biggest early influence on his playing: nonjazz players Rudy Wiedoeft and Rudy Vallee, and jazzmen Frank Teschemacher, Jimmy Dorsey, and Bud Freeman. He definitely surpassed all of these players.

In 1936, Parker used to stand around in the alley behind the Reno Club in Kansas City and listen to the Basie band. At fifteen years of age he was learning in the same way that most jazz players learned their trade: he listened and attempted to imitate. Parker was always curious about advanced harmony, and he worked for and studied with a graduate of the Boston Conservatory, Tommy Douglas, who was ahead of his time in this direction in 1935. Parker's study with pianists and guitarists furthered this knowledge. He became intensely interested in the use of the higher harmonies of chords as structures on which to improvise new melodies. This approach became one of the mainstays of the bop movement, and many new tunes were created from old chord progressions.

When saxophonist Budd Johnson heard eighteen-year-old Parker in Chicago, he noted that Parker already had some of the elements of bop—such as double time—in his repertoire.

Parker first came into New York in 1939 where he searched out jam sessions and every other opportunity to listen and learn, supporting himself by washing dishes and doing other menial jobs. The first combo job that Parker played in New York City was at Clark Monroe's Uptown House on 134th Street. He left town afterward with the Jay McShann band. The first recorded solos of Charlie Parker are on transcriptions made by the Jay McShann band in 1940 at a Wichita, Kansas, radio station. The McShann band, besides being blues-based, was also riff-oriented like Basie. It was McShann who brought Parker back to New York in 1942, this time as a mature musician. Today it is hard to locate recordings of Parker with McShann. Folkways pressed "Hootie Blues," recorded in Dallas in 1941, and Decca pressed "Sepian Bounce," recorded in New York in 1942.[6]

By 1942, because of jam sessions at Minton's Playhouse mainly, Charlie Parker and Dizzy Gillespie had become the most talked about musicians in the new style of jazz called bop.

In 1942, saxophonist Budd Johnson was urging Earl Hines to hire Charlie Parker from the blues-oriented band of Jay McShann. In December 1942, Johnson himself left Hines. Billy Eckstine then talked Hines into hiring Parker and buying a tenor sax for him even though Parker much preferred to play alto sax. The Hines band collapsed, but Eckstine held most of the avant-garde players together by hiring them for his own band. In 1944, as this band started a tour toward St. Louis, a trumpeter became ill and was replaced temporarily by a young teenager named Miles Davis. Thus the association between Davis and Parker began.

The key musicians each produced certain ideas independently and when they came together in New York they discovered their affinities and stimulated each other to further effort. Over a period of several years this produced a synthesis of new elements based on old that became known as modern jazz, or bop.[7]

Parker's first job as leader was at the Spotlight Club on New York's Fifty-second Street in 1944 after he had left Eckstine. His most mature jazz statements are generally conceded to be those recorded in 1945 under his own name as leader: "Koko," "Now's the Time," "Billie's Bounce," "Meandering," "Warming Up a Riff," and "Thriving from a Riff." On these records he shows a rich, expressive tone and unprecedented rhythmic freedom in his phrasing.

Parker's success was demonstrated by the fact that after World War II he was sometimes paid $1,200 a week by the same people who had hired him earlier for $2 a night.

Parker spent seven months in Camarillo State Hospital in California in 1946. By 1949, due to a combination of ulcers, drugs, and alcohol, his playing began to decline. He was not considered reliable by booking offices, so employment began to be a problem. Some musicians never see the dope and alcohol problems affecting them, but Parker was very much aware of the fact that his career had been ruined by these mistakes.

6. Jay McShann, "Hootie Blues," *Folkways Jazz*, vol. 10; Jay McShann, "Sepian Bounce," *Encyclopedia of Jazz*, vol. 3, Decca Records, DL 8400 and *Encyclopedia of Jazz on Records*, vol. 3.

7. Max Harrison, *Charlie Parker* (New York: A. S. Barnes & Co., 1961), p. 17.

He constantly advised against such indulgence. Sonny Rollins tells of conversations along this line with Parker:

Bird befriended quite a few guys. Sonny Stitt before me. With us and a few other cats, especially saxophone players, it was like a father thing. When we were hung up personally, we went just to talk to him, just to see him. The purpose of his whole existence was music and he showed me that music was the paramount thing and anything that interfered with it I should stay away from. Later on I was able to take advantage of his advice, but he died before I had a chance to see him and tell him I had.[8]

In 1950, Parker (as did Gillespie) recorded with strings. It was the fulfillment of a dream for Parker, but his fans screamed that he had "gone commercial."

When Parker's young daughter Pree died of pneumonia, he seemed to decline for the last time both musically and physically. He died March 12, 1955, less than thirty-five years old.

One of the trying aspects of Parker's career is that he knew that even among contemporary musicians only a few understood his music. Parker's abilities and contributions have, of course, been finally recognized. In fact, it would be extremely difficult to find a musician who is more recognized and so little understood. In 1973, a group called Supersax was featured on an album called *Supersax Plays Bird*.[9] For this album, saxophonist Med Flory and bassist Buddy Clark put together a library of Parker's recorded solos. But Flory and Clark harmonized all of these wonderful improvisations and played them using five saxophones—an almost overwhelming sound. The album won a Grammy Award from the National Academy of Recording Arts and Sciences (NARAS) for the best jazz record performed by a group (as opposed to a large band). Supersax has extended these efforts further since their first recording. In 1974, Onyx Records released an album of the very first works recorded by Parker going back to his work with Jay McShann.[10] This album, called *Original Recordings*, also won a NARAS award for the best solo jazz album. Such public recognition came nearly twenty years after Parker's death.

Most young saxophonists feel that Parker's style and melodic and rhythmic thoughts are the "correct" ways to play. Furthermore, in 1969 a Charlie Parker Center for the Performing Arts was established by a group of teachers, musicians, and civic leaders to provide free music instruction for young players.

In February 1942, one *Down Beat* reporter stated that Parker had a tendency to play too many notes. In July of that same year, another reporter from the same magazine noted that Parker used a minimum of notes. To say that there was controversy and a lack of understanding of Parker's work even among his peers would be a gross understatement. Some who write and talk about jazz feel that Parker was the most important catalyst in the advancement of jazz. Surely there can be no doubt that he brought to culmination the many innovations of the 1940s and 1950s, more changes than had previously occurred in the history of jazz.

Parker was one of the rare musicians who could play slow blues very well but was also comfortable at extremely fast tempos. A great percentage of what Parker played was based on the blues—"Now's the Time," "Cool Blues," and others.

One of Parker's most impressive assets was his use of rhythmic nuances. "Relaxin' at Camarillo" shows how beautifully these can be applied to the standard blues form. Of course, Parker had an impeccable ear and virtuosity on the alto saxophone that could be exploited unconsciously instead of contrived. When a musician realizes what Parker was able to invent within the six-note phrase in "Embraceable You," the musician hears developments leading to Sonny Rollins and others. Parker used the phrase repeatedly, but he also changed each time, demonstrating a creativeness worthy of Mozart, Beethoven, and others who composed great music from motifs. Most musicians agree that as advanced as Parker's style was, he never seemed to lose sight of the early jazz roots. Some casual observers seem surprised that Parker could appreciate all kinds of music that were performed well, classical music as well as early jazz.

Parker thought that there must be something in jazz improvisation that had not been done before because he thought that he could hear things that he could not play. By working over and over his favorite tune "Cherokee," he finally found that he could play what he had been hearing by developing melodic lines from the higher harmonies of the chords (as described in chapter 10). Parker freed the solo aspect of jazz not only melodically and harmonically but also rhythmically. Those who follow him can benefit from the freedom, not necessarily from copying his actual phrases.

8. Harrison, *Charlie Parker*, pp. 64–65.

9. *Supersax Plays Bird*, Capitol Records, ST 11177.

10. Charlie Parker, *Original Recordings*, Onyx Records, 221.

It is true that drummers Kenny Clarke and Max Roach developed new rhythmic approaches; Thelonious Monk, new harmonic approaches; Dizzy Gillespie, new solo directions; and so on. But it did seem to be Charlie Parker who brought all of these elements to maturity in the style known as bop. Parker's playing was the realization of the potential of what was available; Parker's influence, like Armstrong's earlier, extended to all instruments.

Parker's achievements are unique and for a continually sick man almost incredible. It is hard to imagine what he would have accomplished given a long and healthy life. In many ways his admirers got more out of his life than Parker did himself but, in the end, he is not a man to be pitied. On all but his darkest days he experienced the joy of creation that is given few men to know and he enriched the lives of all those who could respond to his work.[11]

John Coltrane (1926–1967)

Saxophonist John Coltrane combined great emotion with excellent musicianship, and discipline with freedom. Like Parker, he did not have an extensive career compared to Armstrong and Ellington. His career lasted about twelve years, from 1955 to 1967.

John Coltrane was born in Hamlet, North Carolina, September 23, 1926. He studied saxophone in Philadelphia and began playing professionally in that city. Coltrane started to attain recognition while playing with Miles Davis from 1955 to 1960. In 1960 he formed his own quartet. In 1965 Alice McLeod (Mrs. John Coltrane) joined the group. Coltrane's short career ended with his death on July 1, 1967, at the age of forty.

Musicians disagree about other contemporary players such as Ornette Coleman, but there were few disagreements about John Coltrane. Coltrane was a fine saxophone player (tenor and soprano) in every sense. The prime concern of most musicians is the tone that a player produces. There is no way to imagine a musical sound without considering the quality of the tone. Coltrane produced a large, dark, lush sound from his instrument. A brief listen to "Ogunde" verifies this fact.[12] On the album *Giant Steps* (Coltrane's first album under his own name) his beautiful, solid tone is most evident in "Naima."[13] This record shows his confidence at this time in his career and reveals deeper feeling and conviction than when he worked for Davis. His drive is very apparent on "Cousin Mary."

Coltrane's chief legacy was his beautiful tone and his control of the upper register. (He had equal strength in all registers of the instrument—an unusual trait.) Wayne Shorter, Charles Lloyd, Pharoah Sanders, and Eddie Harris all show traces of this legacy. The influence of Coltrane's very passionate approach appears in unlikely places, like in an occasional near scream from cool saxophonist Stan Getz. Coltrane said that Sidney Bechet was an important influence on his own playing.

As stated in chapter 13, Coltrane advanced jazz improvisation harmonically through long excursions into the higher harmonics of chords on an instrument that is sounded where a trombone, or a man's voice, is pitched (the tenor saxophone).

Coltrane had great coordination between his fingering of the saxophone and his tonguing. This coordination allowed him such fast technique that he played arpeggios so rapidly that they are referred to as Coltrane's "sheets of sound." His sheets of sound can be heard as early in his career as "All Blues" with Miles Davis, and a little in "Cousin Mary" with his own quartet. Coltrane's creativity with his sheets of sound was actually homophonically constructed music which had been carried to a higher level. He thought of these runs as if they were chords on top of chords. His fast arpeggios have great emotional impact, and he was an expert in the use of sequences.

A logical starting place for those uninitiated in Coltrane's music is Miles Davis's recording of *Kind of Blue*.[14] On "All Blues," "So What," and "Freddie Freeloader," the listener can hear Coltrane when he was working for a fairly conservative leader. Therefore he had not expanded his directions very much and is quite easy to understand and appreciate immediately. It is interesting to compare the Coltrane of this album with Cannonball Adderley. On both "So What" and "Freddie Freeloader," Adderley shows a more direct association with Parker and at the same time plays some very funky-type phrases not to be found in Coltrane's playing. In "Freddie Freeloader," Coltrane is blowing aggressively and melodically at the same time.

Coltrane played rhythmically but counter to that which was being played by what would normally be the rhythm section; so the music became arhythmic. This effect freed the rhythm players to play whatever

11. Harrison, *Charlie Parker*, p. 74.

12. John Coltrane, "Ogunde," *Expression*, Impulse Records, A–9120.

13. John Coltrane, *Giant Steps*, Atlantic Records, 1311.

14. John Coltrane (Miles Davis album), *Kind of Blue*, Columbia Records, CL 1355.

John Coltrane. Courtesy of Ray Avery.

Eventually, Coltrane turned toward emphasizing the melodic line above all else. Chords were used only as they related to the melody. Instead of melody being improvised out of harmony, melody was improvised from melody—an approach used by classical composers quite early in the history of music but seldom by jazz performers. Coltrane had the advantage of working with Thelonious Monk. From Monk, he was able to establish a mature, consistent relationship between the chords and his melodic thoughts. Monk stimulated Coltrane's interest in wide intervals, while it is very possible that his interest in various types of scales came from his time with the Miles Davis group.

Coltrane broke away from the format of theme, solos, theme. On his recording of "The Father and the Son and the Holy Ghost," there is no real theme before his solo, and the ensemble portion has no theme at all. This is very disturbing to jazz listeners who expect only traditional approaches to jazz. In "Countdown," Coltrane shows his great coordination. The work sounds free; yet when chords are brought in under his solo, he is exactly where he should be harmonically.

An example of Coltrane's innovation is a selection called "India," recorded before the Beatles received credit for discovering Ravi Shankar. In this album one hears influences such as Indian scales and rhythms.

Coltrane opened the path for others like Archie Shepp through his conviction that improvisation could continue past all existing melodic considerations, harmonic considerations, and rhythmic flow. Free form seemed to need another leader besides Ornette Coleman. Coltrane became this leader with his long improvisations (sometimes 40 minutes), his sheets of sound, his tone, and his technique. He was looked upon as a spiritual leader. Coltrane and his followers have often been criticized for playing solos that were too long, but their answer was that they needed the time to explore the music in depth.

At first, Coltrane was admired more as a technically complete musician than as a creative artist. He showed speed as he cascaded chords with his powerful moving tone. But his recording *A Love Supreme* seemed to change the attitude toward his playing.[16] It is a very emotional record that does away with some earlier excesses and is more a work of art than an exhibition. Coltrane tried to explain (in his music) the

occurred to them according to the melodic thoughts they were hearing. Coltrane could play "on top of the beat" whenever he wanted to, but he liked to play differently from the rhythm players with the idea that this freed them from having to play with him. His counterrhythms can be heard on both "Countdown" and "Spiral" on *Giant Steps*. He seemed to fuse melody and rhythm in "The Father and The Son and The Holy Ghost,"[15]

15. John Coltrane, "The Father and The Son and The Holy Ghost," *Meditations*, Impulse Records, A–9110.

16. John Coltrane, *A Love Supreme*, Impulse Records, A–77.

wonderful things that the universe meant to him. Playing jazz was a spiritual experience to Coltrane, and he always felt that he should share his feelings with his listeners. There is no doubt about his strong religious motivation.

Coltrane continually experimented. Even when listeners were well acquainted with Coltrane's recordings, they would still be constantly surprised and amazed at each live performance. His fans learned to expect only the unexpected.

"Coltrane came, and he made music. He built on existing foundations. He and his music lived in inexorable relation to other lives, other ideas, other musics. But how he built! The musical structures are changed forever because of him."[17]

Additional Reading Resources

Louis Armstrong

Armstrong, Louis. *Swing That Music.*
Jones, Max, and Chilton, John. *Louis: The Louis Armstrong Story.*
Jones, Max. *Salute to Satchmo.*
Panassie, Hughes. *Louis Armstrong.*
Sanders, Ruby W. *Jazz Ambassador Louis Armstrong.*

Duke Ellington

Dance, Stanley. *The World of Duke Ellington.*
Ellington, Duke. *Music Is My Mistress.*
Ellington, Mercer, and Dance, Stanley. *Duke Ellington in Person: An Intimate Memoir.*
Gammond, Peter, ed. *Duke Ellington: His Life and Music.*
Gleason, Ralph. *Celebrating The Duke.*
Schuller, Gunther. *Early Jazz: Its Roots and Musical Development.*
Shapiro, Nat, and Hentoff, Nat, eds. *The Jazz Makers.*
Ulanov, Barry. *Duke Ellington.*

Charlie Parker

Gitler, Ira. *Jazz Masters of the Forties.*
Harrison, Max. *Charlie Parker.*
Reisner, Robert. *The Legend of Charlie Parker.*
Russell, Ross. *Bird Lives. The High Life and Hard Times of Charlie (Yardbird) Parker.*
Note: Complete information including name of publisher and date of publication is provided in the Bibliography.

Additional Record Resources

Louis Armstrong

Autobiography. Decca Records, DX–155.
Best of Louis Armstrong. Audio Fidelity Records, 6132.
Essential Louis Armstrong. Verve Records, V–8569.
Folkways Jazz. vols. 2, 4, 5, 7.
Hello Dolly. Kapp Records, 3364.
Louis Armstrong. Audio Fidelity Records, 6241.
Louis Armstrong. RCA Victor Records, VPM–6044.
Louis Armstrong and Earl Hines. Columbia Records, CL 853.
Louis Armstrong in Memoriam. Everest Records, 3312.
Louis Armstrong in the Thirties and Forties. RCA Victor Records, LSP 2971.
Louis Armstrong Jazz Classics. Decca Records, 8284.
Louis Armstrong Plays W. C. Handy. Columbia Records, CL 591.
Louis Armstrong Story, vols. 1, 2, 3, 4. Columbia Records, CL 851–52–53–54.
Louis Armstrong, V.S.O.P. Epic Records, EE 22019.
Rare Batch of Satch. RCA Victor Records, LPM 2322.
Rare Items. Decca Records, 79225.
Satchmo at Pasadena. Decca Records, 8041.
Satchmo at Symphony Hall. Decca Records, DXS 7195.
Satchmo on Stage. Decca Records, 8330.

17. Gordon Kopulos, "John Coltrane: Retrospective Perspective," *Down Beat* 38, no. 14 (July 1971): 40.

Smithsonian Collection of Classic Jazz. Columbia Special Products, P6 11891.

Young Louis Armstrong: The Sideman. Decca Records, 79233.

Duke Ellington

And His Mother Called Him Bill. RCA Victor Records, LSP–3906.

At His Very Best. RCA Victor Records, LPM–1715.

Best of Duke Ellington. Capitol Records, SM–1602.

Birth of Big Band Jazz. Riverside Records, 129.

Duke's Big 4. Pablo Records, 2310703.

Duke Ellington, the Beginning. Decca Records, DL–9224.

Duke Ellington's Concert of Sacred Music. RCA Victor Records, LPM–3582.

Duke Ellington's Greatest Hits. Reprise Records, S–6234.

Duke Ellington, 70th Birthday Concert. Solid State Records, SS 19000.

Early Ellington. Brunswick Records, 54007.

Ellington at Newport. Columbia Records, CS 8648.

Ellington Era. Columbia Records, C3L 27.

Ellington '66. Reprise Records, 6154.

Historically Speaking, the Duke. Bethlehem Records, BCP 60.

New Orleans Suite. Atlantic Records, SD 1580.

Smithsonian Collection of Classic Jazz. Columbia Special Products, P6 11891.

This Is Duke Ellington. RCA Victor Records, VPM–6042.

This One's For Blanton. Pablo Records, 2310721.

Togo Brava Suite. United Artists Records, UXS–92.

Benny Goodman

All Time Greatest Hits. Columbia Records, PG–31547.

Benny Goodman. Archive of Folk and Jazz Music Records, 277.

Carnegie Hall Concert. Columbia Records, OSL–160.

From Spirituals to Swing. Vanguard Records, VRS–8523/4.

Great Benny Goodman. Columbia Records, CS–8643.

Greatest Hits. Columbia Records, CS 9283.

Small Groups. RCA Victor Records, LPV 521.

Smithsonian Collection of Classic Jazz. Columbia Special Products, P6 11891.

This Is Benny Goodman. RCA Victor Records, VPM 6040.

Charlie Parker

Bird and Diz. Verve Records, V6–8006.

Bird Symbols. Charlie Parker Records, PLP–407.

Charlie Parker. Everest Records, FS–254.

Charlie Parker. Prestige Records, 24009.

Charlie Parker. Savoy Records, S5J5500.

Charlie Parker in Historical Recordings. Le Jazz Cool Records, JC102.

Charlie Parker Memorial. Savoy Records, MG–12000.

Charlie Parker Story, vols. 1, 2, 3. Verve Records, V6–8000–1–2.

Echos of an Era. Roulette Records, RE–105.

Essential Charlie Parker. Verve Records, V–8409.

Genius of Charlie Parker. Savoy Records, MG–12014.

Greatest Jazz Concert Ever. Prestige Records, 24020.

Jazz at Massey Hall. Fantasy Records, 6003.

Original Recordings. Onyx Records, 221.

Smithsonian Collection of Classic Jazz. Columbia Special Products, P6 11891.

John Coltrane

Ascension. Impulse Records, A–95.

Ballads. Impulse Records, S–32.

Best of John Coltrane. Atlantic Records, S–1541.

Impressions. Impulse Records, AS 42.

John Coltrane. Prestige Records, 24003.

My Favorite Things. Atlantic Records, 1361.

Selflessness. Impulse Records, AS–9161.

Smithsonian Collection of Classic Jazz. Columbia Special Products, P6 11891 (12 sides).

The Mastery of John Coltrane. Volume 1, *Feeling Good*. Impulse Records, 129345/2. Volume 2, *To the Beat of a Different Drum*. Impulse Records, 129346/2. Volume 3, *Jupiter Variation*. Impulse Records, 1A–9360.

Appendix A

Scores

Chapter 5: Early New Orleans Dixieland (1900–1920)

Example 15

(Side 1, Band 4)

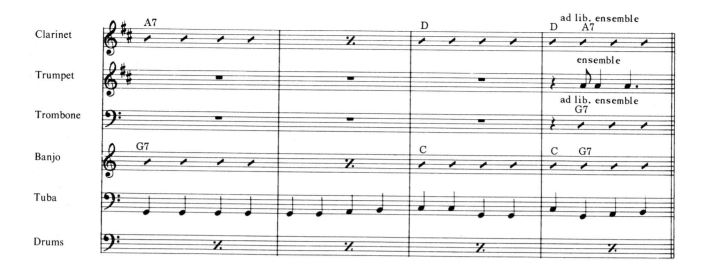

Chapter 7: Chicago Style Dixieland (the 1920s)

Example 18
(Side 1, Band 6)

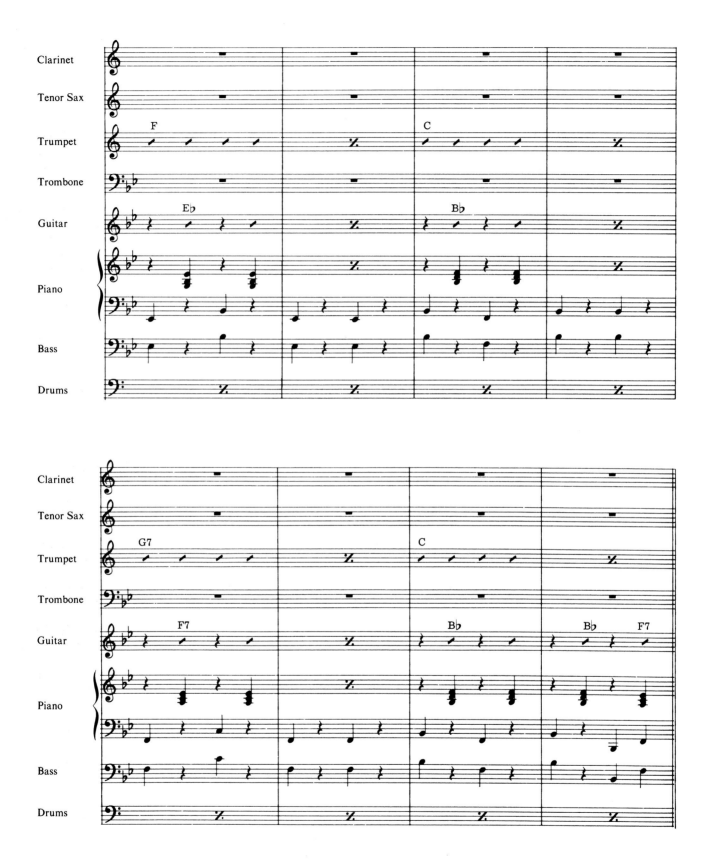

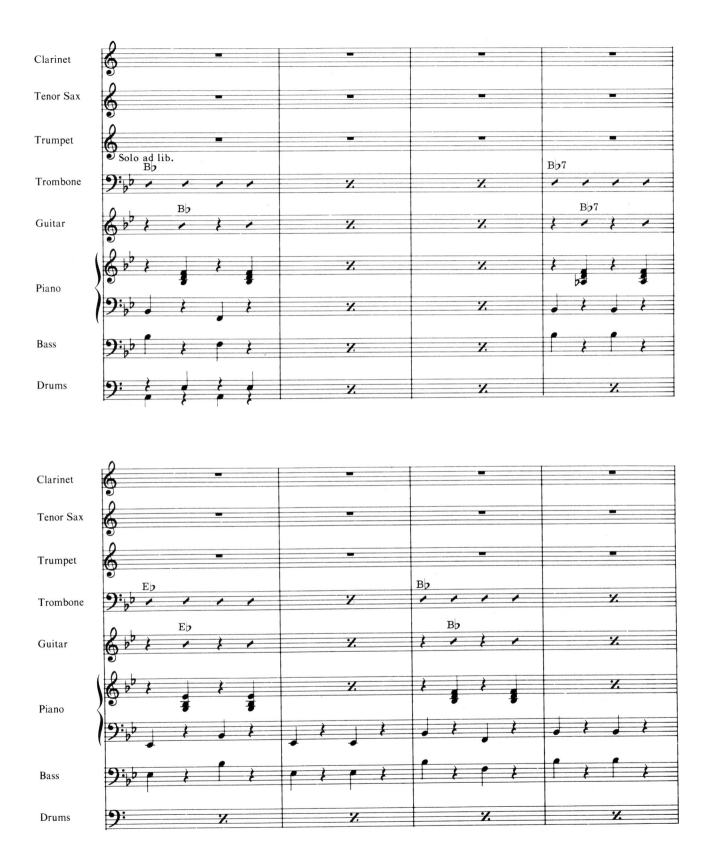

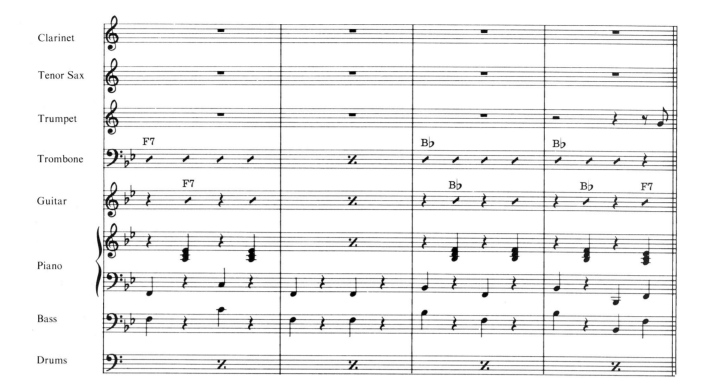

Chapter 9: Swing (1932–42)

Example 27
(Side 2, Band 2)

1st Alto Sax
1st Tenor Sax
2nd Tenor Sax
Baritone Sax
1st Trumpet
2nd Trumpet
3rd Trumpet
1st Trombone
2nd Trombone
3rd Trombone
4th Trombone
Guitar
Piano
Bass
Drums
B♭7
E♭7

1st Alto Sax
1st Tenor Sax
2nd Tenor Sax
Baritone Sax
1st Trumpet
2nd Trumpet
3rd Trumpet
1st Trombone
2nd Trombone
3rd Trombone
4th Trombone
Guitar
B♭
F7
Piano
Bass
Drums

Change to Clarinet
1st Alto Sax
1st Tenor Sax
2nd Tenor Sax
Baritone Sax
1st Trumpet
2nd Trumpet
3rd Trumpet
1st Trombone
open
2nd Trombone
open
3rd Trombone
open
4th Trombone
open
Guitar
B♭
Piano
Bass
Tom-Tom Solo
Drs.
Drums

F
C
1st Alto Sax
1st Tenor Sax
2nd Tenor Sax
Baritone Sax
1st Trumpet
2nd Trumpet
3rd Trumpet
1st Trombone
2nd Trombone
3rd Trombone
4th Trombone
Guitar
E♭7
B♭
Piano
Bass
Drums

1st Alto Sax
1st Tenor Sax
2nd Tenor Sax
Baritone Sax
1st Trumpet
2nd Trumpet
3rd Trumpet
1st Trombone
2nd Trombone
3rd Trombone
4th Trombone
Guitar
F
F
C
C
C
G7
Piano
Bass
Drums
2
2

1st Alto Sax
1st Tenor Sax
2nd Tenor Sax
Baritone Sax
1st Trumpet
2nd Trumpet
3rd Trumpet
1st Trombone
2nd Trombone
3rd Trombone
4th Trombone
Guitar
G7
G7
C
C
C
Db
Piano
Bass
Drums
2
2

1st Alto Sax
1st Tenor Sax
2nd Tenor Sax
Baritone Sax
1st Trumpet
2nd Trumpet
3rd Trumpet
1st Trombone
2nd Trombone
3rd Trombone
4th Trombone
Guitar
Piano
Bass
Drums
D♭
D♭7
G♭
2
2

1st Alto Sax
1st Tenor Sax
2nd Tenor Sax
Baritone Sax
1st Trumpet
2nd Trumpet
3rd Trumpet
1st Trombone
2nd Trombone
3rd Trombone
4th Trombone
Guitar
Piano
Bass
Drums
G♭
G♭
D♭
D♭
D♭
A♭7
2
2

1st Alto Sax
1st Tenor Sax
2nd Tenor Sax
Baritone Sax
1st Trumpet
2nd Trumpet
3rd Trumpet
1st Trombone
2nd Trombone
3rd Trombone
4th Trombone
Guitar
Piano
Bass
Drums
Change to Clar.
Solo
A♭7
A♭7
D♭
D♭

Chapter 10   Bop (1940–50)

Example 31
(Side 2, Band 3)

Chapter 11 Cool (1949–55)

Example 33
(Side 2, Band 4)

Chapter 12   Funky (circa 1954–63)

Example 36
(Side 2, Band 5)

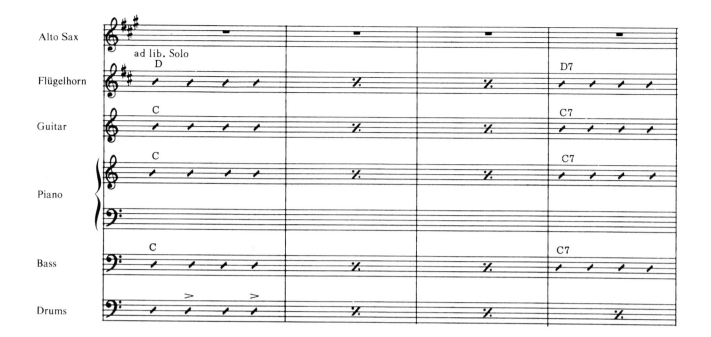

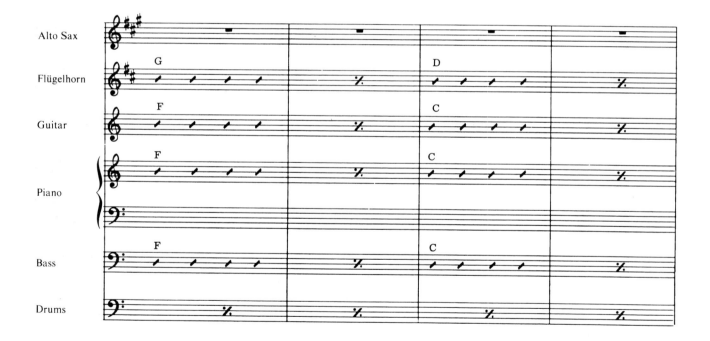

Appendix B
Awards and Films

National Academy of Recording Arts and Sciences Awards for Jazz

The award is given annually for the best jazz record of the year as voted by the National Academy of Recording Arts and Sciences (NARAS).

1966 Wes Montgomery. *Goin' Out of My Head.* Verve Records, V–8642.

1967 Cannonball Adderley. *Mercy, Mercy, Mercy.* Capitol Records, T 2663.

1968 Duke Ellington. *And His Mother Called Him Bill.* RCA Victor Records, LSP–3906.

1969 Quincy Jones. *Walkin' in Space.* A & M Records, SP 3023.

1970 Miles Davis. *Bitches Brew.* Columbia Records, GP 26.

1971 Bill Evans. *The Bill Evans Album.* Columbia Records, 30855.

1972 Gary Burton. *Alone at Last.* Atlantic Records, 1598 (solo).

1972 Freddie Hubbard. *Hub of Hubbard.* BASF Records, 20726 (group).

1972 Duke Ellington. *Togo Brava Suite.* United Artists Records, UXS, 92 (big band).

1973 Art Tatum. *God Is in the House.* Onyx Records, 295 (solo).

1973 Supersax. *Supersax Plays Bird.* Capitol Records, 11177 (group).

1973 Woody Herman. *Giant Steps.* Fantasy Records, 9432 (big band).

1974 Charlie Parker. *Original Recordings.* Onyx Records, 221 (solo).

1974 Oscar Peterson. *The Trio.* Pablo Records, 2310–701 (group).

1974 Woody Herman. *Thundering Herd.* Fantasy Records, F9452 (big band).

1975 Phil Woods and Michel Legrand. *Images.* RCA Victor Records, BGL 1–1027 (big band).

1975 Return to Forever (Chick Corea). *No Mystery.* Polydor Records, 6512 (group).

1975 Oscar Peterson and Dizzy Gillespie. *Oscar Peterson and Dizzy Gillespie.* Pablo Records, 2310740 (solo).

1976 Duke Ellington. *The Ellington Suites.* Pablo Records, 2310–762 (big band).

1976 Chick Corea. *The Leprechaun.* Polydor Records, PD6062 (group).

1976 Count Basie and Zoot Sims. *Basie and Zoot.* Pablo Records, 2310–745 (solo).

1976 Ella Fitzgerald and Joe Pass. *Fitzgerald and Pass . . . Again.* Pablo Records, 2310–772 (vocal).

1977 Count Basie. *Prime Time.* Pablo Records, 2310–797 (big band).

1977 Phil Woods. *Live from the Showboat.* RCA Victor Records, BGL 2–2202 (group).

1977 Oscar Peterson. *The Giants.* Pablo Records, 2310–796 (solo).

1977 Al Jarreau. *Look to the Rainbow.* Warner Brothers Records, 2BZ–3052 (vocal).

1978 Thad Jones and Mel Lewis. *Live in Munich.* Horizon Records, SP–724 (big band).

1978 Chick Corea. *Friends.* Polydor Records, PD1–6160 (group).

1978 Oscar Peterson. *Montreux '77.* Pablo Records, 2308–208 (solo).

1978 Al Jarreau. *All Fly Home.* Warner Brothers Records, BSK–3229 (vocal).

1979 Weather Report. *8:30.* ARC-CBS Records, PC2–36030, C3603 (jazz/rock).

1979 Duke Ellington. *At Fargo, 1940 Live.* Book of the Month Club (big band).

1979 Gary Burton and Chick Corea. *Duet.* EMC-Warner Brothers Records, 1–1140 (group).

1979 Oscar Peterson. *Jousts.* Pablo Records, 2310817 (solo).

1979 Ella Fitzgerald. *Fine and Mellow.* Pablo Records, 2310829 (vocal).

National Academy of Recording Arts and Sciences Hall of Fame Awards
Honoring Recordings of Lasting Historical or Qualitative Significance Released before Inception of the Grammy Awards in 1958

The following recordings have been voted as winners since the first Hall of Fame Awards were given in 1974:

Bach: The Well-Tempered Clavier (Complete). Wanda Landowska. RCA Victor, 1949–54.

Bach-Stokowski: Toccata & Fugue in D Minor. Leopold Stokowski conducting Philadelphia Orchestra. Victrola, 1927.

Ballad for Americans. Paul Robeson. Victor Records, 1940.

Beethoven: Piano Sonatas (32). Artur Schnabel. Beethoven Sonata Society/RCA, 1932–1938.

Beethoven: Symphonies (9). Arturo Toscanini conducting the NBC Symphony. RCA Victor, 1950–53.

Begin the Beguine. Artie Shaw. Bluebird, 1938.

Body & Soul. Coleman Hawkins. Bluebird, 1939.

Carnegie Hall Jazz Concert. Benny Goodman. Columbia, 1950.

Christmas Song. Nat "King" Cole. Capitol, 1946.

The Genius of Art Tatum, vols. 1–13. Art Tatum. Verve, 1954–1955.

Gershwin: Porgy & Bess (Opera). Lehman Engel, conductor; Cast: Lawrence Winters, Camilla Williams, and others. Columbia, 1951.

Gershwin: Rhapsody in Blue. Paul Whiteman with George Gershwin. RCA Victor, 1927.

God Bless the Child. Billie Holiday. Okey, 1941.

How High the Moon. Les Paul & Mary Ford. Capitol, 1951.

I Can Hear It Now, vols. 1–3. Edward R. Murrow. Columbia, 1948–1950.

I Can't Get Started. Bunny Berigan. Victor, 1937.

In a Mist. Bix Beiderbecke (piano). Okey Records, 1927.

Jelly Roll Morton: The Saga of Mr. Jelly Lord. Circle Records, 1938.

Leoncavallo: Pagliacci. Act I: Vesti La Giubba. Enrico Caruso. Victrola, 1907.

Mood Indigo. Duke Ellington. Brunswick, 1930.

My Blue Heaven. Gene Austin. Victor, 1928.

My Fair Lady. Original Broadway cast with Rex Harrison & Julie Andrews. Columbia, 1956.

Oklahoma! Original Broadway cast with Alfred Drake; orchestra and chorus directed by Jay Blackton. Decca, 1943.

One O'Clock Jump. Count Basie. Decca, 1937.

Rachmaninoff: Piano Concerto No. 2 in C Minor. Sergei Rachmaninoff (Piano), Philadelphia Orchestra, Leopold Stokowski, conductor. Victrola, 1929.

Rachmaninoff: Rhapsody on a Theme of Paganini. Sergei Rachmaninoff (piano), Philadelphia Orchestra, Leopold Stokowski, conductor. RCA Victor, 1935.

Singin' the Blues. Frankie Trumbauer & His Orchestra featuring Bix Beiderbecke on cornet. Okey, 1927.

Strange Fruit. Billie Holiday. Commodore, 1939.

Take the "A" Train. Duke Ellington & His Orchestra. Victor, 1941.
West End Blues. Louis Armstrong. Okey, 1928.
White Christmas. Bing Crosby. Decca, 1942.

Authors' Note

It is quite obvious that many of these recordings are jazz or at least jazz oriented.

Films

The following are suggested films about jazz.

Audio-Visual History of Jazz (filmstrips). Orrin Keepnews. Educational Audio Visual.
Discovering Jazz (16 mm.). Paul Tanner. Bailey Film Associates, a Division of Columbia Broadcasting System.
An Introduction to Electric Music Synthesizers (filmstrips). Don Muro. Belwin-Mills Publishing Company.

Appendix C

Discography

The Bass. Impulse Records, 9284 (6 sides).

Capital Jazz Classics. Capitol Records.

Volume 1 Miles Davis

Volume 2 Stan Kenton

Volume 3 Art Tatum

Volume 4 Gerry Mulligan

Volume 5 Coleman Hawkins

Volume 6 Various Artists: All Star Sessions

Volume 7 Serge Chaloff

Volume 8 Nat King Cole Trio

Volume 9 Woody Herman

Volume 10 Various Artists: Swing Exercise

Collector's History of Classic Jazz. Murray Hill Records, 927942.

The Definitive Jazz Scene, vols. 1, 2, 3. Impulse Records, A–99, A–100, A–9101.

The Drums. Impulse Records, 9272 (6 sides).

Encyclopedia of Jazz on Records. Decca Records, DXSF–7140 (8 sides).

Folkways Jazz Series. Folkways Records, FJ2801–2811.

Volume 1 The South

Volume 2 The Blues

Volume 3 New Orleans

Volume 4 Jazz Singers

Volume 5 Chicago No. 1

Volume 6 Chicago No. 2

Volume 7 New York (1922–34)

Volume 8 Big Bands

Volume 9 Piano

Volume 10 Boogie-Woogie

Volume 11 Addenda

History of Classic Jazz. Riverside Records, SDP–11.

Volume 1 Backgrounds

Volume 2 Ragtime

Volume 3 The Blues

Volume 4 New Orleans Style

Volume 5 Boogie-Woogie

Volume 6 South Side Chicago

Volume 7 Chicago Style

Volume 8 Harlem

Volume 9 New York Style

Volume 10 New Orleans Revival

Jazz Odyssey. Columbia Records, C31–30, 32, 33.

Volume 1 The Sound of New Orleans (1917–47)

Volume 2 The Sound of Chicago (1923–40)

Volume 3 The Sound of Harlem

Jazz Piano Anthology. Columbia Records, PG 32355 (4 sides).

The Jazz Story. Capitol Records, W2137–41.
    Volume 1 New Orleans
    Volume 2 North to Chicago
    Volume 3 The Swinging Years
    Volume 4 The Big Bands
    Volume 5 Modern and Free Form

The Saxophone. Impulse Records, 9253 (6 sides).

Smithsonian Collection of Classic Jazz. Columbia Special Products, P6 11891.

Three Decades of Jazz. Blue Note Records, LA 158–60.
    1939–49
    1949–59
    1959–69

Albums

African Drums. Folkways Records, FE 4502.

Anatomy of Improvisation. Verve Records, 8230.

Art of Jazz Piano. Epic Records, 3295.

The Art Tatum Touch (Paul Smith). Outstanding Records, vols. 1 and 2, 004 and 007.

Basic Miles. Columbia Records, C 32025.

The Be-Bop Era. RCA Victor Records, LPV–519.

The Best of Dixieland. RCA Victor Records, LSP–2982.

Bix Beiderbecke and the Chicago Cornets. Milestone Records, M–47019 (4 sides).

The Blues in Modern Jazz. Atlantic Records, 1337.

The Blues Roll On. Atlantic Records, 1352.

Boogie-Woogie Rarities. Milestone Records, MLP 2009.

Carnegie Hall Concert. Columbia Records, OSL–160.

Chicagoans (1928–30). Decca Records, 79231.

Chicago Jazz Album. Decca Records, 8029.

A Child's Introduction to Jazz. Wonderland Records, 2435.

Classic Jazz Piano Styles. RCA Victor Records, LPV–543.

Classic Piano Styles. RCA Victor Records, LPV–546.

Energy Essentials. Impulse Records, ASD–9228 (6 sides).

From Spirituals to Swing. Vanguard Records, VRS–8523/4.

The Golden Age of Ragtime. Riverside Records, 12–110.

The Great Band Era. RCA Victor Records, RD4–25 (RRIS–5473).

Great Blues Singers. Riverside Records, 121.

The Greatest Jazz Concert in the World. Pablo Records, 2625704.

The Greatest Names in Jazz. Verve Records, PR 2–3.

Guide to Jazz. RCA Victor Records, LPM 1393.

Jazz of the 1920s. Merry Makers Records, 103.

The Jazz Makers. Columbia Records, CL 1036.

Jazz at the Santa Monica Civic '72. Pablo Records, 2625701.

The Jazz Scene. Verve Records, 8060.

Jazz Scene I. Epic Records, LA–1600.

Kansas City Jazz. Decca Records, 8044.

Mainstream Jazz. Atlantic Records, 1303/S.

A Musical History of Jazz. Grand Awards Records, 33–322.

Never Before . . . Never Again (Joe Venuti/Tony Romero). Dobre Records, DR 1066.

New Orleans Jazz. Decca Records, 8283.

New Orleans: The Living Legends. Riverside Records, 356–57 (s).

The New Wave in Jazz. Impulse Records, A–90.

New York: Fall 1974 (Anthony Braxton). Artista Records, AL 4032.

Piano Roll Hall of Fame. Sounds Records, LP 1202.

Ragtime Piano Roll. Riverside Records, 126.

The Roots of American Music. Arhoolie Records, 2001–2.

Saxophone Revolt. Riverside Records, 284.

The Soul of Jazz. Riverside Records, S–5.

The Story of the Blues. Columbia Records, G 30540.

Thesaurus of Classic Jazz. Columbia Records, C4L 18.

This Is Benny Goodman. RCA Victor Records, VPM 6040.

Authors' Note

The authors have often suggested more than one example for the convenience of the instructors and the student. Also it should be mentioned that most large metropolitan areas have collectors' record stores that attempt to locate the records that are not easily obtainable. For example, in the Los Angeles area, the authors rely heavily on the services of an outlet called Ray Avery Rare Records, 417 E. Broadway, Glendale, California 91205. All of these outlets are most happy to operate by mail.

Glossary

accompanying To perform with another performer or performers usually in a less prominent role; for example, to play the piano accompaniment for a trombone soloist.

appoggiatura A musical ornament consisting of a single tone moving to an adjacent tone which is harmonized.

arpeggio In which the individual tones of a chord are not sounded simultaneously but performed like a melody (single tones), nearly always starting at the bottom or lowest tone.

arrangement An adaptation of a musical composition (often called *charts* in musical slang). In a written arrangement, the musical arranger writes out the notes he wants each performer to play. In a head arrangement, the arrangement is made up out of someone's head, not written down.

arranger One who writes musical compositions for particular groups of performers.

attack The manner in which the tone or tones are first sounded.

ballad A simple song, usually romantic in nature, which uses the same melody for each stanza.

bar line A vertical line drawn down a music staff dividing it into bars or measures.

bar of music A means of dividing music; also called a measure of music.

bass (brass) The member of the brass family sounding the lowest tones; generally referred to as the *tuba*.

bass (string) An instrument that looks like a very large violin; also called the *bass violin*. The string bass is played either by plucking the strings with the fingers (*pizzicato*) or by bowing (*arco*).

block chords Usually chords with many notes that move in parallel motion.

blue tonalities The alteration of the third and seventh tones of the major scale by a flatting inflection.

bombs Spontaneous punctuations by the drummer.

break A short interruption in the flow of the music; an interlude in which a solo player improvises or an accompanying group interpolates.

bridge The name given to the third eight-bar section in the most common construction of a thirty-two bar chorus. AABA—the B is the bridge.

call-and-response pattern A musical pattern common to much jazz and African music in which a "call," usually by a solo singer or instrumentalist, is followed by a "response" from one instrument, an ensemble, or the assembled participants in a ritual. In religious ceremonies the congregation may respond to the "call" of the preacher.

chamber music Music intended for small groups performing in intimate surroundings, as distinct from large groups performing in concert halls, theaters, and the like.

Charleston A dance form that was extremely popular during the 1920s.

chord The simultaneous sounding of three or more tones.

chord changes A series of successive chords; also called *chord progression*.

chorus The main body or refrain of a song as distinct from the verse, which comes first. Very often an arrangement contains many choruses played by individual instrumentalists.

chromatic Refers to the scales or the alteration of scale tones by using half-steps.

collective improvisation A situation in which all members of a small group improvise simultaneously.

combo A small instrumental group consisting of three to eight players.

concerto grosso A composition consisting of interplay between a large body of instruments (orchestra) and a small group of instrumentalists (combo).

Congo Square A large field in New Orleans where slaves gathered to sing and dance.

contrived Music that is planned beforehand.

Creole A person with Negro and French or Spanish ancestry.

crossover A style of music that appeals to more than one type of listener; usually refers to jazz/rock (*fusion*).

cross-rhythm Two or more rhythmic patterns played simultaneously.

diatonic Pertains to the precise arrangement of tones as found in the major and minor scales.

digital recording Computer method of recording sound through the use of numbers.

Dorian mode The arrangement of tones found in the scale using only the white keys of the piano from D to D.

double-stop Two tones stopped by the fingers on a stringed instrument and sounded simultaneously.

double time When the tempo of the music becomes twice as fast.

eleventh chord A chord consisting of six different tones, each separated by an interval of a third.

ensemble Usually a small group of performers as distinct from an orchestra or choir.

extended harmony Tones added to a chord.

field hollers A secret means of communication between slaves while they worked in the fields; sometimes called *field cries*.

fill-in Originally, a short interlude in a song (such as a blues song) played by an instrumentalist.

flatted fifth Lowering by a half step the fifth degree of the scale or chord.

flatted tone Used to lower the pitch one half step.

flügelhorn A type of brass instrument with valves, similar to a trumpet.

form Refers to the design of a composition, its repeated and contrasting parts.

frontline Instrumentalists who are placed along the front of an ensemble.

fugue A type of contrapuntal composition for a given number of parts. Each part is introduced individually, and successive parts are heard in imitation.

fusion A style of music that appeals to more than one type of listener; usually refers to jazz/rock (*crossover*).

gospel song A song whose lyrics recount passages from scripture.

guitorgan A guitarlike instrument with an organ sound.

harmony Simultaneous sounding of two or more tones.

higher harmony See *extended harmony*.

homophonic A single melody, usually in the highest voice part, with harmony in the lower voices acting as an accompaniment.

horizontal thinking Polyphonic texture; a simultaneous combination of melodies; the opposite of homophonic texture, which consists of a single melody with harmonic accompaniment.

hymn A congregational song, whose words are not taken directly from the Bible, sung in praise of God.

iambic pentameter A type of poetry consisting of an unaccented syllable followed by an accented one, with five of these combinations in each line of poetry.

improvise To perform music that is made up (created) at the moment, not from memory or from written music; a manner of playing extemporaneously.

instrumentation The different types of instruments making up an ensemble.

jam session An informal gathering of musicians playing on their own time and improvising just for the "fun of it."

key A classification given to a particular arrangement of tones in a scale. The first degree of the scale is the tonal center or key name, and the necessary flats or sharps for a particular key form the key signature.

liturgical Pertaining to the rites and services of a religious service.

Mass The principal service of the Roman Catholic Church. The part that does not vary is called the Ordinary, or Common, of the Mass and consists of the Kyrie, the Gloria, the Credo, the Sanctus with Benedictus, and the Agnus Dei.

measure See *bar of music*.

melisma A melodic ornamentation; one syllable sung on more than one tone of a song.

melody A succession of single tones varying in pitch and rhythm and having a recognizable musical shape.

meter The division of beats into accented and unaccented groupings of two, three, or more.

middle register The middle part of the complete range of the voice or instrument.

mixolydian The arrangement of tones found in the scale using only the white keys of the piano from G to G.

monophonic A single melody with neither an accompanying melody nor harmony.

mordent A rapid movement from one tone to an upper or lower scale tone and back again to the principal tone.

ninth chord A chord consisting of five different tones, each separated by an interval of a third.

obligato An accompanying or free melody played by a second instrument, less prominent and secondary to the main melody played by the lead instrument.

ostinato A clear melodic and/or rhythmic figure that is persistently repeated.

overtone series Tones that are related to the first (fundamental) tone sounded. A series of higher tones, or upper partials, which, when the first or fundamental is sounded, make up a complex musical tone.

pedal point A tone sustained below while harmonies change.

pentatonic A scale consisting of only five tones as represented by the five black keys of the piano.

phrase A small unit of a melody.

pizzicato A manner of playing stringed instruments by plucking rather than by bowing.

plagal cadence A specific chord progression, namely, the IV chord resolving to the I chord; example, amen chords.

polymeters Simultaneous use of several meters.

polymodal The simultaneous sounding of several different modes.

polyphonic The simultaneous sounding of two or more melodies of equal importance.

polytonal The simultaneous sounding of tones in more than one key.

portamento The movement from one tone to another higher or lower tone without any break in the sound.

quadrille A square dance of five figures that was popular in the nineteenth century.

raga A particular scale in Eastern music.

reggae A Jamaican style of rhythm and blues.

rhythm section The section of an instrumental ensemble that provides the most prominent rhythmic feel of the music, usually consisting of drums, piano, bass, and guitar.

riff A short pattern of sounds repeated and played by a soloist or group.

rim shots Produced by striking the edge or rim of the drum and drum head simultaneously.

rondo A musical form in which one section of a composition recurs intermittently with contrasting sections coming between each repetition, for example, ABACADA.

root tone The lowest note or tone of a chord when that chord is in its basic, or root, position.

rubato A fluctuation in the tempo of the music for the purpose of giving music an additional element of expression.

salsa A combination of jazz and Afro-Cuban rhythms.

scale A precise progression of single tones upward or downward in steps. Chromatic scale: a twelve-tone scale with intervals of a half step. Diatonic scale: an eight-tone scale with a repetition of the eighth degree, pertaining to the major and minor scales. Pentatonic scale: consisting of five tones.

Schoenberg's twelve-tone system A technique of composition in which all twelve half steps in an octave are treated as equal. A method used by Schoenberg in the form of a "tone row," in which all the twelve tones are placed in a particular order forming the basis of a musical composition. No tone is repeated within a row. The tone row becomes a "tonal reservoir" from which the composition is drawn.

sharped tone Raises the pitch one half step.

sideman A player in the musical ensemble as differentiated from the leader.

soulsa A combination of Latin jazz and "soul" music.

speakeasy A nightclub in the 1920s.

spiritual A name given to a type of religious folk song of the American Negro, usually of a solo-and-refrain design.

standard tunes Familiar, well-established popular or jazz tunes. Copyright can be renewed for a certain number of years after the death of the composer.

stock arrangement A published commercial arrangement, usually simplified and standardized.

Storyville Red-light district in New Orleans which figured in the origin of jazz.

symmetrical Exhibiting a balance of parts.

syncopation To accent a normally weak beat or weak part of a beat.

tack piano A piano with thumb tacks on the felts of the piano hammers to make it sound older and more authentic for playing ragtime and similar music.

tag A short addition to the end of a musical composition.

tailgate trombone A name deriving from the practice of early trombone players sitting on the tailgate of a wagon so that their slides could operate freely out the rear. The phrase became associated with the trombone part in a dixieland ensemble.

tango A dance of Spanish-American origin commonly in 4/4 meter.

tempo Refers to the speed of the underlying beat. The speed is determined by the number of beats counted over the span of sixty seconds.

theme and variation A musical form in which the theme is introduced and successive repetitions of the theme, changed or altered in some manner, follow.

thirteenth chord A chord consisting of seven different tones each separated by an interval of a third.

time signature Sign at the beginning of a composition indicating the grouping of beats for each measure. The meter signature ¾ means that there are three beats in a measure and that a quarter note gets one beat.

Tin Pan Alley Refers to the industry centered in New York that published popular music.

tonal clash Tones played simultaneously that produce a discordant or clashing effect.

tonal sonorities The overall effect of the juxtaposition of tonal sounds.

trading fours Two solo instrumentalists alternating in playing four measures each.

twelve-bar strain A composition or a part of a composition consisting of twelve measures.

unison Two or more instruments or voices sounding on the same pitches (tones) or an octave apart.

up-tempo Fast tempo.

vamp A transitional chord or rhythmic progression of indefinite duration used as a filler until the soloist is ready to start or continue on.

verse The introductory section of a popular song as distinguished from the chorus. The latter consists commonly of thirty-two bars, while the verse may have an irregular number of bars and may be sung or played in a free tempo.

vertical thinking Block chords that accompany a melodic part; opposite of horizontal thinking.

vibrato   Refers to the artificial wavering of a tone; rapidly recurring fluctuations of pitch. Most jazz uses vibrato for warmth and interpretation in imitation of the human voice.

vocoder   An electronic musical device that allows the player to choose the pitch of any syllable that he sings.

walking bass   The bass part that was originally introduced in boogie-woogie in ostinato form. It concisely spells out the notes in the chords being used and is usually played in eighth notes.

well-tempered scale   Refers to the tuning system found on a keyboard.

Bibliography

Albertson, Chris. *Bessie*. New York: Stein & Day Publishers, 1972.

Allan, William Francis; Ware, Charles Pickard; and Garrison, Lucy McKim. *Slave Songs of the United States*. New York: Peter Smith, 1867.

Allen, Walter C. *Hendersonia: The Music of Fletcher Henderson and His Musicians, Jazz Monograph no. 4*. Highland Park, N.J.: Walter C. Allen, 1973.

Apel, Willi. *Harvard Dictionary of Music*. Cambridge, Mass.: Harvard University Press, 1955.

Armstrong, Louis. *Swing That Music*. New York: Longmans, Green & Co., 1936.

————. *Louis Armstrong: A Self Portrait*. New York: Eakins Press, 1971.

Baird, David. *From Score to Tape*. Boston: Berklee Press Pub., 1973.

Balliett, Whitney. *Dinosaurs in the Morning*. Philadelphia: J. B. Lippincott Co., 1962.

————. *The Sound of Surprise*. New York: E. P. Dutton & Co., 1959.

Bechet, Sidney. *Treat It Gentle: An Autobiography*. New York: Hill & Wang, 1960.

Berendt, Joachim. *The New Jazz Book*. Translated by Dan Morgenstern. New York: Hill & Wang, 1962.

————. *Jazz Book: From New Orleans to Rock and Free Jazz*. New York: Lawrence Hill & Co., 1974.

Bernstein, Leonard. *The Joy of Music*. New York: Simon & Schuster, 1959.

Berton, Ralph. *Remembering Bix: A Memoir of the Jazz Age*. New York: Harper & Row, 1974.

Blesh, Rudi. *Classic Piano Rags*. New York: Dover Publications, 1973.

Blesh, Rudi, and Janis, Harriet. *They All Played Ragtime*. New York: Grove Press, 1959.

Bloom, Eric, ed. *Grove's Dictionary of Music and Musicians*. Nine vols. New York: St. Martin's Press, 1959.

Brask, Ole, and Morgenstern, Dan. *Jazz People*. New York: Harry N. Abrams, Inc., 1976.

Budds, Michael J. *Jazz in the Sixties*. Iowa City, Iowa: University of Iowa Press, 1978.

Buerkle, Jack V. and Barker, Danny. *Bourbon Street Black*. London: Oxford University Press, 1973.

Buszin, Walter E., ed. *Anniversary Collection of Bach Chorales*. Chicago: Hall McCreary, 1935.

Charters, Samuel B., and Kunstadt, Leonard. *Jazz: A History of The New York Scene.* New York: Doubleday & Co., 1962.

Charters, Samuel. *Jazz: New Orleans (1885–1963).* New York: Oak Publishers, 1964.

Chilton, John. *Billie's Blues.* New York: Stein & Day Publishers, 1975.

Cole, Bill. *Miles Davis.* New York: William Morris and Co., 1976.

Collier, James Lincoln. *The Making of Jazz.* New York: Dell Publishing Co., Inc., 1978.

Coryell, Julie, and Friedman, Laura. *Jazz-Rock Fusion.* New York: Delta Books, 1979.

Dance, Stanley. *The World of Duke Ellington.* New York: Charles Scribner's Sons, 1970.

———. *The World of Swing.* New York: Charles Scribner's Sons, 1975.

Dankworth, Avril: *Jazz: An Introduction to Its Musical Basis.* London: Oxford University Press, 1968.

Davis, Nathan. *Writings in Jazz.* Dubuque, Iowa: Gorsuch Scarisbrick Publishers, 1978.

Dexter, Dave. *The Jazz Story.* Englewood Cliffs, N.J.: Prentice-Hall, 1964.

Drake, Russell; Herder, Ronald; and Modugno, Anne D. *How to Make Electronic Music.* Pleasantville, New York: EAV Inc., 1975.

Ellington, Duke. *Music Is My Mistress.* New York: Doubleday & Co., 1973.

Ellington, Mercer, and Dance, Stanley. *Duke Ellington: An Intimate Memoir.* New York: Houghton Mifflin, 1975.

Feather, Leonard. *The Book of Jazz.* New York: World Publishing Co., Meridian Books, 1959.

———. *Inside Jazz.* New York: J. J. Robbins & Sons, 1949.

———. *The New Edition of the Encyclopedia of Jazz.* New York: Horizon Press, 1960.

———. *The Encyclopedia of Jazz in the Sixties.* New York: Horizon Press, 1966.

———. *From Satchmo to Miles.* New York: Stein & Day Publishers, 1974.

———. *Pleasures of Jazz.* New York: Horizon Press, 1976.

Finkelstein, Sidney. *Jazz: A People's Music.* New York: Da Capo Press, 1975.

Flower, John. *Moonlight Serenade.* New Rochelle, N.Y.: Arlington House, 1972.

Francis, André. *Jazz.* Translated and revised by Martin Williams. New York: Grove Press, 1960.

Friend, David; Perlman, Alan R.; and Piggott, Thomas G. *Learning Music with Synthesizers.* Winona, Minn.: Hal Leonard Pub. Corp., 1974.

Gammond, Peter, ed. *Duke Ellington: His Life and Music.* New York: Roy Publishers, 1958.

———. *Scott Joplin and the Ragtime Era.* New York: St. Martin's Press, 1975.

Gillespie, Dizzy, and Fraser, Al. *To Be, or Not . . . to Bop.* Garden City, New York: Doubleday Pub. Co., 1979.

Gitler, Ira. *Jazz Masters of the Forties.* New York: Macmillan Co., 1966.

Gleason, Ralph. *Celebrating the Duke.* New York: Dell Publishers, 1975.

Goffin, Robert. *Jazz: From the Congo to the Metropolitan.* New York: Da Capo Press, 1975.

Gold, Robert S. *A Jazz Lexicon.* New York: Knopf, 1964.

Goldberg, Joe. *Jazz Masters of the Fifties.* New York: Macmillan Co., 1965.

Gridley, Mark C. *Jazz Styles.* Englewood Cliffs, N.J.: Prentice-Hall, 1978.

Hadlock, Richard. *Jazz Masters of the Twenties.* New York: Macmillan Co., 1965.

Harris, Rex. *Jazz.* Baltimore, Md.: Penguin Books, 1956.

Harrison, Max. *Charlie Parker.* New York: A. S. Barnes & Co., 1960.

Hentoff, Nat. *Jazz Life.* New York: Da Capo Press, 1975.

———. *Jazz Is.* New York: Random House, 1976.

Hentoff, Nat, and McCarthy, Albert. *Jazz: New Perspectives on the History of Jazz.* New York: Da Capo Press, 1975.

———, eds. *Jazz.* New York: Holt, Rinehart & Winston, Inc., 1959.

Hodeir, André. *Jazz: Its Evolution and Essence.* Translated by David Noakes. New York: Grove Press, 1956.

———. *Toward Jazz.* New York: Grove Press, 1962.

Holiday, Billie, and Dufty, William. *The Lady Sings the Blues.* New York: Doubleday & Co., 1965.

James, Michael. *Dizzy Gillespie.* New York: A. S. Barnes & Co., 1959.

Jewell, Derek. *Duke: A Portrait of Duke Ellington.* New York: W. W. Norton & Co., 1977.

Jones, LeRoi. *Black Music.* New York: William Morrow & Co., 1965.

————. *Blues People.* New York: William Morrow & Co., 1963.

Jones, Max. *Salute to Satchmo.* London: Longacre Press, 1970.

Jones, Max, and Chilton, John. *Louis: The Louis Armstrong Story.* New York: Little, Brown & Co., 1971.

Jost, Ekkehard. *Free Jazz.* Wien, Austria: Universal Edition, 1975.

Keepnews, Orrin, and Grauer, Bill, Jr. *A Pictorial History of Jazz.* New York: Crown Publishers, 1955.

Keil, Charles. *Urban Blues.* Chicago: University of Chicago Press, 1966.

Kinkle, Roger D. *The Complete Encyclopedia of Popular Music and Jazz.* New Rochelle, N.Y.: Arlington House, 1974.

Leonard, Neil. *Jazz and the White Americans.* Chicago: University of Chicago Press, 1962.

Lomax, Alan. *Mr. Jelly Roll.* New York: Grosset & Dunlap, Universal Library, 1950.

McCarthy, Albert. *Louis Armstrong.* New York: A. S. Barnes & Co., 1959.

————. *Big Band Jazz.* New York: G. P. Putnam's Sons, 1974.

Marquis, Donald. *In Search of Buddy Bolden: First Man of Jazz.* Baton Rouge, La.: Louisiana State Univ. Press, 1979.

Martin, John H., and Fritz, William F. *Listening to Jazz.* Fresno, Calif.: University of California Press, 1969.

Meeker, David. *Jazz in the Movies: A Guide to Jazz Musicians, 1917–1977.* New Rochelle, N.Y.: Arlington House, 1978.

Mehegan, John. *Jazz Improvisation.* New York: Watson-Guptill Publications, 1959.

Miller, Hugh Milton. *History of Music.* New York: Barnes & Noble Books, 1957.

Muro, Don. *An Introduction to Electronic Music Synthesizers.* Melville, New York: Belwin-Mills Publishing Corp., 1975.

✓ Nanry, Charles. *The Jazz Text.* New York: D. Van Nostrand, 1979.

Oliver, Paul. *Bessie Smith.* New York: A. S. Barnes & Co., 1961.

————. *The Meaning of the Blues.* New York: Macmillan Co., Collier Books, 1960.

————. *The Savannah Syncopators.* New York: Stein & Day Publishers, 1970.

Ostransky, Leroy. *The Anatomy of Jazz.* Seattle: University of Washington Press, 1960.

————. *Jazz City.* Englewood Cliffs, N.J.: Prentice-Hall, 1975.

✓ ————. *Understanding Jazz.* Englewood Cliffs, N.J.: Prentice-Hall, 1977.

Panassie, Hughes. *Louis Armstrong.* New York: Charles Scribner's Sons, 1971.

————. *The Real Jazz.* Translated by Anne Sorrelle Williams. New York: A. S. Barnes & Co., 1960.

Pleasants, Henry. *Serious Music and All that Jazz.* New York: Simon & Schuster, 1969.

Roach, Hildred. *Black American Music: Past and Present.* Boston: Crescendo Publishing Co., 1973.

Roberts, John Storm. *Black Music of Two Worlds.* New York: William Morrow and Co., 1974.

Reisner, Robert G. *Bird: The Legend of Charlie Parker.* New York: Citadel Press, 1962.

————. *The Jazz Titans.* New York: Doubleday & Co., 1960.

✓ Russell, Ross. *Jazz Styles in Kansas City and the Southwest.* Berkeley: University of California Press, 1971.

————. *Bird Lives: The High Life and Hard Times of Charlie (Yardbird) Parker.* New York: Charterhouse Books, 1973.

Russell, Tony. *Blacks, Whites and the Blues.* New York: Stein & Day Publishers, 1970.

Sanders, Ruby W. *Jazz Ambassador Louis Armstrong.* Chicago: Childrens Press, 1973.

Schuller, Gunther. *Early Jazz: Its Roots and Musical Development.* London: Oxford University Press, 1968.

Scott, Allen. *Jazz Educated, Man.* Silver Springs, Md.: Institute of Modern Languages, 1973.

Schafer, William J. et al. *The Art of Ragtime.* Baton Rouge, La.: Louisiana State Univ. Press, 1973.

Shapiro, Nat, and Hentoff, Nat., eds. *The Jazz Makers.* New York: Grove Press, 1957.

Simpkins, C. O. *Coltrane: A Biography.* New York: Herndon House, 1975.

Simon, George T. *The Big Bands.* New York: Macmillan Co., 1967.

————. *Simon Says.* New Rochelle, N.Y.: Arlington House, 1971.

———. *Glenn Miller*. New York: Thomas Y. Crowell Co., 1974.

Southern, Eileen. *Music of Black Americans*. New York: W. W. Norton & Co., 1971.

Standifer, James A., and Reeder, Barbara. *African and Afro-American Materials for Music Educators*. Washington, D.C.: Music Educators National Conference, 1972.

✓ Stearns, Marshall. *The Story of Jazz*. London: Oxford University Press, 1958.

Stewart, Rex. *Jazz Masters of the '30s*. New York: Macmillan Co., 1972.

Stewart-Baxter, Derrick. *Ma Rainey*. New York: Stein & Day Publishers, 1970.

Strange, Allen, *Electronic Music: Systems, Techniques, and Controls*. Dubuque, Iowa: Wm. C. Brown Company Publishers, 1972.

Sudhalter, Richard M., and Evans, Philip R. *Bix: Man and Legend*. New York: Harper & Row, 1974.

Talmadge, William. *Afro-American Music*. Washington, D.C.: Music Educators National Conference, 1957.

Thomas, J. C. *Chasin' the Trane*. New York: Doubleday & Co., 1975.

✓ Tirro, Frank. *Jazz: A History*. New York: W. W. Norton & Co., 1977.

Ulanov, Barry. *Duke Ellington*. New York: Farrar, Strauss & Young, 1946.

✓ ———. *Handbook of Jazz*. New York: Viking Press, 1959.

Ulrich, Homer. *Music: A Design for Listening*. 2d ed. New York: Harcourt, Brace, & World, 1962.

Walker, Leo. *The Wonderful Era of the Great Dance Bands*. New York: Doubleday & Co., 1972.

Williams, Martin T. *Jazz Masters of New Orleans*. New York: Macmillan Co., 1965.

✓ ———. *Jazz Masters in Transition (1957–69)*. London: Macmillan Co., 1970.

✓ ———. *The Jazz Tradition*. London: Oxford University Press, 1969.

———. *King Oliver*. New York: A. S. Barnes & Co., 1960.

✓ Williams, Martin T., ed. *The Art of Jazz*. London: Oxford University Press, 1959.

Wilson, John S. *The Collector's Jazz: Modern*. Philadelphia: J. B. Lippincott Co., 1959.

———. *The Collector's Jazz: Tradition and Swing*. Philadelphia: J. B. Lippincott Co., 1958.

Index